Strategic Studies Institute Book

LEARNING BY DOING:
THE PLA TRAINS AT HOME AND ABROAD

Roy Kamphausen
David Lai
Travis Tanner
Editors

November 2012

*****

Comments pertaining to this report are invited and should be forwarded to: Director, Strategic Studies Institute, U.S. Army War College, 47 Ashburn Drive, Carlisle, PA 17013.

*****

All Strategic Studies Institute (SSI) publications may be downloaded free of charge from the SSI website. Hard copies of this report may also be obtained free of charge while supplies last by placing an order on the SSI website. SSI publications may be quoted or reprinted in part or in full with permission and appropriate credit given to the U.S. Army Strategic Studies Institute, U.S. Army War College, Carlisle Barracks, PA. Contact SSI by visiting our website at the following address: *www.StrategicStudiesInstitute.army.mil.*

*****

The Strategic Studies Institute publishes a monthly e-mail newsletter to update the national security community on the research of our analysts, recent and forthcoming publications, and upcoming conferences sponsored by the Institute. Each newsletter also provides a strategic commentary by one of our research analysts. If you are interested in receiving this newsletter, please subscribe on the SSI website at *www.StrategicStudiesInstitute. army.mil/newsletter/.*

ISBN 1-58487-552-6

CONTENTS

FOREWORD

Learning by Doing: The PLA Trains at Home and Abroad is the latest volume in a series on the PLA produced by the Strategic Studies Institute (SSI), The National Bureau of Asian Research (NBR), and the United States Pacific Command (USPACOM). The papers presented here are a timely and critical look at an evolving and expanding Chinese military and provide context for the changes we may yet see as the PLA continues to modernize.

As the USPACOM Commander, I seek to better understand China in aspects that further our ability to find common areas of interest, reduce miscalculation, and contribute to regional stability. Greater insight into the PLA is essential to this effort. As the Chinese military matures, grows, and ventures farther from China's territory, the regional and global implications for the United States and USPACOM, as well as our allies and partners will be complex, yet critical to our understanding of China's evolving international role and influence. Therefore, accurate and timely assessments of the changes taking place within the PLA are essential to understanding how the Chinese are matching military power with their broader policy aims. The outstanding scholarship in this jointly-sponsored study by SSI, NBR, and USPACOM is an important contribution toward this end.

The judgments in this volume provide unique and valuable insights on how the PLA is adapting its training to its perception of the security environment. This does not just include how it is resourcing, organizing, and training its forces, but also how the PLA thinks about warfare and the threats they currently face. Through participation in international military exercises, as well as peacekeeping operations

(PKO) and humanitarian assistance and disaster relief (HADR) missions abroad, the PLA is gaining greater experience in carrying out a broader spectrum of missions. For example, the lessons learned from counter-piracy missions in the Gulf of Aden as well as internal, transregional deployment exercises are impacting the way China responds to issues ranging from domestic natural disasters to cooperative security efforts requiring the projection and sustainment of military power beyond China's borders. Monitoring these developments is not only key to our understanding of China's perceptions of the security environment, but also to identifying opportunities to further develop cooperative capacity in the areas of nontraditional security threats—a growing area of cooperation between our two militaries.

The outstanding analysis provided by SSI and NBR, will inform the decisions that affect our operations and relations throughout the Asia-Pacific region. Both organizations have again demonstrated their commitment to excellence with the release of this volume, and it is therefore my pleasure to introduce it to you. *Learning by Doing: The PLA Trains at Home and Abroad* is an essential source for those seeking to understand the changes that are taking place within the Chinese military. But more importantly, it sets the stage and helps us prepare for the opportunities that lie ahead.

SAMUEL J. LOCKLEAR III
Admiral, USN
Commander, U.S. Pacific Command

CHAPTER 1

INTRODUCTION:
PLA LESSONS LEARNED FROM
INCREASINGLY REALISTIC EXERCISES[1]

Roy Kamphausen
Travis Tanner

For more than 2 decades, the annual People's Liberation Army (PLA) Conference has been a premier source of original analysis on China's military development. Each conference results in an edited volume consisting of the papers presented that year by top PLA scholars.[2] This volume represents the 2011-12 iteration of the event, a workshop titled "Learning by Doing: The PLA Trains at Home and Abroad," held on February 18, 2012. This year's event was unique in that it marked the first time the event was held at Marine Corps University (MCU) in Quantico, Virginia. The workshop was convened by The National Bureau of Asian Research (NBR), the Strategic Studies Institute (SSI) of the U.S. Army War College (USAWC), the United States Pacific Command (USPACOM), and MCU.

In an effort to better understand the PLA's ability to employ its developing capabilities in a variety of potential scenarios, this year's workshop examined how the PLA learns by doing, specifically through its exercises and noncombat operations at home and overseas, and through key logistical and theoretical developments. In many ways, this year's workshop was the second installment of an examination of how the PLA has sought to gain experience in the practice of modern warfare despite lacking recent combat experience of its own. Though some Chinese sources assert that the current Gulf of Aden anti-piracy mission involves "combat-like" conditions, most PLA observers cite the 1979 Sino-Vietnamese clash as the last instance of Chinese military involvement in a major armed conflict with a foreign foe. Consequently, the previous volume in the annual series—*Chinese Lessons from Other Peoples' Wars* (2011)—examined what the PLA has learned from its observation of the armed conflicts of foreign nations. Key insights included the following: (1) the lessons the PLA learns from foreign conflicts are colored by China's domestic politics and ideology; (2) most of the lessons learned take place at the high operational and strategic levels of war, we suspect because there is no current tactical or operational context to which they might apply; and, (3) the PLA tends to focus its attention on U.S. military institutions such as USPACOM, both as models for its own development and as sources of information on how it might effectively fight against the U.S. military in a potential conflict. In addition, an assumption undergirding much of the conference's analysis—namely, that the PLA would have more leeway to criticize openly the conduct of wars in which it was not involved—was mostly borne out.

This volume seeks to build on these findings and examine how the PLA follows Mao Zedong's maxim to learn by doing ("in war, study war" ["在战争中学习战争"]) by analyzing another major source of the PLA's practical knowledge, namely its exercises and noncombat operations. Moreover, exercises and military operations other than war (MOOTW) have recently become a vital area of PLA studies due to the increasing pace and scope of China's military exercises as well as the formal integration of MOOTW into PLA doctrine.[3] Thus, the 2012 workshop aimed to fill a void within the literature, assessing the PLA's progress by examining recent exercises and noncombat operations in the following areas: PLA Navy (PLAN) exercises and operations, PLA ground force exercises within China's borders, multinational exercises in international settings, and systems and strategy reform.

In analyzing each of these areas of development, the workshop explored the following key questions: What PLA capabilities have been enhanced as a result of recent exercises and noncombat operations? What lessons about military doctrine, strategy, and training were learned? Are there observable adjustments that the PLA has made in response to these lessons learned? And, what are the implications of these developments for the United States? The focus on the PLA's own exercises and operations was accompanied by the assumption that these assessments would be less frank than those involving foreign conflicts.

The book's key findings can be summarized as follows. First, recent PLAN exercises and operations point to an increasing interest in developing expeditionary naval capabilities and a presence in distant seas, suggesting that a move beyond the current "near seas" focus is both possible and an extension of existing efforts. Second, PLA ground force exercises — rather than aiming to intimidate others by demonstrating the ability to project power beyond China's borders — focus on moving military power within China, both to defend China's borders and perhaps as a prelude to military restructuring in which smaller but more mobile formations could replace larger and more static ones. Third, through its participation in international military exercises as well as peacekeeping operations (PKO) and humanitarian aid and disaster relief (HADR) missions, the PLA is gaining greater capabilities to deploy outside of China's borders for a variety of missions. Finally, PLA operations are increasingly supported by a modern, civilian-integrated military logistics network, though a lack of overseas bases continues to limit the effectiveness of this network as it pertains to overseas power projection capabilities.

PLAN EXERCISES AND OPERATIONS

In many ways, the PLAN has been the most visible branch of the Chinese military on the global stage through its port calls, exercises with international partners, and participation in overseas operations such as the Gulf of Aden anti-piracy mission. Of these international engagements, the anti-piracy deployment in particular has led to important lessons. Admiral Michael McDevitt's chapter examines what the PLAN has learned from its interactions with foreign navies, focusing in particular on the anti-piracy deployments. One highlighted lesson is the importance of logistics during extended deployments. Due to China's long-held stance of not establishing overseas military bases, the PLAN relies on commercial ports and agreements for its replenishment and support operations. Additionally, the Gulf of Aden mission has led to the improvement of the PLAN's emergency medical evacuation and major engineering repair capabilities, due to specific events that have occurred during the deployments. More generally, these ongoing deployments have contributed to the PLAN's ability to maintain itself at sea for longer periods of time, allowed it to develop realistic exercises based its operational experiences, and given it the opportunity to absorb best practices through its interactions with other major navies in a real world "battle laboratory." In short, these operations have contributed to the PLAN's learning how to operate in distant seas, an area of ever-expanding importance, because of China's increased interests and presence abroad. These operations will continue to carry the PLAN beyond "offshore defense" and into becoming a more global, expeditionary navy.

Dr. Bernard Cole's chapter examines recent initiatives on the domestic side of the PLAN's evolution, including unilateral training exercises. The complexity, length, and multi-unit participation of Chinese naval exercises have been continuously increasing. These exercises are part of the PLAN's developing training regime, which must balance the competing requirements of both indoctrinating sailors ideologically and ensuring their loyalty to the Communist Party while also ensuring their ability to work in the high-technology environment of modern warfare. Despite struggling to perfect this balance, the PLAN continues to make progress in joint training, MOOTW, civilian integration in military operations, training according to doctrine, and training under "real-war" conditions. This training regime has led to improvements in professionalism and the PLAN's ability to perform in all the standard areas of naval warfare, especially informatized warfare at sea. Furthermore, naval exercises are increasingly being employed to send political signals to the United States and others in the Asia-Pacific through demonstrating an increased PLAN presence in the region. This trend will continue in the near future as the PLAN continues to develop its training and exercise regimen, and becomes more capable in carrying out modern naval operations and contributing to the protection and advancement of China's national interests.

As with the other volume authors, Admiral McDevitt and Dr. Cole draw out a series of implications for the United States from their analyses of recent PLAN developments. First, both authors underscore the move to a greater emphasis on "distant or far seas" activity as a factor that increasingly challenges U.S. interests. Dr. Cole specifically highlights the increasing sophistication and length of training exercises as important indicators of a large-scale move toward this "far seas" approach. Additionally, despite the potential for conflict, both authors note prospects for convergent interests in some areas. Admiral McDevitt mentions the PLAN becoming more "integrated" into naval activities near the Strait of Hormuz and the convergence of Chinese and U.S. interests in the region as potentially leading to a greater opportunity for the two nations to work together on supporting regional peace and stability. Admiral McDevitt also notes that increasing PLAN capabilities confirm the necessity and timeliness of the recently announced U.S. strategic rebalancing, including an increased focus on the Asia-Pacific region. Finally, both authors stress the PLAN's increasing capability to support the protection of China's national interests, with Dr. Cole citing the "three seas" ("三海") formulation as an indication that China's vital maritime interests are focused in the Yellow, South China, and East China Seas.

DOMESTIC GROUND FORCE EXERCISES

Representing another key area of development for China's military exercises and noncombat operations, domestic exercises by ground forces, including trans-military region (MR) exercises and related activities conducted by the People's Armed Police (PAP) force, are another focus of this volume. Trans-MR exercises, the focus of Mr. Dennis Blasko's chapter, mainly feature PLA ground forces and carry important implications for the PLA's overall development and modernization, as well as its power projection capabilities. These exercises have been growing in size and complexity in recent years and are aimed at improving the PLA's ability to send forces to border regions to repel attacks on China. Within this framework, the Jinan MR is particularly relevant, given its geographic location and role as a strategic reserve. Consequently, Jinan has played a central role in many of the trans-MR exercises. The reliance on civilian support and transportation by rail in these exercises further emphasizes their domestic, mainland focus. In addition, these exercises have allowed the PLA to experiment with operational techniques in areas such as command and control for joint operations, operations in a complex electromagnetic environment, the formation of combined arms battalion task forces, and logistics support. Thus, trans-MR exercises contribute not only to PLA capabilities but also to China's overall deterrence posture and are important signifiers of overall PLA development and modernization.

Another element of China's ground forces development involves the exercises of the PAP, the focus of Cortez Cooper's analysis. The PAP is unique among China's armed forces in that, in contrast to the PLA, it *often deploys* to conduct its primary mission, namely, responding to domestic crises and ensuring domestic security. Given these circumstances, even more so than other elements of China's armed forces, the PAP is forced to balance the need to always be prepared to immediately fulfill its role as a ready response force with the need to develop its capabilities through training and exercises. Recently, in part due to lessons learned from past deployments, the PAP has stepped up its training on counterterrorism as well as on riot control, border control, and natural disaster response operations. A series of events that occurred between 2008 and 2010 — including the Beijing Olympics and the major earthquake in Sichuan Province, combined with force modernization efforts — have led to better training and equipment, the integration of new operational concepts, and a historically high state of readiness. The main areas of PAP development include administrative adjustments, joint integration, informatization, and equipment modernization, as well as logistics and infrastructure enhancement. Going forward, China's central leadership will place great emphasis on the PAP's ability to respond quickly and effectively in anti-terror and riot control missions while coordinating its role with that of the PLA and other elements of China's forces. During wartime, the PAP's importance will lie in supporting the PLA at the national level while providing local crowd control in the face of the domestic civil unrest that may accompany an external crisis — a mission of great concern for China's leadership.

The implications of these chapters are far-reaching. Mr. Blasko notes that the domestic focus of these ground force exercises indicates that they were not designed to intimidate Taiwan. In addition, trans-MR exercises may eventually prove that out-of-region forces supported by reserves and civilians can sufficiently reinforce border areas during a conflict. This development could justify cuts in main force ground units that could, in turn, free up resources for a range of other uses, including transportation assets that could supplement the PLA's lagging long-distance power projection capabilities. Finally, Mr. Blasko explains that these exercises were carried out in a relatively transparent manner and included significant domestic media coverage, which contradicts common assumptions regarding PLA secrecy. Mr. Cortez Cooper also touches on the transparency issue, noting that the promotion of increased transparency could be one of the main advantages of bilateral U.S. engagement with the PAP on initiatives such as policing, disaster relief, and counterterrorism and multilateral engagement on peacekeeping, humanitarian assistance, and disaster relief operations. This advantage would need to be balanced with other considerations, including the potential to increase inadvertently the PAP's ability to quell peaceful domestic protests. Mr. Cooper concludes that, in general, the advantages of these forms of engagement outweigh the negatives.

MULTINATIONAL EXERCISES IN INTERNATIONAL SETTINGS

Since the PLA continues to increase its participation in exercises and operations outside China's borders, this volume also examines the level and depth of interactions between the PLA and the militaries of other nations. Specifically, the 2010 iteration of the *Peace Mission* exercise is the focus of Mr. Daniel Hartnett's chapter. This multilateral military exercise, organized under the auspices of the Shanghai Cooperation Organization (SCO), aimed to test the interoperability of SCO forces as they simulated scenarios modeling how to provide assistance to a member state facing an attack. *Peace Mission 2010* involved a 2-week phased exercise in Kazakhstan in which a simulated terrorist attack was repelled by a force made up of SCO member states, including China, Kazakhstan, Kyrgyzstan, Russia, and Tajikistan. Participating PLA forces included approximately 1,000 troops, mostly from the Beijing MR. These forces were divided into army, air force, and logistics groups accompanied by heavy equipment and vehicles such as tanks, helicopters, and fighter jets. Despite providing an opportunity for the PLA to train with international partners on coordinated air strikes, joint operations, rapid assaults, and nonlinear operations, the exercise's scripted nature, lack of realism, and dearth of coordination among the various national forces detracted from the value of potential lessons learned by the PLA. In addition, the nature of the exercise reflects the SCO's primarily role as a political, not military, institution.

Mr. Chin-Hao Huang's chapter analyzes an important element of the continued development and expansion of the PLA's mission scope, namely, the increased emphasis on MOOTW and nontraditional security threats. This development has led to increased PLA participation in international PKOs and HADR operations in the past decade. In order to improve its MOOTW capabilities, seen as important in ensuring stable domestic and international environments for China's continued development, the PLA has been improving its training methodology, its operational command system, and its integrated support capabilities. While PLA contributions to international PKO and HADR missions to date have consisted of noncombat roles for Chinese troops in areas such as logistics, engineering, and transportation, they have provided a number of benefits for China and the PLA. These include reducing external suspicion and mistrust of China's intentions and the PLA's rapid development, improving the PLA's ability to deal with domestic emergencies and increasing the professionalism and capabilities of PLA troops through real operations and interactions with foreign militaries.

Regarding the implications of these international exercises and operations, Mr. Hartnett emphasizes that, despite *Peace Mission 2010's* shortcomings, the PLA did draw important lessons from transporting troops and equipment over long distances and international borders. In addition, the PLA Air Force (PLAAF) had the opportunity to practice a long-range air strike outside China's borders. These experiences reinforce and contribute to the growing notion of the PLA as an expeditionary force more willing and confident to dispatch its assets overseas. Of most relevance to the United States is the increasing potential for PLA forces to be dispatched in the event of a regional crisis. Mr. Huang notes that the PLA's continued participation in international PKO and HADR provides the United States and its allies with the opportunity to engage the PLA, institutionalize these operations, continue to integrate China into the international system, and emphasize the importance of reciprocity and transparency. Despite concerns that these engagements could lead to an improvement in PLA capabilities, which could then potentially be employed against the United States and its allies, Mr. Huang emphasizes that building trust with the PLA will reduce the potential for misunderstanding and miscalculation and will give the United State a greater understanding of actual PLA capabilities.

SYSTEMS AND STRATEGY REFORM

The volume's final area of focus includes an explanation of recent developments related to PLA systems and strategy. Mr. Abraham Denmark's chapter examines how PLA logistics have been forced to keep up as the demands placed on the PLA have increased in terms of the diversity and geographic scope of its missions. The chapter describes recent advancements in logistics as seen through PLA exercises and foreign and domestic security challenges. The improvement and modernization of PLA logistics have included introducing complex information systems, incorporating market forces, improving civil-military and inter-service logistical integration, enhancing readiness for diverse military roles, and ensuring logistical support for operations conducted in the domains of land, sea, air, space, and electronics. In particular, the integration of civilian capabilities, as well as the modernization of the logistics system, has led to marked improvements in PLA logistics, which are now able to support more extended, mobile, and long-distance deployments both at home and abroad. However, these still-limited capabilities are dependent on a relatively stable external environment, given the PLA's immature power projection capabilities and its lack of external basing. The acquisition of aerial refuelers and replenishment ships, as well as the institution of conceptual frameworks such as "system of systems" and "multidimensional" capabilities, may mitigate the problem, but will not solve it, as PLA assets remain quite vulnerable beyond China's territory.

In terms of China's strategic thinking, Dr. David Lai argues in his chapter that, despite the PLA's internalization of U.S. military concepts such as integrated joint operations (IJO), the PLA continues to adhere to its own unique views on the nature of war, the justification of the use of force, and the ways to conduct war. The "Chinese way of war" is made up of classical Chinese military and political thought, traditional Chinese strategic culture, and Mao Zedong's espoused military principles. Additionally, China abides by the Confucian view that war is a means to restore order both externally and internally, which is especially relevant in terms of China's justification for reclaiming disputed territories: "recovering" what has been taken from it. In deciding when to employ force, the Chinese have developed the concept of "post-emption," meaning that China will not initiate wars but may employ preemptive strikes once a certain threshold has been crossed. Finally, China still references Sun Zi's call to "subjugate the enemy without fighting" through the use of strategy, stratagems, and deception. Thus, the introduction of modern concepts and equipment to the PLA has only amplified the tenets of the "Chinese way of war," while calling into question the applicability of some past concepts such as "People's War."

The main implication of Mr. Denmark's chapter on PLA logistics is that, despite its progress in this area, continued shortcomings and a lack of overseas bases imply that the PLA will be only able to project and sustain power beyond its immediate periphery if its external environment is relatively pacific and accommodating. Dr. Lai's chapter points out that China's military capabilities will continue to develop and be influenced by Western concepts while its core traditions, values, institutions, and unique way of waging war will ensure a certain level of divergence with the United States. This level of divergence with the United States will continue to present challenges, especially in terms of the potential for meaningful engagement between the two nations' militaries.

IMPLICATIONS

Workshop participants set out to examine what developments can be seen from the PLA's domestic and international exercises as well as its noncombat operations. The increasingly expeditionary nature of the PLA was a recurring theme. Whether it be through the PLAN's participation in anti-piracy missions, the PLA ground force's and PLAAF's participation in multinational exercises abroad, PLA participation in MOOTW operations, the development of PLA logistics, or even ground force's transregional domestic exercises, all of these operations and exercises reveal a PLA that is more comfortable with a modest projection of power outside China. In this regard, the "New Historic Missions," in place since at least 2004, are instructive. Recent developments could enable the PLA to conduct more "combat-like" operations in the future, given China's expanding interests and presence, and outside observers must continue to analyze the PLA's intentions and capabilities. The lessons the PLA draws from these simulations and noncombat situations and the ways it translates them into real capabilities bear attention. In particular, observers should closely monitor how the PLA plans to overcome its lack of overseas bases when projecting power abroad. In addition, the assumption that the PLA demonstrates greater reticence in discussing its own shortcomings received a mixed review. Mr. Blasko demonstrates that the PLA is relatively comfortable discussing the challenges it faces as it proceeds on a modernization path. Dr. Cole, on the other hand, describes a PLAN that rarely recounts less-than-successful drills.

Aside from the stand-alone value of these implications, an evaluation of them in conjunction with the implications derived from the 2010 conference on PLA lessons from foreign conflicts adds an entirely new level of analysis and significance to the conclusions of the two events. When put together, the 2010 conference and the 2012 workshop present two views of how the PLA learns without fighting. Within this framework, there is a natural tendency to examine whether the lessons the PLA has learned from foreign conflicts are being implemented in the conduct of its own exercises and noncombat operations. The introduction to the 2010 conference volume noted that drawing a direct line between PLA analyses of foreign conflicts and lessons learned is fraught with analytical gaps, due to the limited information available, and many of the same challenges apply to connecting these lessons with developments in China's military exercises and operations. However, it does not seem unreasonable to conclude that the PLA has applied some lessons from foreign conflicts to its own exercises, even if only to help portray a more realistic "threat" military within the exercise construct.

As an example of the connections that can be drawn, Christopher D. Yung's 2010 chapter on the PLA's study of the Malvinas War notes that there were valuable lessons for the PLA regarding a self-reliant resupply system, expeditionary force projection, foreign base and access facilities, and well-protected supply lines.[4] In this volume, many of these same areas are touched on in the context of recent PLA exercises and operations. Specifically, Admiral McDevitt's chapter analyzes developments in the PLAN's resupply systems, while Mr. Denmark's chapter examines how the PLA is improving its long-distance logistics support capabilities. Additionally, Martin Andrew's 2010 chapter on PLA observations regarding U.S.

counterinsurgency operations in Afghanistan notes a focus on helicopter assault, close air support, and precision strike operations.[5] Subsequently, Mr. Hartnett's chapter in this volume details the PLAAF's unprecedented exercising of its strike capabilities outside China's borders as well as assault exercises involving PLA helicopters in *Peace Mission 2010*. More generally, the 2010 conference volume noted PLA lessons related to command and control, national mobilization, informatization and electronic warfare, and troop readiness, all of which emerge in this new volume in the context of recent PLA exercises and operations. Thus, despite the impossibility of ascertaining the exact level of causality between lessons learned by the PLA and its exercises and operations, some level of correlation appears to exist.

It also appears that experimentation in PLA exercises might have the most salience when it comes to new types of operations. For instance, the technical improvements that shape how the PLA ground forces move within China are in the service of national defense missions that have not changed in 60 years. These improvements reflect enhancements of current abilities to accomplish long-standing missions. However, in the maritime domain, a nascent PLA "far seas" effort is entirely new, and thus calls for studies and exercises that will inform how the new missions will be executed.

A final and inescapable conclusion is that the PLA is modernizing at a rate and scale of its own choosing. The absence of alliance relationships, the existence of a self-restricting policy and posture on the employment of military force overseas, and a still risk-averse strategic culture — in conjunction with a strategic and regional environment in which Chinese territory (if not all of its claimed sovereignty) is not at risk—afford the PLA strategic space in which to modernize in line with Chinese priorities and not in reaction to external pressure. In part, this flexibility is reflected in modernization timelines—fully mechanized (digitized) force by 2020; informatized force by 2050—that speak to a measured, large-scale modernization. Ultimately, the question will remain how Chinese policy options—and their implied decisions about the use of military power—might change as ever-newer capabilities come on line.

ENDNOTES - CHAPTER 1

1. This chapter draws extensively from the 2012 workshop summary, Anton Wishik II, "Colloquium Brief: Learning by Doing: The PLA Trains at Home and Abroad," May 2012.

2. More information about previous years' conferences is available from *www.nbr.org/placonference*.

3. See Andrew Scobell, David Lai, and Roy Kamphausen, *"Introduction,"* in Andrew Scobell, David Lai, and Roy Kamphausen, eds., *Chinese Lessons from Other Peoples' Wars,* Carlisle, PA: Strategic Studies Institute, U.S. Army War College, 2011, p. 3.

4. Christopher D. Yung, "Sinica Rules the Waves? The People's Liberation Army Navy's Power Projection and Anti-Access/ Area Denial Lessons from the Falklands/Malvinas Conflict," Andrew Scobell, David Lai, and Roy Kamphausen, eds., *Chinese Lessons From Other Peoples' Wars,* Carlisle, PA: Strategic Studies Institute, U.S. Army War College, and National Bureau of Asian Research, 2011, pp. 75-114.

5. Martin Andrew, "The Influence of U.S. Counterinsurgency Operations in Afghanistan on the People's Liberation Army," Andrew Scobell, David Lai, and Roy Kamphausen, eds., *Chinese Lessons From Other Peoples' Wars,* Carlisle, PA: Strategic Studies Institute, U.S. Army War College, and National Bureau of Asian Research, 2011, pp. 237-275.

CHAPTER 2

CHINA'S NAVY PREPARES:
DOMESTIC EXERCISES, 2000-10

Bernard D. Cole

This chapter reflects the author's views alone and not those of the National War College nor any other agency of the U.S. Government.

EXECUTIVE SUMMARY

This chapter examines Chinese naval modernization demonstrated during a decade of training ashore and exercising at sea.

MAIN ARGUMENT

During the 10 years between 2000 and 2010, the People's Liberation Army Navy (PLAN) conducted a series of carefully planned exercises designed to advance its capability to execute assigned missions across the spectrum of naval operations. These exercises focused on all the standard naval warfare areas, with a concentration on preparing for informationalized warfare at sea. Many specific exercise objectives were achieved; the end result was a PLAN more capable both of dealing with modern naval operations and of serving its nation as an effective instrument in safeguarding vital security interests.

POLICY IMPLICATIONS

The 10 years of exercises examined for this chapter demonstrate that the PLAN is getting better. This must be a consideration for American policymakers evaluating the use of the navy in supporting national security policies. The United States still has maritime dominance in East Asian waters, but two factors have emerged. First, the PLAN is posing the most serious challenge to the U.S. Navy since 1945; second, maintaining U.S. maritime dominance in East Asia may now require exerting power not just at sea, but also projecting power ashore, against targets on the Asian mainland.

Beijing is modernizing its navy for publicly announced maritime interests vital to its national security; these are most simply stated in the phrase "san hai" or "three seas," denoting the Yellow Sea and the East and South China Seas.

The United States also defines vital national security interests in East Asian waters; first is the requirement for access to those waters, required by both commercial trade and by the need to fulfill the responsibilities of U.S. security treaties with Japan, South Korea, the Philippines, and Australia, as well as lesser commitments to Taiwan, Singapore, and Thailand.

Where these two sets of perceived vital maritime interests coincide or conflict define the points of contention between China and the United States in this century.

INTRODUCTION

Discussion of PLAN modernization typically focuses on hardware—on new ships, submarines, missiles, and airplanes. That emphasis too often overlooks the key factor in naval effectiveness: the people who maintain and operate the hardware. Their capabilities are determined to a significant extent by their education and training, most explicitly demonstrated in the exercises in which they participate.

This chapter addresses that topic: What do we know about, and what has the PLAN learned from, its exercises during the past decade or so? This includes questions about personnel, education, and training; the structure and types of exercises; and, most importantly, the results of those exercises in terms both of immediate accomplishments and long-range implications for PLAN capability and the importance to China's leaders of the Navy as an instrument of national security policy.

That instrument made impressive strides during the decade between 2000 and 2010. Particularly notable is increased PLAN personnel education and professional development, training facilities modernization, and more complex exercise scenarios.

The sources for this survey are primarily Chinese-generated reports of training and exercises, mostly accessed through the Open Source Center. Other reports were either published in English or translated by National Bureau of Research (NBR) Fellows Anton Wishik II and Alan Burns (for whose assistance I am very grateful). I must also acknowledge the continued guidance of my "sea daddy," Lao Gao, as well as expert advice received from Ken Allen, Dennis Blasko, and Ed O'Dowd.

I am aware that my understanding of Chinese naval history, doctrine, and strategy are couched in my experience as a U.S. Navy officer. That said, I think talk of a unique Chinese strategic or doctrinal way of thinking must be approached very cautiously; the commander of a Chinese task group conducting a multimission exercise in the North Arabian Sea during the Southwest Monsoon is confronted with the same problems and the same limited courses of action as those of a U.S. or other foreign commander — it is not chess vs. *wei qi*.

After a brief background discussion, this chapter addresses the PLA's *Outline of Military Training* (OMTE) and *China's National Defense* in 2008 and in 2010 white papers, all authoritative documents. Personnel requirements and professional military education (PME) will then be discussed, followed by a view of training prioritization in the PLAN. The heart of the chapter follows, with naval exercises viewed by warfare area. A brief conclusion sums up the paper's findings.

BACKGROUND

China's Navy in 2011 numbers approximately 290,000 personnel, including the Marine Corps, but not the maritime elements of the People's Armed Police (PAP), reserve forces, militia, or coast guard organizations.[1] Personnel issues are addressed in the PLAN's 10-year plan for "Capable Personnel Development," which aims to foster personnel "for winning sea operations under informatized conditions." Future naval personnel are to be capable in "joint operations command, informatization management, information technology, and the operation and maintenance of new equipment."[2]

Exercise experience is emphasized as a development criterion, as is service in other arms, development of noncommissioned officers (NCOs), and "senior officers involved in foreign military relations who have received training to handle sensitive issues."[3] Addressing the Chinese Communist Party's (CCP) Central Military Commission (CMC) in 1999, then-Chairman Jiang Zemin stated that, "We must [develop] high-quality talented military people." Jiang reemphasized this rather obvious observation in 2001, when he noted that, "though we're unable to develop all high-technology weapons and equipment within a short period of time, we must train qualified personnel first, for we would rather let our qualified personnel wait for equipment than the other way round."

Three seminal documents addressing training have also been issued during the past 5 years. The first two are China's 2008 and 2010 *Defense White Papers*; the third is the *Outline of Military Training and Evaluation* (OMTE), written in 2008 and effective as of January 1, 2009. The PLAN plans its training and exercise year from the OMTE, which is issued by the PLA General Staff Department's (GSD) Military Training and Service Arms Department in Beijing.

The new regulations emphasize standardized training relying on science and technology to prepare for "modern warfare," a general theme that was often repeated in 2008. The 2008 *Defense White Paper* and OMTE both repeatedly emphasize several key concepts and requirements for PLA training and exercising. These are:

- Scientific and high-tech;
- Informatization (or informationization);
- Joint, integrated (sometimes linked);
- Complex, electromagnetic environments;
- Combat-like conditions: "real war;" and,
- Concern for objective evaluations of exercises.

The 2008 white paper also prioritized the creation of "a scientific system for military training in conditions of informationization," a theme repeated in the 2010 white paper.[4]

The Chinese Navy appears to be striving to meet the dictates of these directives in its exercises. Advances in personnel education and training are important ingredients in the success of unit and multi-unit exercises. These efforts were spurred in part by the loss of the crew of the *Ming* class submarine *Hull #361* in 2003, probably due to inadequate training and shoddy equipment maintenance.[5] This accident led to a major leadership turnover in the PLAN, including dismissal of the service's commander and political commissar; the commander and political commissar of the North Sea Fleet, of which *Ming 361* was a unit; and at least eight other senior officers, including the commander of the Lushun Naval Base, who apparently was responsible for the maintenance work performed on the submarine shortly before its loss. The new PLAN commander following the incident, Vice Admiral Zhang Dingfa, was a career submarine officer whose appointment suggested CMC dissatisfaction with accepted navy maintenance and training practices and concern about the operational readiness of China's submarine force.[6]

Assessing current PLAN education, training, and exercise practices indicates that the Navy's leadership has implemented "lessons learned" from the *Ming 361* accident and other experiences that have occurred during the PLAN's post-1990 operations. One step was redefinition of the operational and maintenance responsibilities of the Navy's shore establishment. Discussions with senior PLAN officers indicate that these changes, while not always welcomed by shipboard officers, have regularized, centralized, and most likely improved Navy-wide maintenance, supply, and training processes.[7]

OUTLINE OF MILITARY TRAINING AND EVALUATION

The OMTE is the defining training document, with specific directives for each service and for service elements. It delineates procedures for drafting training plans, organization, and assessment. Seven OMTEs are provided for the PLAN, each addressing a specific class of vessels:

1. Units for each class of naval submarine and surface vessel;

2. Units for each type of naval aviation aircraft, anti-aircraft artillery (AAA), and surface to air missiles (SAM);

3. Naval coastal defense coastal artillery and coastal missile units;

4. Marine Corps;

5. Reconnaissance units and subunits;

6. Observation units and subunits; and,

7. Communications units and subunits.[8]

The current OMTE emphasizes that training must be "scientific," focusing on developing operational proficiency at the tactical level, combined arms tactics, and individual and unit training, before addressing joint training.[9]

The 2009 OMTE represents more continuity than change from the previous training plan, which also emphasized training under "informatized conditions" and a "complex electromagnetic environment," though the current document lays special emphasis on the need to exercise and improve in joint operations. It also demonstrates dissatisfaction with some aspects of the previous exercise regime: in 2007, Vice Chairman of the CMC, General Guo Boxiong, urged "great efforts to uplift the combat effectiveness of the Army under the informationalization conditions," while concern remains about "formalism" in training — criticized in 2006 in the newspaper of the Shenyang Military Region (MR) Political Department — and defined as "a major obstacle," characterized by training and exercises:

- Limited to traditional courses and not acknowledging informationized conditions;
- Conducted only in ordinary conditions;
- Aimed only at passing examinations; and,
- Aimed at special performances along preset plans.

Instead, the article stipulated that training should be "strictly organized" to meet "strict standards, and should be subject to stringent evaluation."[10]

Guo followed in 2008 with a by-then-standard call for training to focus on joint and integrated operations in "complex electromagnetic environments" to "enhance combat capabilities." As an example of this, Exercise Vanguard-2009 was dedicated to advancing joint capabilities. Army units conducted its field phase, but observers were present from the Navy, Air Force, Second Artillery, and PAP. The PLA reportedly described the exercise as the "first time" it engaged in joint operations planning, joint command and control (C2) capabilities, joint intelligence processing, and joint combat decisionmaking under conditions of "informatization."[11] If accurate, this report marks the PLA's ability to operate jointly as being at a surprisingly rudimentary level in light of the fact that joint operability has been a goal of its education-training-exercise paradigm for more than a decade.

The outline's objectives also include the regularization and accurate assessment of training; realistic training in specific operational and tactical tasks, including "various kinds of security threats" and "diverse military tasks"; "basic and integrated training" to incorporate new equipment operation and maintenance; command-and-staff training; military operations other than war (MOOTW); joint training; an increased prevalence of OMTE training objectives in civilian officer candidate education programs; and increased training support.[12]

At the fleet level, these directions are applied to the globally accepted naval warfare mission areas. These are primarily anti-surface warfare (ASUW); anti-submarine warfare (ASW); anti-air warfare (AAW); amphibious warfare (AMW); mine warfare (MIW); command and control, including intelligence, communications, and computers (C4ISR); and information warfare (IW), which includes electronic warfare (EW). Exercising this last warfare area — usually phrased by the PLAN as being able to operate in the electromagnetic spectrum — is one of the most important to the PLAN, appearing as an objective not only in reports of almost every exercise and training evolution, but also in almost every PLA training directive and in speeches by senior Chinese military and civilian leaders.

CHINA'S 2008 DEFENSE WHITE PAPER

China's 2008 *Defense White Paper*, issued in January 2009, addresses the "strategic project for talented people," highlighting the "training of commanding

officers for joint operations and high-level technical experts." In April 2008, the CMC had also issued
"Opinions on Strengthening and Improving the Officers' Training Work of the Armed Forces." Interestingly, this directive addressed linking "institutional
education" with operational training. The repeated
emphasis on preparing to operate under conditions
of information warfare, including a "complicated
electromagnetic environment," and the focus on joint
warfare evince what the PLAN believes are lessons
learned from its observations of recent U.S. operations
and a conviction that the United States is the opponent it is most likely to face. These apparent conclusions are sometimes included under a general training
rubric, such as the 2009 recommendations by officers
of all three PLA services on "drilling on joint operations . . . under informatized conditions."[13]

Navy exercise responsibilities were delineated by
the PLAN's commander, Admiral Wu Shengli, when
he addressed the Navy's Military Training Conference
in January 2008 while the OMTE was no doubt being
constructed, though not yet promulgated. He emphasized the need for reforming the training system, with
closer supervision from above and the need to "promote education and training" in the "three warfares":
public affairs, psychological, and legal. He also noted
the importance of "training exercises in wartime political work." Wu reportedly did not discuss joint or
integrated training, although he did characterize the
PLAN's "training mission for 2008" as "scientific," in
"complex electromagnetic environments," and "realistic to actual war." Wu mentioned this last requirement no less than 10 times, and stated that the "situation is grave." Significantly, he used the phrase "with
an eve-of-battle posture," which is reminiscent of the

U.S. Navy's aphorism during the Cold War that the fleet had to train for a "come-as-you-are" war with the Soviet Union, due to the belief that war at sea would begin with a surprise attack by the Russian Navy.[14]

Most of these same points were highlighted in the PLA General Staff Department (GSD) announcement of new training guidance for 2009. The GSD emphasized the importance of improving joint and integrated training, and improving the performance of command and staff personnel.[15]

PERSONNEL REQUIREMENTS

The PLAN was organized in 1950 with an initial strength of 450,000 personnel, but soon began declining in size, reaching 225,000 in 2001. Numbers since then have increased to approximately 290,000, reflecting the Navy's modernization. The PLAN's manning challenge is not numbers, however, but the education and intellectual capability required of its personnel, who must be able to cope with and benefit from complex training evolutions on equally complex engineering, sensor, and weapons systems.

The PLAN recognizes that the evolution of Chinese military philosophy from Mao Zedong's original concept of manpower-intensive "People's War" to "Revolution in Military Affairs" (RMA) warfare has not reduced the importance of the human element in deploying combat-capable forces. "People's War" remains a mantra.

Increased personnel expertise, in conjunction with technologically advanced systems and effective training, is apparent in the importance attached to "the organic integration of man and weaponry." President Jiang Zemin argued in 2002 that "manpower is a decisive factor in determining the outcome of war." His successor, Hu Jintao, has laid even greater emphasis on the centrality of personnel performance to military effectiveness as part of the Scientific Development concept[16] and expanded on this theme in 2009 on the 82nd anniversary of the founding of the PLA.[17]

Presdient Hu also delivered an important speech at the 2006 PLA training conference urging the acceleration of "innovation and reform in military training" to make it comprehensive, noting that "vigorously and satisfactorily conducting military training is beneficial for advancing comprehensive army building." This commentary on the importance of comprehensive training reinforces the PLAN's apparent lack of U.S. Navy-style "type commanders"—admirals with large staffs dedicated to ensuring that ships and aircraft of a particular class or type are maintained and their personnel trained to meet Navy-wide standards of operational excellence.[18]

PROFESSIONAL MILITARY EDUCATION

The Navy's school structure has passed through four broad phases since it was established in 1950; the most recent began in 1975 when Deng Xiaoping stated that "peacetime education and training should be considered a matter of strategic importance."[19] In addition, the founding of the National Defense University (NDU) in Beijing in 1985 marked the professionalization of military education in China.

The PLA initiated further major changes in the organization and curricula of its educational system in 1998, in the belief that "warfare is changing from a traditional mechanical war to an informationalized one," and that the "key in competing for strategic initiatives in the new century [is] the establishment of a new military educational system."[20] In April 2000, the CMC published the *Essentials for Reform and Development of Military Universities and Schools* to define military education for the 21st century.[21] This plan applies to military schools and to civilian universities participating in officer candidate programs and includes undergraduate degree programs for officer trainees, continuing education in engineering for serving officers, and "reading-for-degree" and postgraduate courses, also for active-duty officers.

The call for transformation has continued, marked, for instance, by a speech by General Guo Boxiong in 2006 and a speech by Genera Xu Caihou in 2010, in which he "called for continued efforts to transform military training based upon mechanized warfare to that based on information warfare," which demanded "strength[ening] training and enhancing [its] leadership."[22]

As for the PLAN, in 1999 Admiral Shi Yunsheng ordered it to build "a new education system" covering combat command tactics, engineering technology, logistics management, political work, and rank and file education. He wanted a "naval commander training system at four levels": technological, tactical, joint tactical, and campaign. Shi's successors, Admirals Zhang Dingfa in 2003 and Wu Shengli in 2009, have continued that theme.[23]

The Navy has participated in the overhaul of PLA service academies during the past decade, including the campaign to ensure that academy education contributes to "strengthening the military through science and technology" and to support the CCP.[24] At midpoint in their careers (as lieutenant commanders or commanders), naval officers are expected to attend the Naval Command School in Nanjing, which concentrates on courses in technical subjects but also addresses naval operations analysis, strategy, and campaign planning—all supported by a wargaming center. This school maintains a "practice base" with the East China Sea Fleet, where students presumably apply their studies in an operational setting.[25]

PLAN officers must satisfy educational requirements in technological, tactical, joint tactical, and campaign categories before taking command; both practical and theoretical examinations are required, including "a wide range of professional knowledge and skills on 34 professional and academic subjects." The campaign to increase commanding officer qualifications—and, by inference, performance—was proclaimed in an extravagant October 2008 claim that "100 percent of frontline captains of the Navy are graduates of specialized academies."[26]

Commanding officers are now subject to new standards laid out in the July 2008 *Guideline of the Chinese People's Liberation Army for the Evaluation of Commanding Officers* and supporting instructions, which evaluate commanders "in accordance with the requirements of scientific development." The Navy has moved to link classroom education and operational exercises to address combat command tactics, engineering technology, logistics management, political work, and enlisted education and training.[27]

Although the emphasis of recent revisions and innovations has focused on officer education, improved enlisted educational opportunities center on technical capability and include officer accession programs. Additionally, the All-Army Propaganda and Cultural Information Network was recently established, using Internet technology to enable centralized education among different bases and units, including standard-ized political education for enlisted personnel.[28] Politi-cal reliability—"the improvement of ideological and political qualities"—is emphasized in the 2010 *Defense White Paper*, which lists it ahead of joint operations, in-formationization, information technology, and NCO training "as the foundation" of increasing the number of "new-type and high-caliber military personnel."[29]

IDEOLOGY AND PROFESSIONALIZATION: POLITICS AT SEA

The emphasis on training military personnel who are both ideologically "sound" and professionally competent becomes a question of allocating training hours; to exaggerate a bit, how many hours each week does a newly commissioned naval officer aboard a *Luzhou* class destroyer spend studying Marxism-Le-ninism-Maoism, and how many hours studying the maintenance and operation requirements of the com-plex radar system for which he is responsible?[30] How-ever, any ideological struggle in the PLA between po-litical reliability ("red") and professional knowledge ("expert") apparently has reached a viable compro-mise: professionally qualified naval officers who are dedicated to both China and its Communist Party.

Training.

Navy enlistments have been shortened from 4 years to 2 years as part of the 1999 *Military Service Law of the People's Republic*. The PLAN, however, still re-quires a 3- or 4-year obligation for recruits who attend a technical training course before or immediately after reporting to their first operational unit, prepared to engage in the full spectrum of individual, work center, crew, and multiship exercises. This policy illustrates the Navy's need for extensive technical training for many of its personnel.[31]

PLAN "boot camp" focuses on physical training and basic military orientation. Enlisted training and education typically occurs aboard the first operational unit or is conducted by a naval base command within one of the three geographic fleets. "Floating schools" exist in such specialties as engineering, medical, surface warfare, aviation, and submarine warfare. Each fleet command has a training directorate with responsibilities that likely include training standardization and prioritization.

Crew training traditionally has occurred almost entirely aboard ship, and while this remains the PLAN's focus, more centralized facilities have been created during the past decade to teach personnel how to operate modern shipboard systems. These new schools/training centers are operated by each fleet to teach engineering, surface warfare, ship handling, aviation operations, submarine warfare, and medical operations in addition to addressing specific equipment systems.[32] However, a centralized training command able to delineate and enforce standards throughout the PLAN appears to be lacking.

The increasing availability of sophisticated shore-based trainers that accurately simulate real-time operational conditions has to some degree reduced required at-sea time. The PLAN is placing emphasis on a realistic shore-based training infrastructure, to include online training.[33] An extensive series of articles in *Jiefangjun Bao* shows concern with combined training and promotes the use of training simulators as a means both to save money and to enhance training, although there seems to be some uncertainty regarding how to go about this.[34]

Operating effectively at sea is physically demanding and requires a substantial amount of actual training at sea, especially for complex, integrated joint operations. PLAN surface ships are spending more time underway each year, and pilots are flying approximately 140 hours per year, substantially more than 10 years ago.

China's 1985 shift in strategic focus to "high-tech wars on the periphery" implied a concomitant shift in PLAN training and exercising. Offshore defense requires training in open-ocean navigation, seamanship, logistics, and operations—especially surveillance, command and control, and multiship training. Coordinated training among subsurface, surface, and aviation units recognizes the increasing role played by technological advances in maritime operations based on automation and integrated operations. Hence, the PLAN has been expanding its exercise infrastructure and regimen to include more multi-unit operational training, although the degree to which the above requirements are actually exercised is not clear.

The PLA explains its training paradigm in a historical context: "Each major mass-scale military training campaign has invariably [been] accompanied . . . by the study of new knowledge [including] studying cultural knowledge in the 1950s and 1960s; studying science in the 1980s; and studying high technology at present. . . . The ongoing mass-scale campaign of military training with science and technology [makes it] . . . imperative to let [soldiers] practice using their equipment."[35] The emphasis on "science and technology" and on "scientific" training continues in numerous exhortations by military and civilian leaders.

One PLAN commander justified "long-distance training in the oceans" when it was still a rare event by stating that "the Navy belongs to the sea. . . . [I]t is necessary to undergo training [on] the oceans, [and] become adapted to a life at sea for long periods of time." However, General Fu Quanyou elaborated on a possible conflict between realistic exercises and budgetary concerns by noting the importance of "simulated training," "on-base training," and "training management," as opposed to training under battlefield conditions.[36]

The PLAN has joined its sister services in emphasizing training to improve logistics performance; exercises have continued to draw on civilian resources as part of the "socialization of logistics," representing current examples of People's War. These include civilian involvement in "advanced scientific-technological" achievements in "military research projects," civilian longshoremen supporting submarine rearming, and civilian vessels and facilities resupplying PLAN units. China's Navy in 2011 appears capable of supporting its operating forces despite the complexity of its disparate platforms and systems. The three fleets include, for example, 16 different destroyer and frigate classes.[37]

Individual ship training is a prerequisite for effective multiship training exercises. Crews of all ships joining the fleet following construction or extensive shipyard periods receive training and certification from their parent fleet's training center before assuming combat duties with the operating forces. A sampling of individual and small-unit training indicates a "building-block" approach, with training progressing in both complexity and scope until a unit is qualified to join fleet-level operations. Such building-block events include training in small-craft maneuvering, sea-lane interdiction, reconnaissance, submarine positioning and navigation, landing ship formation steaming, Marine Corps landing drills, weapons and sensor systems exercises, and aviation unit familiarization with new equipment. This training is conducted by shore-based teaching staff that both train and evaluate operational personnel, including commanding officers.[38]

The PLAN is trying to make its training more realistic. The Nanjing and Guangzhou military regions (MRs), for instance, are credited with conducting "in-depth studies" on joint amphibious operations, with the Navy emphasizing "naval blockade, underwater surprise-defense, and mining of harbor piers," and the Air Force including in its training "low-altitude maritime attack" against ships. Throughout, the concern is to ensure that "training is as close to real combat as possible."[39]

PLAN efforts to modernize training facilities and processes are marked by three characteristics. First, post-exercise analysis is used to evaluate standardized exercises and derive doctrinal and tactical improvements. Second, joint and combined arms operations are emphasized, often with "blue" (i.e., enemy) and "red" forces opposing each other. Third, despite the assertions about the RMA and the importance of injecting "science and technology" into training, the PLAN continues to emphasize the importance of people over machines and technology. In addition, the PLA seems uncertain how best to mix the human element with "the application of science and technology," so that its forces can operate "under informatized conditions."[40]

Various articles emphasize information warfare (IW) and what the U.S. Navy calls "network-centric warfare," but most simply repeat buzzwords without offering realistic links between concept and operational practice. For example:

> The main contents of training . . . are: basic theory, including computer basics and application, communications network technology, the information highway, digitized units and theaters, electronic countermeasures, radar technology, . . . together with . . . IW rules and regulations, IW strategy and tactics, and theater IW and strategic IW; information systems . . . information weapons . . . simulated IW . . . protection of information systems, computer virus attacks and counterattacks, and jamming and counterjamming of communications networks.

Long-range communications are also exercised as part of higher command's directives to ensure that exercises are "informatized."[41]

On a more prosaic level, PLAN training has focused on "multidimensional attacks against targets on the ground from the air and sea," with classroom courses addressing amphibious landings. Technical training has been modified to include logistical and other exercises.

EXERCISES

China's concern about secrecy hinders efforts to identify and analyze PLAN exercises. One source claims that the Navy "successively held as many as 100 large-scale blue-water combined training programs and exercises" between 1979 and 1999.[42] An excellent 1996 study identifies 96 significant (brigade-size or larger) PLA training exercises conducted between January 1990 and November 1995 — about 16 per year. The Navy participated in 36 of these, with half of that number also involving the Army, the Air Force, or both.[43] Of these, 15 are characterized as "combined arms exercises," and 15 involved amphibious training.

These exercises were conducted fairly equally among the three geographic fleets, with the North Sea Fleet conducting 13 and the East Sea and South Sea fleets conducting 10 each. Some of this training probably involved units from more than one of the fleets operating together, but that cannot be confirmed. One interesting facet is that despite appearing to be oriented primarily toward amphibious warfare, the South Sea Fleet engaged in approximately the same number of amphibious training exercises (six) as did the East Sea and North Sea fleets (five each).

The Marine Corps' two brigades are assigned to the South Sea Fleet, as is the PLAN's first large amphibious vessel, the Type 071 landing platform dock (LPD). This indicates that the Marines' primary mission focuses on the land features in the South China Sea, in addition to the presence in the Nanjing and Guangzhou MRs of two Army amphibious infantry divisions and an amphibious armored brigade apparently training to operate against Taiwan. Dedicated amphibious warfare training areas have been established in the East Sea Fleet's area of responsibility (AOR).

The Navy does not appear to have engaged in many complex, joint interfleet exercises. The most sophisticated exercise examined in the 1996 study was conducted in November 1995 on Dongshan Island and coincided with Taiwan's legislative elections. Reportedly, "a ground force element of at least regimental size conducted an amphibious landing supported by perhaps a battalion of amphibious tanks and six or more transport helicopters with assault troops." The exercise included air support by Su-27 and A-5 aircraft, airborne operations, PLAN fire support, and multiple landing beaches, and demonstrated a "viable command and control system." The authors of the study perceptively noted, however, that the exercise was a public relations event that demonstrated the PLA's limitations as well as its capability for conducting joint and combined arms warfare. Nonetheless, large-scale Dongshan exercises were conducted each year from 2000 to 2004.[44]

Analysis of the Dongshan reports indicates that the PLA actually administered a series of discrete exercises, some joint, some not, by units of the three services. These were conducted over periods of several weeks and lacked the continuity and command and control attributes of true joint and integrated operations.

China has on several occasions reported amphibious exercises by division-sized units, but the number of troops actually engaged is not provided; China's amphibious force is believed capable of landing at least one infantry division on a beach, depending on the mix of equipment and stores for immediate resupply. If China were to use its merchant fleet, its capacity to move forces would increase, although inadequate air defense, inexperience in formation steaming, and lack of ability and training in cross-beach movement of forces, would be critical shortcomings.[45]

THE PAST DECADE

President Hu Jintao has continued his predecessor's emphasis on science and technology in military exercises; *Lianhe* (Joint) *2008* was a particularly complex PLAN operation with sea- and shore-based elements.[46] The PLAN's exercise program during the past 15 years evidences an attempt to incorporate the "science and technology" motto into meaningful exercises. The 2008 Navy Military Training Working Conference focused on this problem, touting the development of "analogous" multifunctional training systems for surface and subsurface warfare, to include simulated missile, gun, and torpedo targets that are "increasingly more scientific and closer to the requirements for actual combat."

The PLAN exercise during the past 10 years seems designed to train all three fleets from individual unit drills through complex joint exercises. Militia and reserve forces reportedly are included in some of the exercises, at least once a year.[47] However, the size and capabilities of the "maritime militia" remain difficult to evaluate.

All warfare areas—particularly ASUW, ASW, AAW, AMW, MIW, EW, and submarine—are included in the exercise program, as are logistics, combined arms, navigation, and C4ISR. ASW exercises have been most often reported as evidence of the progress being made in naval warfare proficiency—evidence that seems convincing, in terms both of the technology employed and the personnel performance demonstrated.

Also notable are the exercises focused on incorporating civilian maritime resources into PLAN missions. Other exercise subjects have included base defense, emergency maintenance, medical care, and damage repair by both shore- and sea-based units. The PLAN is emphasizing joint exercises in a multiple-threat environment, operating at greater distances and for longer periods of time at sea, and operating in bad weather and at night.

These attributes were noted in April 2009 when Admiral Wu Shengli summed up the PLAN's exercise program: "In the past decade the People's Navy has organized more than 30 combat operations group campaign exercises at sea. . . . [T]he Navy has focused on comprehensively boosting its overall combat operations capabilities," concentrating on testing new tactics, operating in joint exercises in all warfare areas in "a complex electromagnetic environment," and "training far out at sea," although he did not delineate the distances involved.[48] This number of exercises would mean one major annual exercise for each of the PLAN's three fleets, which is a respectable number.

Recent PLAN activities near Japan indicate its ambitions for developing both operational joint capabilities and geographic reach. Chinese maneuvers in 2010 in Japan's exclusive economic zone (EEZ) were acknowledged by a Japanese analyst to have been in compliance with international law, but were reported in *Jiefangjun Bao* in more strident terms, as "the multiple arm joint formation of the East China Sea Fleet consisting of submarines, destroyers, frigates, comprehensive supply ships, and several ship-based helicopters" carrying out "warship-helicopter cross-day-and-night consecutive confrontation exercise," but also noted that "open-sea training is rare in recent years."[49]

A report of a complex exercise in March 2010 stated that "a joint mobile formation" including ships and aircraft from all three PLAN fleets "embarked on a long-distance training voyage" through the Bo, Yellow, and East and South China Seas, and "the Pacific Ocean." The "confrontations" — presumably the individual exercise events — reportedly involved "over 50 aircraft . . . nearly 60 warships . . . and close to 10 submarines." This undoubtedly was a challenging exercise period and seems to have marked the PLAN's

42

most advanced, effective conduct of the command and control necessary for operating large numbers of fleet units.[50]

WARFARE AREAS

Surface Warfare (ASUW).[51]

Surface warfare is the most basic naval warfare area and a PLAN core competency, but doctrinally takes second place to submarine warfare.[52] Rarely does a surface combatant in any navy exercise train in just one mission area during time at sea. Several factors dictate making the most effective use of underway hours. These include fuel cost and availability, personnel and equipment limitations, limited training services, weather, and the multimission character of most combatants.

Hence, almost all reports of PLAN exercises, or even routine periods at sea, include some mention of seamanship and navigation training. These are valid exercise evolutions, required simply for a ship to unmoor, navigate out of harbor, perhaps conduct flight operations with an embarked helicopter, replenish fuel or supplies while underway, steam in formation with other ships, and communicate with shore stations and other ships. The PLAN's exercises are inherent to more specific warfare mission exercises, such as those focusing on ASUW, AAW, or ASW. Most exercise reports issued by the PLAN concern more glamorous events, such as missile and torpedo firings.[53]

Additionally, certain drills, such as those involving information warfare (IW), electronic warfare (EW), and communications may easily be conducted during night or other "down times," or concurrently with other events that require a greater portion of the ship's crew. Finally, reports of exercises conducted "in rough sea conditions" are not particularly meaningful without knowing the ship type and the actual weather conditions involved; shipboard sensor and weapons systems are designed with movement limitations, and generally speaking, the rougher the weather, the more those personnel and equipment limitations take effect.[54]

Damage Control (DC)—training personnel to control damage and effect repairs to ship and equipment while at sea—is an unglamorous but extremely important exercise area. Again, these drills are easily conducted at night, in port and at sea, where they often occur as part of a wider exercise scenario.[55]

Published exercise reports do not often recount unsuccessful drills; for example, a 2007 report of "land-air-sea" exercises in the Yellow Sea typically contains the key words found in OMTE and the white paper: the exercise was joint, informatized, and "achieved training . . . close to actual combat."[56] No evaluation is provided of the degree of success achieved by exercise participants.

An often overlooked area important to effective exercises is the role of personnel assigned to various training centers to train and evaluate operational units' crews. Since it was founded, the PLAN has focused on establishing effective, objective centers. These are the units that must carry out the frequent calls for ensuring that exercises closely approximate combat conditions and meet the other keyword requirements so frequently found in training directives, a task made more difficult by the lack of a central, authoritative, PLAN training establishment.[57]

A very special mission area for the PLAN is defense of sovereignty claims, focusing on the Yellow,

East, and South China Seas. The concept of "anti-access/area denial," often found in foreign (but not Chinese) reports, means that the PLAN must possess the capability to preclude or at least significantly slow intervention into these seas by foreign naval forces — principally those of the United States.

Chinese analysts and naval officers have written often of ways to defeat U.S. carriers. This concern has influenced several major fleet exercise scenarios during the past decade.[58] The anti-carrier mission, tasked primarily to the PLAN and the Second Artillery, currently focuses on employing submarines and shore-based anti-ship ballistic missiles (ASBMs), essentially an ASUW mission.

While Chinese submarines remain the most effective means of deterring, slowing, and possibly destroying aircraft carriers' effectiveness, Beijing has been striving for the more technologically innovative and challenging ASBM system.[59] China's ASBM, probably a version of the CSS-5 (in NATO terminology) medium-range ballistic missile, would have to be capable of being targeted against a target at sea prior to launch; able to adjust trajectory after reentering the atmosphere to refine its targeting against a moving target; able to differentiate an aircraft carrier from other navy, merchant, and fishing craft; able to overcome electronic and other countermeasures; and actually hit the desired target in a manner sufficient to achieve at least a mission kill. The joint/integrated exercises the PLA will have to conduct to obtain acceptable results for the ASBM — presumably with PLAN participation — have yet to be reported.

Amphibious Warfare (AMW).

No naval operation is more complex than an amphibious assault. Success requires precise timing; closely coordinated operations among surface ships, landing craft, aircraft, and ground troops; and a complex command relationship among officers of at least two different branches or services. The operation is especially complicated when Air Force support and Army troops, rather than Marines, are part of the assault. PLAN amphibious exercises have been a constant in annual training plans, but bounded in number and scope by the limited troop lift deployed by the Navy and the small size of the Marine Corps.[60]

Deploying the PLAN's first large class of amphibious ships, the Type 071 LPDs, shows increased attention to the AMW mission, but also indicates Beijing's determination to participate more actively in humanitarian assistance and disaster relief (HADR) operations. The first of these ships, *Kunlunshan*, has deployed to the Gulf of Aden as a warship conducting anti-piracy missions, but future HADR assignments are likely.

The "main armament" of amphibious ships is the troops that they embark and then land at an objective, via either landing craft or helicopters. China exercises its two Marine Corps brigades and two amphibiously trained Army divisions (approximately 10,000 personnel each) on a regular basis. The most notable amphibious exercises of the past decade were those of the Dongshan series, discussed above.

These have been succeeded by regular, less dramatically designed exercises intended to ensure that the PLA has the ability to land against opposition in the South and East China Seas, where sovereignty dis-

46

putes are present, as well as offering an option in a Taiwan scenario.[61] The largest PLAN exercises, involving units from all three fleets, may include an amphibious phase in addition to other warfare mission areas, as did the PLA's major exercises *Lianhe 2006* and *Lianhe 2008*, conducted in the Yellow Sea.[62]

Anti-Submarine Warfare (ASW) and Submarine Operations.

Amphibious warfare may be the most complex operationally, but no warfare task is more difficult than ASW. This issue is particularly germane when evaluating Chinese naval capabilities, for several reasons. The first is China's remarkable submarine acquisition program during the past 15 years. During that period, the PLAN has added 12 *Kilo* class submarines purchased from Russia, completed its program of building 18 *Ming* class boats, built an inventory of at least 13 *Song* class submarines, and maintained three or four of its old *Han* class nuclear-powered attack (SSN) boats in its operating forces. Ongoing today are construction programs for a new class of SSN, the *Shang* class — two of which have joined the fleet — with a follow-on class (the Type 095) of SSNs apparently on the way; the first class of promising fleet ballistic missile submarines, the *Jin* class, of which two have been completed; and the *Yuan* class, a conventionally powered submarine probably equipped with an Air Independent Propulsion (AIP) cell; eight *Yuan*s are in the water.

Second, the fact that since 2000 China has acquired more than 30 new submarines leads to the conclusion that Beijing has decided that submarines offer the best way to slow or defeat U.S. naval intervention in a Taiwan scenario involving PLAN operations against the island. Third, the conventionally powered submarines acquired by the PLAN are relatively inexpensive.[63] Fourth, the U.S. submarine fleet has declined from 100 to less than 50 boats during the past 20 years; these are more capable than their predecessors, but are stretched thin.

The PLAN devotes significant effort to training and exercising its submarine force. Simulation and shore-based trainers are employed, but the emphasis is on exercising at sea.[64] Available reports of exercises range from methodology, to ensuring safety and objectivity, to counterattacking surface combatants and launching missiles.[65] PLAN submarine bases also seem to have been playing a more prominent role in at-sea training and exercises, as have evaluation efforts, perhaps spurred by the factors leading to the loss of the *Ming 361* crew in 2003.[66]

Chinese ASW exercises during the past several years have demonstrated increased free-play scenarios in deeper water, which requires greater personnel expertise and a willingness to rely more on commanding officers' judgment and initiative. There have also been reported exercises during which officers from the different warfare communities—surface, submarine, and aviation—have exchanged positions, to gain wider experience in naval operations.[67]

ASW exercises have occurred among units from different fleets; others involve helicopter operations, while several reports note an ability to operate in bad weather or at night. These last points must be kept in perspective: naval exercises are not deliberately scheduled to occur during periods of bad weather—which is not defined in available exercise reports (Sea state four? Eight? Visibility 20 miles or 200 yards? Winds 20 knots (kts) or 60 kts?).

The PLAN is serious about ASW and obviously concerned about threats from U.S. and possibly other submarine forces. Significant exercises are conducted several times a year with actual submarine participation and increasingly including aircraft.[68]

Anti-Air Warfare (AAW).

AAW is the third core naval mission, along with ASUW and ASW. It has expanded since the early fixed-wing aircraft days of World War I, when Great Britain deployed the first air-capable warship, to now include coping with cruise and ballistic missiles as well as space-based systems. These latter two changes have altered the character of the military use of the "air," for both offensive and defensive purposes.

Hence, reports of all major PLAN exercises during the past decade have included AAW exercises, ranging from the daily operability tests required for ships' missile systems, to complex exercises involving fixed-wing aircraft from Naval Aviation or the People's Liberation Army Air Force (PLAAF). Earlier AAW exercises by all three fleets emphasized joint defense in coastal waters.[69]

AAW exercises include use of guns and missiles to destroy airborne threats, following their detection and localization. A key capability is area defense: the ability of a ship to defend units other than itself against hostile aircraft and missiles. The Chinese Navy has acquired an area defense capability only in recent years, with its acquisition of *Luyang II* class destroyers. Two of these ships were commissioned in 2004 and 2005, respectively, and at least two more are under construction. They are equipped with a phased array radar that seems to resemble the American Aegis system, which would allow true area defense against air threats to a group of ships.

The other side of the coin for PLAN AAW is the ability to employ its own aviation assets effectively, an ability limited by the Navy's paucity of both fixed- and rotary-wing aircraft. All naval warfare missions profit from the inclusion of air assets; ASUW, ASW, and AAW require them for maximum effectiveness. Joint exercises involving PLAAF assets have occurred, but these are not as important for evaluating Navy capability as are exercises involving its ships' embarked helicopters.

The PLAN deploys approximately 40 helicopters among its approximately 60 air-capable ships (less than 50 of which have hangars); the one aircraft carrier, the ex-*Varyag*, is capable of embarking on some combination of approximately 40 fixed- and rotary-wing aircraft.[70] PLAN advances in helicopter employment have been demonstrated in exercises involving mid-air refueling, sea-air rescue, ASUW, ASW, and support of troops ashore, but the number of rotary-wing aircraft remains extremely low in the Navy, as it does in the PLA generally. Army helicopter participation in maritime exercises has also occurred.[71]

Less frequent are reports of Naval Aviation exercises involving fixed-wing aircraft.[72] This is not surprising, since these aircraft are based ashore and the PLAAF dominates China's military aviation. In fact, there appear to be no reports of Naval Aviation fixed-wing aircraft flying combat air patrol missions in support of surface ships.

PLAN interaction with space-based assets, both its own and those of others, particularly the United States, has rarely been reported as part of an AAW exercise. The Chinese Navy depends on these assets for communications, navigation, and intelligence, as is to be expected of a modernizing force. Admiral Wu Shengli reportedly demanded "comprehensive coverage, all-time linkage, and full-course support" from space-based systems for the ships deploying to the Gulf of Aden.[73]

Command, Control, and Coordination (CCC).

No words may appear more frequently in statements by China's civilian and military leaders' discussions of training and exercises than informatization and informationization. Either formally or informally, they are part of every PLAN exercise. The Navy is determined to take advantage of state-of-the-art information operations (IO)—the naval mission summarized by C4ISR, the acronym for Command, Control, Communications, Computers, Intelligence, Surveillance and Reconnaissance. IO is simply a modern version of the basis for any successful naval operation: knowing where I am, where the opponent is, and how to kill him before he kills me.

Effective IO underlays single-ship, joint, integrated, comprehensive, and combined operations. A 2008 exercise by an East Sea Fleet "destroyer flotilla" involved electronic warfare (EW) exercises, with participation by submarine, aviation, and shore-based communications units. It appears to have embodied all of the words used above, but at an IO minimum, required effective communications among the participants.[74] The PLAN is aware of the U.S. Navy's concept of net-centric warfare, which was developed in the early 1990s and has been exercised in its application since at least 2003.[75]

CONCLUSION

There is much we still need to know about the conduct and efficacy of PLAN exercises. In 2005, Blasko noted that "for at least the past 4 or 5 years, PLA exercises have become more complex, longer in duration, and expanded to more units than in the 1990s."[76] He was addressing primarily Army exercises, but research indicates that the Navy has shared in the PLA's intensifying exercise complexity, length, and multiunit participation—a paradigm that has continued during the past half-decade.

That pattern continued during 2011. In January, one U.S. analyst predicted a continuation of the themes discussed above, and delineated in both the 2008 and 2010 *Defense White Papers* as well as in the 2009 OMTE.[77] That analysis has been borne out by observed PLAN exercises, although an increase in MOOTW has also been demonstrated by the Navy's new hospital ship, which conducted its first mission in northeast China before deploying to the Indian Ocean in 2011 and to the Caribbean in early-2012.

The PLAN serves a nation with a rapidly expanding economy and an increasingly well-educated population. The provides a pool of better-educated and intellectually more-qualified personnel from which officers and enlisted personnel may be drawn for a Navy that is increasingly dependent on sophisticated technology. The situation also has negative aspects, however, given the reduced motivation for young men and women to elect naval service rather than entry into the booming economy.

Once in the PLAN, personnel are subject to an apparently logical, progressive structure of education and training. The education-training-exercise system established by the Chinese Navy is coherent on paper, but hampered by the short service term of recruits, the relatively decentralized administration of training, and the dynamism of the developing operational PLAN. Furthermore, though the priority assigned ideological training in the Navy is unclear, it certainly affects professional development.[78]

An undertone of dissatisfaction is apparent in the PLAN's public announcements reporting training and exercises, including frequent admonitions to educate, train, and exercise in accordance with the dictates of high technology and modern methods. The account by two senior captains who served as on-scene observers of one of the U.S. Navy's most advanced complex exercises, RIMPAC 98, remains significant: these officers were unable to restrain their enthusiasm for the operational expertise they witnessed, especially as applied to equipment and systems such as advanced automation, information-processing technology, and night-vision systems.

The officers particularly emphasized the "rigorous and regular personnel training"; the ability to operate at sea for extended periods; "whole-staff, whole-system, whole-function, and whole-course training"; the ability of equipment to operate continuously for long periods; personnel and equipment safety awareness and programs; frequent and continuing personnel education and training; systematic equipment maintenance procedures and practices; delegation of responsibility to lower-ranking officers and enlisted personnel; and shipboard cleanliness. Perhaps most telling was the officers' emphasis on having witnessed the consistency of "specific efforts in a down-to-earth manner instead of shouting empty slogans." PLA representatives also observed the U.S.-led *Valiant Shield* exercise, conducted in waters near Guam in June

2006, but a similarly enthusiastic report has not been published.[79]

Open-source reports during the past decade illustrate substantial progress in becoming a modern navy. PLAN training and exercises highlight joint training, MOOTW exercises, integrating civilian support into military operations, training according to doctrine, and perhaps most important, training under "real-war" conditions.[80]

The performance of China's naval task groups operating in the Gulf of Aden since December 2008 is the clearest demonstration of the PLAN's strides in becoming an effective 21st-century force. Significant self-awareness exists; naval officers grade their service and personnel relatively harshly both in person and in press reports. This may in turn impart a degree of caution on the part of Beijing in employing the Navy in pursuit of national security goals.[81] One PLAN "lesson learned" from the U.S. Navy is indicated in a 2009 description of junior officer ship-handling training—emphasizing decisiveness and professional knowledge—that could have been written by the commanding officer of a U.S. destroyer.[82]

China is also using naval exercises to send political signals in addition to those inherent in exercising the naval mission of "presence." Two recent examples occurred in June and July 2011. The first took place shortly after the incidents in the South China Sea between Chinese and U.S. vessels, when nominally civilian-manned boats interfered with a U.S. hydrographic survey vessel, and PLAN exercises were then conducted in those same waters. The second was a PLAN live-fire exercise in the northern waters of the East China Sea, shortly after plans were announced for U.S.-South Korean naval exercises in response to the North Korean provocations that spring.[83]

Strong implications for future exercise scenarios may be seen in a speech by Admiral Wu Shengli in 2009, when he noted that "transformation building" would create a navy able to deal with "multiple security threats [while] accomplishing diversified military tasks." Significantly, he stated that these would include tasks beyond China's "territorial integrity [such as] maritime rights and development interests" and would include "the ability to go deep into the ocean." He also said the PLAN would "incorporate the capacity for nonwar military actions to the integrated construction of the Army's power, especially emergency offshore search and rescue and anti-terrorism activities."[84]

This delineates an ambitious program. The PLAN's training and exercise program during the past decade has increased in complexity and sophistication. An evaluation program is in place, but the high command is not happy. This is evidenced in at least two relatively public ways. The first is ideological uncertainty, reflected in the constant stream of admonitions to the Navy and the other services by civilian and military leaders about loyalty to "the party." The second is obvious concern about substandard performance demonstrated in exercises and, the command apparently fears, in the case of potential conflicts. Official statements carry a stream of concern for the objective evaluation of exercises and exhortations to units throughout the PLAN to embrace informatization, science and high technology, joint and integrated operations, complex electromagnetic environments, and combat-like conditions ("real war").

The repeated emphasis in PLAN training and exercises on IW, including EW, leads to two conclusions. First, that proficiency in IW/EW is considered vital to effective naval operations, and second, that this is seen as a U.S. naval vulnerability and a weakness to be attacked. Despite the concerns expressed by Chinese officers and officials in the public documents that constituted the bulk of research for this chapter, the PLAN's exercises clearly indicate progress in professionalism and the ability to perform operationally in all the standard naval warfare areas. The PLAN is getting better.

This should be a factor for American policymakers considering the use of the Navy in supporting national security policies. The United States dominates East Asian waters, but two factors have emerged. First, the PLAN is posing the most serious challenge to the U.S. Navy since 1945; second, maintaining U.S. maritime dominance in East Asia may now require exerting power not just at sea, but also projecting power ashore, against targets on the Asian mainland.

China's emerging maritime power requires reconsideration by American policymakers of when and how to employ the Navy. Beijing has delineated maritime interests vital to its national security; these are most simply stated in the phrase "san hai" or "three seas," denoting the Yellow Sea, and the East and South China Seas. The United States also defines vital national security interests in East Asian waters; first is the requirement for access to those waters, required by both commercial trade and by the need to fulfill the responsibilities of U.S. security treaties with Japan, South Korea, the Philippines, and Australia, as well as lesser commitments to Taiwan, Singapore, and Thailand. Where these two sets of perceived vital maritime interests coincide or conflict may well define the most dangerous points of diplomatic and naval conflict between China and the United States in this century.

ENDNOTES - CHAPTER 2

1. The 2010 *Defense White Paper*, p. 2 ff., addresses reserve and militia forces. The most authoritative personnel figure is the 290,000 in *The People's Liberation Army Navy*, Washington, DC: Office of Naval Intelligence, 2007, p. 32. The U.S. Navy, by comparison, in January 2011, numbered 328,516 uniformed and 199,000 civilian personnel, as well as 101,689 reserves. The PLA also maintains "up to another 15 ship groups," likely small landing craft. See Dennis J. Blasko, "PLA Amphibious Capabilities: Structured for Deterrence," *China Brief*, Vol. 10, Issue 17, Jamestown Foundation, August 19, 2010, available from *www.jamestown.org/programs/chinabrief/single/tx_ttnews[tt_news]=36770&tx_ttnews[backPid]=25&cHash=5c40a5009d*. Also worth noting that the PLAN is an overwhelmingly male-dominated organization; a great reserve of human capital is yet untapped by Beijing.

2. It is useful to note that "joint" in the PLA refers to two or more of the four services—Army, Air Force, Navy, and Second Artillery—operating together, while "combined arms" refers to two or more of a single service's branches operating together. The PLAN, for example, has five branches: surface, subsurface, aviation, coastal defense, and Marine Corps. Coastal defense is shared with PLA coastal defense units, however, and with personnel and weapons—principally, anti-air and anti-surface missile batteries—manned at specific points along China's long coast. See James C. Bussert, "China Taps Many Resources for Coastal Defense," *Signal*, Vol. 56, No. 11, November 2002, available from *www.afcea.org/signal/articles/templates/SIGNAL_Article_Template.asp?articleid=311&zoneid=30*, which offers a general description of China's coastal defense organization. More specific information is provided in Dennis J. Blasko, "PLA Ground Force Modernization and Mission Diversification: Underway in All Military Regions," Roy Kamphausen and Andrew Scobell, eds., *Right Sizing the People's Liberation Army: Exploring the Contours of China's Military*, Carlisle, PA: Strategic Studies Institute, U.S. Army War College, 2006); also see "Coastal Defense/Counter-terror Exercise by PLA, Police, Militia, and Reserves," *Xinhua*, September 22, 2002, available from *www.highbeam.com/doc/1P2-13323874.htm*, which reports a related exercise. A similar drill is reported in Zhang Shengzhong

and Zhou Yawen, "The Return of the Naval Infantry,"*PLA Daily*, February 10, 2009, available from *www.worldaffairsboard.com/rise-china/49652-return-pla-naval-infantry.html*. Jointness remains one of the most often mentioned goals in the 2010 *Defense White Paper*.

3. Described in "PLA Navy Publishes Capable Personnel Development Plan Outline for Period Up to 2020," *People's Navy*, July 5, 2011, in "China: PLA Activities Report August 1-15, 2011, Item 9," in OSC-CPP20110815563001.

4. Jiang is quoted in "Opening Up New Prospects for Ideological, Political Building of China's Military Academies," *Jiefangjun Bao*, May 23, 2000, in Foreign Broadcast Information Service (FBIS)-CPP20000523000043 and in "Jiang Zemin's Book on Technology, Army Building Viewed," *Yangcheng Wanbao* (Guangzhou) February 13, 2001, in CPP20010221000077; the 2008 *Defense White Paper* (quote is from Sec. III) is available from *news.xinhuanet.com/english/2009-01/20/content_10688124_4.htm*; the 2010 edition is available from *news.xinhuanet.com/english2010/china/2011-03/31/c_13806851_12.htm*. I am indebted to Kenneth Allen and Dennis J. Blasko for several documents dealing with the OMTE, including OSC-FEA20080909767592 "Analysis: Revised PRC Military Training Guidance Codifies Joint Operations," September 8, 2008, which lists 30 articles in the Chinese press that concern the OMTE. OMTEs have been promulgated in 1957, 1978, 1980, 1989, and 1995, in addition to those of 2001 and 2008. Blasko also noted that Jiang's admonition was consistent with the Strategic Project for Talented People, initiated in 2003 and explained in China's 2004 *Defense White Paper*, with goals out to 2020.

5. The normal *Ming* crew is 55; hull number 361 apparently embarked its squadron commander and staff, as well as some cadets from the Naval Academy at Dalian. "Mechanical malfunction" was the official Chinese explanation for the accident; the submarine was semi-submerged when found, indicating that the accident probably involved a failure in ventilation and safety systems that resulted in the absence of internal oxygen when the submarine's diesel engine was started, killing all onboard. See William Foreman, "Chinese Submarine Accident Kills 70," Associated Press report available from *www.dcfp.navy.mil/mc/articles/other/MingSub.htm*; author's interviews with U.S. submarine officers.

6. Two of the many accounts of this personnel upheaval are Ray Cheung, "Leaders Are Replaced in Naval Shakeup," *South China Morning Post*, Hong Kong, June 13, 2003, passed to me by Cheung; "CMC Appoints New PLA Navy Commander, Political Commissar," *Xinhua*, June 12, 2003, in OSC-CPP20030612000174.

7. Author's interviews with senior (0-6 and higher) PLAN officers between 1998 and 2009. Also see Zhang Weiran, "PLA Becomes Smaller in Size but Stronger in Battle Effectiveness," *China Military Online*, September 2, 2009, available from *eng.chinamil.com.cn/news-channels/china-military-news/2009-09/02/content_4032392.htm*.

8. Zhang Xushan, ed., *Navy Dictionary*, Shanghai: Shanghai Dictionary Publishing House, October 1993, cited by Kenneth W. Allen; "Military Training Guidance Thought," paper provided to the author, August 2011. In the PLA, units (*budui*) include corps, division, brigade, and regiment organizations. Subunits (*fendui*) which are also called grassroots (*jiceng*) organizations, include battalion, company, and platoon organizations.

9. Information provided by Frederic Vellucci, restatement on "Recent Trends in PLA Navy Training and Education," Testimony before the U.S.-China Economic and Security Review Commission, Washington, DC, June 11, 2009, available from *www.uscc.gov/hearings/2009hearings/transcripts/09_06_11_trans/09_06_11_trans.pdf#x*. This OMTE was promulgated in July 2008; see "New Outline of Military Training and Evaluation Promulgated," *PLA Daily*, July 25, 2008, available from *english.chinamil.com.cn/site2/news channels/2008/07/25/content_1379311.htm*. Military operations other than war (MOOTW) are also featured, an element of direct concern to the PLAN in view of China's relative inability in the past to respond to foreign disasters such as the 2006 tsunami that struck Southeast Asia. Construction of the Type 071 landing platform dock (LPD) provides the PLAN with a capable platform for such missions. Also see the 2010 *Defense White Paper*, p. 13.

10. Cited in "Shenyang MR Commentator Urges Units to Train to Strict Standards," *Shenyang Qianjin Bao*, September 18, 2006, p. 1, in OSC-CPP20061025318007, September 18, 2006, p. 1 (Note: daily newspaper published by the political department of the Shenyang MR). Guo is cited in Wang Xibin, "Guo Boxiong

Urges Stepping Up Transformation of Military Training," *Jief-angjun Bao*, January 18, 2007, available from *english.chinamil.com. cn/site2/militarydatabase/2007-01/19/content_710755.htm.*

11. Guo is quoted in Ding Haiming, "When Meeting With the Representative to the PLA Military Training and Appraisal Outline Session," *Jiefangjun Bao*, July 30, 2008, p. 1, in OSC-CPP20080730710004. Also see "PLA Field Tests New Joint Operations Unit at 2009 Exercise," OSC-FEA20091116975239, November 13, 2009. Also see the 2010 *Defense White Paper*, p. 25.

12. The 2010 *Defense White Paper* is especially rich in addressing these nontraditional military missions. Also see "GSH Arranges PLA's Military Training Work in 2009," *english.chinamil. com.cn*, January 7, 2009, available from *english.chinamil.com.cn/ site2/news-channels/2009-01/07/content_1610805.htm.* The author is indebted to Dennis J. Blasko for this translation of the GSD directives. Also see Wu Dilun and Liu Feng'an, "Highlights of Military Training in First Half of 2009," *PLA Daily*, July 9, 2009, available from *eng.mod.gov.cn/DefenseNews/2009-07/09content_4002936.* An unusual program in the Nanjing MR required East Sea Fleet "commanders of services and branches" to exchange with Army officers in the MR. See "East Sea Fleet/Nanjing MR Command Exchange," *People's Daily*, April 19, 2002.

13. Qin Jun, "Provisions Officers' of the Three Services Acquire Masterly Skills through Online Joint Training," *Jiefangjun Bao*, March 30, 2009, in OSC-CPP20090410088001.

14. Xu Xinlei, "Wu Shengli, Hu Yanlin Attend Navy Conference on Year's Military Training, Deliver Important Speeches," *Renmin Haijun*, Beijing, January 22, 2008, p. 1, in OSC-CPP20080314318003, January 23, 2008. I am indebted to David Chen for drawing my attention to this report. I think Wu's statement that "the situation is grave" more likely referred to his perception of the state of training in the PLAN rather than to the proximity of war breaking out.

15. Wu Dilun, "The GSD of the PLA Makes Overall Plans for 2008 Military Training," *Jiefangjun Bao*, 20 January 2008, in OSC-CPP20080121708005, January 21, 2008, p. 1.

16. Jiang is quoted in Fu Quanyu, "Vigorously Conduct Military Training of Science and Technology to Strengthen Great Wall of Steel," *Quishi*, Beijing, China, August 1, 1999, pp. 12–17, in FBIS-CHI-99-0902, p. 4; for Hu Jintao on this subject, see James Mulvenon, "Hu Jintao and the 'Core Values of Military Personnel,'" *China Leadership Monitor*, No. 28, Spring 2009, Hoover Institution, available from *www.hoover.org/publications/clm/issues/44612967.html*. For an operational note, see He Yu and Si Yanwen, "A Navy Destroyer Flotilla Realizes Information Interconnections in Offshore Maneuver," *Jiefangjun Bao*, December 17, 2003, in FBIS-CPP20031218000081.

17. "China Reports High Employment for College Graduates," *Xinhua*, April 13, 2000, in FBIS-CPP20000413000172, states that "university graduates are in great demand" and that "postgraduates and students from well-known universities are being actively pursued by employers," according to the Ministry of Education in Beijing. More than 90 percent employment for 2006 college graduates is reported in Cao Yangxia, *Private Higher Education and the Labor Market in China*, Boca Raton, FL: Universal Publishers, 2008, p. 130; a rate of 89 percent is given for 2010 in "Employment Rate for Chinese College Graduates Improving: Survey," *Xinhua* , June 9, 2011, available from *English.news.cn*.

18. Quoted in editorial on PLA Training Conference, *Jiefangjun Bao*, July 1, 2006, p. 3, in OSC-CPP20060629702003. I have seen no evidence that the post-2003 reorganization of various administrative functions in the PLAN included instituting a system of type commanders.

19. Quoted in Mulvenon, *Professionalization of the Senior Chinese Officer Corps: Trends and Implications*, Santa Monica, CA: RAND, 1997, p. 11.

20. "Unify Our Ideas and Actions With Central Commission's Policy Decisions," *Jiefangjun Bao*, June 21, 1999, p. 1, in FBIS-CHI-99-0628.

21. "Basic Military Project for Development in the New Century," editorial in *Jiefangjun Bao*, April 15, 2000, p. 1, in FBIS-CPP20000417000056.

22. Cited in "Senior Chinese Commander Calls for Intensified Military Training," *Xinhua*, August 16, 2010, available from *news. xinhuanet.com/english2010/china/2010-08/17/c_13447805.htm.*

23. Huang Caihong, Chen Wanjun, and Zhang Zhao, "The PLA Navy Has Enhanced Comprehensive Combat Effectiveness," *Xinhua*, April 19, 1999, in FBIS-CHI-99-0423, quotes Shi; Wu is quoted in the *Beijing Review*, May 4, 2009; *China's Navy, 2007* discusses the long trend in educational improvements for PLAN personnel.

24. Quoted in "Put Military Academy Education in a Strategic Position of Priority Development," *Jiefangjun Bao*, June 23, 1999, p. 1, in FBIS-CHI-99-0629.

25. Author's discussions with senior PLAN officers, 1994-2008.

26. Kondapalli, "China's Naval Training Program," 1338, lists these as "microelectronics, PERT [?], CPM [?], navigation, dynamics, telemetering and remote control, and aviation and astro-navigation; "30 Years of PLA's Development, 1978–2008," CCTV-7, October 2008, p. 4, available from OSC-FEA20081215800637.

27. *Defense White Paper*, 2008, sec. III; *Defense White Paper*, 2010, p. 19; Chen Yeong-kang, paper on the PLAN submarine force presented at the April 2000 CNA Conference on the PLAN; also see *China's Navy, 2007*, p. 63, Fig. 19: "Rank and Grade Promotion Cycle." Numbers herein are based on the author's conversations with senior PLA and Taiwan Navy officers and with PLAN commanding officers aboard their ships from 1994 to 2008, with the PLAAF's 24th Air Division chief of staff in 1997 and 9th Air Division commander in 2000; one senior PLAN officer said that a submarine commander may serve in his billet for 6 years but operate at sea for only about 300 days during that period. Also see Xhi Xingchun and Qin Ruoyun, "Aiming Straight at the Future Battlefield at Sea," *Renmin Haijun*, November 12, 2011, p. 3, in OSC-CPP20110125478007. The 2002-2011 deployments to the Gulf of Aden attest to the PLAN's increased operational readiness and, by inference, to the effectiveness of its exercise program.

28. *China's Navy, 2007*, p. 82. Also see "PRC's Yu Yongbo Reviews Military Propaganda Network," *Xinhua*, December 26,

1999, in FBIS-FTS20000120000818; and "PLA Information Network Begins Operations," *Xinhua*, December 28, 1999, in FBIS-FTS19991228000766.

29. "Implementing the Strategic Project for Talented Individuals."

30. "The People's Navy," p. 41, reports an ideological extreme in a 1958 report that the East China Sea Fleet commander "respond[ed] to a call by the CPC Central Committee and the CMC to undergo training as a sailor on Ship 311 [and] wears a sailor uniform with a private's insignia." Bullard, *China's Political-Military Evolution*, p. 27, estimates that at the height of the Cultural Revolution, 70 percent of a soldier's time was devoted to nonmilitary activities; by 1984, 70 percent was devoted to military duties. See Heaton, "Professional Military Education in the People's Republic of China," p. 125, for a description of the ideological character of the PLA as either "Maoist" or "Dengist": Mao stressed the importance of men over machines and held up the PLA as the socialist model that embodied his thought; Deng's concept was described in 1979 by Defense Minister Xu Xiangqian as stressing the importance of expertise and "expert" taking precedence over "red." Despite the consistent exhortations about the PLA being a "Party Army," there is little reason to assume that a zero-sum situation pertains between political indoctrination and technical training. That is, as voiced by Ellis Joffe, there is no reason why a military force cannot be both ideologically reliable and professionally competent.

31. Su Ruozhou, "Major Reform in Our Army's Service System," *Jiefangjun Bao*, July 13, 1999, p. 2, in FBIS-CHI-99-0811, discusses the 2-year requirement; author's discussion with senior PLA officers about longer PLAN enlistments. Technical training schools vary in length, but a recruit may spend an additional 3 to 6 months in school after completing 3 months of "boot camp." By comparison, a technician in the U.S. Navy may spend as many as 24 months in schools before reporting to his/her first ship — after agreeing to extend his/her enlistment from 4 to 6 years. Furthermore, the USN trains sailors to both maintain and operate a system, while most other navies train their sailors to do one or the other. Based on the author's conversations with its officers, the PLAN follows the latter model. Also see Blasko, "New PLA Force

Structure," in James C. Mulvenon and Richard H. Yang, eds., *The People's Liberation Army in the Information Age,* Santa Monica, CA: RAND, 1999, p. 24.

32. Author's discussions with senior PLA officers between 1994 and 2006. *China's Navy, 2007,* p. 90, notes that each of China's three fleets has a training center. Also see Jiang Minjun and Si Yanwen, "A Certain Destroyer Flotilla Designates 'Training Ships; to Train Crew[s]'," *Jiefangjun Bao,* June 14, 2002, p. 2, in FBIS-CPP20020614000045. Particularly useful is Mulvenon, "True Is False, False Is True: Virtual Is Reality, Reality Is Virtual: Technology and Simulation in the Chinese Military Training Revolution," Roy Kamphausen, Andrew Scobell, and Travis Tanner, eds., *The "People" in the PLA: Recruitment Training, and Education in China's Military,* Carlisle, PA: Strategic Studies Institute, U.S. Army War College, 2008. Individual reports include "China's New-Type Submarine Simulator Passes Expert Appraisal," *People's Daily Online,* March 15, 2004, available from *english.peopledaily.com.cn/200403/15/eng20040315_137548.shtml*; and "ESF Warship Training Center Expands Warship Training Capacity," *Jiefangjun Bao,* July 21, 2007, in OSC.

33. Visits by the author and other U.S. observers, 1990–2008, to PLAN training facilities in Dalian, Qingdao, Shanghai, and Guangzhou; and to PLA training facilities in Beijing, NDU, Armored Engineering College, and Air Force Command College, Dalian, Shenyang MR Military Academy, Xi'an, PLAAF Engineering College, and Nanjing, PLA Staff and Command College, showed computerized training facilities that are improving but seemed still analogous to U.S. Navy facilities c. 1990. Online training is addressed in "East Sea Fleet Base Conducts Internal Joint Operations to Enhance On-line Military Training," *Jiefangjun Bao,* August 5, 2004, available from *www.pladailycom.cn/gb/pladaily/2004/08/05/20040805001002.html* and "PLA Navy Base Conducts Joint Exercise With NDU," *Jiefangjun Bao,* August 5, 2004, available from *www.pladaily/com/cn/gb/pladaily/2004/08/05/20040805001023.html*.

34. See, for instance, three *Jiefangjun Bao* articles: Zhang Guoyu and Wang Boming, "Carry Out Scientific and Technological Training and Create Brilliant Historic Achievements," January 19, 1999, p. 6, in FBIS-FTS19990208000125; Li Jianyin, "On Wel-

coming the Cross-Century Military Training Revolution," January 26, 1999, p. 6, in FBIS-FTS19990209000171; and Gao Jianguo, "Change the Pattern of Personnel Training," January 26, 1999, p. 6, in FBIS-FTS19990208000103.

35. Tang Liehui, "Work Hard to Explore Optimal Solution to Man-Weapon Integration," *Jiefangjun Bao*, June 15, 1999, p. 6, in FBIS-CHI-99-0711; author's discussions with senior PLAN officers.

36. Admiral Zhang Lianzhong, quoted in "Navy Chief on Technical, Tactical Upgrading," Beijing Domestic Service, May 5, 1988, in FBIS-CHI-88-090; Fu is quoted in Mao Xiaochun and Chen Hui, "Chief of Staff Fu Quanyou on High-Tech Military Training," *Xinhua*, October 16, 1999, in FBIS-CHI-99-1016.

37. The best current work on PLA logistics is that of Susan Puska, "Taming the Hydra: Trends in China's Military Logistics since 2000;" paper presented at the NBR, U.S. Army War College, and Texas A&M University Conference on "The PLA at Home and Abroad" at Carlisle Barracks, PA, September 25-27, 2009." Specific examples of logistics efficiency are indicated in Wu Ruhui, Jin Zhifeng, and Chen Bingfeng, "Navy's 'Military Representatives' Hard at Work in Supervising Armament Development," *Jiefangjun Bao*, April 10, 2002, p. 10, in FBIS-CHI-2002-0410; Liu Xinmin and Xu Feng, "Chinese Submarine Unit Succeeds for First Time in Making Use of Civilian Port to Load Torpedoes," *Zhongguo Qingnian Bao*, Beijing, June 1, 2002, in: FBIS-CPP20020603000058; "Comprehensive Support Formation of the PLA Navy Service Ship Group Successfully Conducts Non-contact Supply Operation to Submarine," *People's Daily*, June 21, 2003, available from *www.peopledaily.com.cn/GB/junshi/1079/1927053.html*; "PLA Fujian Military District to Conduct Maritime Logistic Replenishment Drill," *Wenweipo News*, Hong Kong, July 23, 2004, available from *www.allacademic.com/meta/p_mla_apa_research_citation/0/7/1/2/1/pages71219/p71219-45.php*; Zhou Yongwei, "Naval Aviation Unit Reforms Support Pattern," *Jiefangjun Bao*, February 13, 2004, in FBIS-CPP20040218000093; "Chinese Local Oil Tanker Replenishes Oil for PLA Navy South Sea Fleet Destroyer," *Military China*, July 11, 2006; "PLA Navy Stages Military-Civilian Integrated Ordnance Support Exercises in Ningbo," *Renmin Tupian Wang*, October 23, 2006; "PLA Navy NSF Repair Battalion Commander

Pursues Submarine Repair," *Jiefangjun Bao,* August 9, 2007. Copies of photographs provided to the author by Dr. Lyle Goldstein, the U.S. Naval War College's China Maritime Studies Institute: "DDG168 Conducting Helo and UNREP," 2009, demonstrate the PLAN's state-of-the-art capabilities in replenishment at sea.

38. Author's conversations with senior PLA officers. Xu Sen "Building a Modern Naval Battlefield," *Jiefangjun Bao,* September 15, 1999, p. 6, in FBIS-CHI-99-0923, describes the North Sea Fleet training center and compares it to similar centers built by the United States, France, Great Britain, and others. Crews are trained in navigation and ship handling, weapons systems, and electronic warfare.

39. Ren Yanjun, "Entire Army Bears in Mind Sacred Mission, Makes Ample Preparations for Military Struggle," *Jiefangjun Bao,* April 12, 2000, p. 1, in FBIS-CPP20000412000032, describes "the army as a whole . . . successively [sending] tens of divisions and brigades into training bases to conduct exercises under simulated and virtual battleground environments with real personnel, real vehicles, real bullets and real explosives to train for actual combat capabilities."

40. In 1999 one of the Deputy Directors of the GSD's Military Training Department described five features of this RMA: 1) changing the components of the armed forces, especially in the campaign formation between different services; 2) introducing new combat means; 3) generating much larger combat space; 4) creating new modes of operations; and, 5) inventing new methods of combat engagement. Major General Chen Youyuan, quoted in You Ji, "The Revolution in Military Affairs and the Evolution of China's Strategic Thinking," *Contemporary Southeast Asia,* Vol. 21, No. 3, 1999, p. 350.

41. The PLAN's concerns with net-centric warfare are discussed in Andrew S. Erickson, "PLA Navy Modernization: Preparing for 'Informatized' War at Sea," *China Brief,* Vol. 8, No. 5, February 29, 2008, available from *www.jamestown.org/programs/chinabrief/single/?tx_ttnews%5Btt_news%5D=4759&tx_ttnews%5BbackPid%5D=168&no_cache=1;* also see Zhang Zhenzhong and Chang Jianguo, "Train Talented People at Different Levels for Information Warfare," *Jiefangjun Bao,* February 2, 1999,

p. 6, in FBIS-FTS19990210001865. Michael Pillsbury, *Chinese Views of Future Warfare, Chinese Views of Future Warfare*, Washington, DC: National Defense University Press, 1997, contains an extensive selection of PLA writings on the RMA and IW; more current is Wang Liuyi, Yang Zongjin, and Wu Jianming, "An Airborne 'Information Fortress'," *Renmin Haijun*, July 13, 2011, p. 1, in OSC-CPP20110811318001, which offers a rare discussion of PLAN employment of UAVs. Also see Yuan Shenwei and Peng Wensong, "Shenyang MR Informationization Leading Group Holds Its Sixth Meeting," *Qianjin Bao*, Shenyang, March 28, 2008, p. 1, in OSC-CPP20080506478019.

42. Si Liang, "Chinese Navy Holds Exercises Again and Again Recently and Stands in Combat Readiness," *Zhongguo Tongxun She*, August 5, 1999, in FBIS-CHI-99-0805.

43. Dennis J. Blasko, Philip T. Klapakis, and John F. Corbett, Jr., "Training Tomorrow's PLA: A Mixed Bag of Tricks," *China Quarterly*, Vol. 146, June 1996, pp. 499–515. This admittedly is an old reference, but highlights the fact that the premier journal in English in the field of China studies has only published this one edition devoted to the military.

44. Shen Hairong and Chen Tangsheng, "Certain Group Army of Nanjing Military Region Makes Fresh Breakthrough in Its Capability of Fighting and Winning Battles at Sea," *Jiefangjun Bao*, August 8, 2000, in FBIS-CPP20000808000036, states that "the group army has built a simulated landing training site for each of its infantry regiments." Also see Liu Demao and Zhang Xianqiu, "Joint Teaching and Training Base of NDU and SAF Established," *PLA Daily*, July 15, 2009, available from *english.chinamil.com.cn/site2/news-channels/2009-07/15/content_1837286.htm*. Specific reports about the Dongshan series include "Dongshan Drill to Enter New Stage," *People's Daily*, August 3, 2001, in FBIS-CPP20010803000050; "Preliminary Discussion Regarding Organizing Fishing Craft for Sea Crossing Operations," *Jianchuan Zhishi*, Beijing, February 1, 2002, in FBIS-CPP20020304000243; "PLA's Annual Military Exercises Focus on Forced Landing Drills," *Wen Wei Po*, Hong Kong, September 23, 2002, in FBIS-CPP20020923000029; Oliver August, "China to Rehearse 'Taiwan Invasion,'" *The Times*, London, July 8, 2004, available from *www.timesonline.co.uk/tol/news/world/article454188.ece*; Bao Daozu,

"Dongshan Set for Military Exercise," *China Daily*, July 13, 2004, available from *www.highbeam.com/doc/1P2-8821314.html*; David G. Brown, "China-Taiwan Relations: Unproductive Military Posturing," available from *csis.org/files/media/csis/pubs/0403qchina_taiwan.pdf*. "Beijing Plans Showdown with Taiwan by Resuming Dongshan Drills," *Ming Pao*, Hong Kong, October 2, 2007, reported that the Dongshan exercise would be resumed in 2007, apparently as a deterrent move against Taiwan's president, Chen Shuibian, but the exercise was not conducted.

45. The 2009 OSD report to Congress cites the one division capability. Also see Zeng Bin *et al.*,"Sword Coming Out of the Scabbard and Shows Its Sharpness," *Zhanshi Bao*, Guangzhou, p. 2, September 16, 2003, in FBIS-CPP20031027000241; "Fujian Military District to Conduct Maritime Logistic Replenishment Drill," *Wenweipo News*, July 23, 2004; "Navy, Army Units Conduct Sea-Land Joint Exercises on 28 April," *Jiefangjun Bao*, June 2, 2008, in OSC-CPP20080502710007; Jeff Chen, More general assessments of PLAN amphibious capabilities are provided in *Xinhui*, "Amphibious Warfare Capabilities of the PLA: An Assessment on Recent Modernizations," *ChinaDefense.com*, December 7, 2008, available from *www.chinadefense.com/pla/plaamphops/plaamphops07.html*.

46. "PLA Navy Completes Highly Difficult Drills," *Jiefangjun Bao* article, January 10, 2000, cited in *Zhongguo Tongxun She*, January 10, 2000, in FBIS-FTS20000112001752; Zhang and Yuqing and Zhang Junlong, "Five-Dimensional Confrontation in Exercise '*Lianhe-2008*' in Bohai Gulf," *Xinhua*, September 22, 2008, in OSC-CPP20080822074019; also see Minnick, "China's Gator Navy Makes Marginal Strides."

47. Chen Wanjun and Wu Dengfeng, "Our Military's First Maritime Reservist Unit Formed," *Xinhua*, May 13, 2005, in OSC-CPP20050513000104. See, for instance, "Haian's Lingao County People's Armed Department Improves Communications With Fishing Vessels Working at Sea," *Zhanshi Bao*, Guangzhou, September 30, 2003; Xu Zhuangzhi and Li Xuanliang "Gratifying Leaping Development of National Defense and Armed Force Construction in 10th Five-Year Plan Period," *Xinhua*, December 6, 2005, I OSC-CPP20051206139021; Xu Ruopeng, Ju Xianzhong, and Chen Xiaojun, "Improving National Defense Mobilization Capabilities and Developing Competence in Maritime Front-

line Support," *Renmin Qianxian*, Nanjing, July 29, 2004, in OSC-CPP20040901000131; Chen Wanjun and Wu Dengfeng, "Our Military's First Maritime Reservist Unit Formed, *Xinhua*, May 13, 2005, in OSC-CPP20050513000104; "Chinese Local Oil Tanker Replenishes Oil for PLA Navy SSF Destroyer," *Military China*; "Guangzhou's Haizhu District Stages Militia Urban Defense Exercises," in *Guoji Xianqu Daobao*, March 30, 2008, in OSC-CPP20080331710015.

48. Wu is quoted in "PRC Navy Head: Military Exercises Boost Combat Power," *Xinhua*, April 15, 2009, in OSC-CPP20090415074018. Significant ASW exercises are reported in "Ocean Observation Laser-Fluorescence Radar Test-Flown Successfully," *Chin.comMilitaryNews*, November 26, 2003, in VIC report, November 27, 2003; Yan Runbo, Tan Jingchun, and Yang Fengjing, "Firsthand On-site Witness Report on the Navy's Continuous Heterotypic Anti-Submarine Drill," *Zhongguo Qingnian Bao* (Beijing) June 25, 2005, in OSC-CPP20050627000021; "North China Sea Fleet's Anti-submarine Unit Conducts Search and Destroy Drills in Designated Waters," CCTV-7 Report, April 10, 2005, in OSC-FEA20051123013669; "PLA Destroyer's Development of Combat Effectiveness," *Jiefangjun Bao*, December 3, 2007, in OSC-CPP20071203710011; "South Sea Fleet Logistics Support Unit Improves Torpedo Testing," *Jiefangjun Bao*, April 25, 2008, in OSC-CPP20080425710006; and Zhang Xiaoqi, Dai Zongfeng, and Zhu Lifang, "Deep Sea Shark Hunting," *Jiefangjun Bao*, March 23, 2009, p. 1, in OSC-CPP20090323710005.

49. "Chinese Fleet's Flag Waving in Miyako Channel International Law, Not Intimidation," *Mainichi Daily News Online* (Tokyo) April 29, 2010, in JPP20100429969031; and "Joint Formation Carries Out Collaboration Training in Distant Waters," *Jiefangjun Bao*, April 12, 2010, in CPP20100413702004. The 2010 *Defense White Paper* offers laws and regulations as one of the most mentioned frameworks within which the PLA operates.

50. "Report [with video] on PLA Navy Enhancing Comprehensive Maritime Operations in 2010," CCTV-7 (Beijing) November 1, 2010, in CPP20110302048003. This may have been the umbrella exercise under which the aforementioned "exercise" in Japan's EEZ was conducted.

51. NATO warfare abbreviations are used.

52. The 2008 *Defense White Paper* also lists submarine warfare first in the PLAN's five branches; no such protocol is identified in the 2010 paper. Liu Xianjun and Luo Hongwang, "Newly Commissioned Artillery Forms Combat Power," *PLA Daily*, August 4, 2011, available from *eng.mod.gov.cn/MilitaryExercises/2011-08/05/content_4288428.htm*, is a recent example. Also see "PLA Tests Container-Based Guns During Exercise," *Renmin Ribao* (Beijing) August 20, 2001, p. 2, in OSC-CPP20010821000070.

53. For instance, see the report of a North Sea Fleet (NSF) ASUW/anti-submarine warfare (ASW)/ anti-air warfare (AAW) exercise in *Renmin Haijun*, October 16, 2009, p. 1, in OSC-CPP20100323090006; missile exercises are described in "The PLA Navy Starts Live-Ammunition Training in West Pacific," *Xinhua*, June 30, 2010, available from *www.china.org.cn/china/2010-06/30/content_20390321.htm*; and Dai Zongfeng, "Guided-Missile Destroyer Flotilla in Attack Drill," *Jiefangun Bao*, August 16, 2011, in OSC-CPP20110816702008. Some nonsuccesses are publicized when a hortatory lesson can be drawn from them, usually in the form of how the unit's personnel recognized their errors and drew on ideological inspiration to improve their performance dramatically. See, for instance, "PRC Shenyang Division Extends Two-day Exercise to Eight Days, 'Replays' and Looks for Problems," *Jiefangjun Bao*, January 24, 2007. Almost all seamanship and navigation evolutions carried out by a ship, submarine, and aircraft is "training," by definition, such as that reported in "PLAN Destroyer Detachment Conducts Post-Typhoon Exercise in ECS," *Jiefangjun Bao*, July 27, 2004, available from *www.pladaily.com.cn/gb/pladaily/2004/07/27/20040727001019.html*; Chen Ji, "ECS Fleet Frigate Squadron Conducts Anti-aircraft Firing Drills," *Jiefangjun Bao*, August 18, 2004, in OSC-CPP20040825000108; and "PLAN Flotilla Holds Exercise in ECS," *Zhongguo Xinwen Wang*, available from *sina.com*, February 23, 2004; both report exercise periods involving evolutions from basic navigation to ASW drills.

54. See, for instance, Li Liu, "Strict Training Underlined in Naval Unit," *PLA Daily*, March 24, 2004; "PLAN NSF Regiment Improves Maneuverability for Emergency Operations," *PLA Daily*, September 8, 2005. There are, of course, three stages to being seasick: 1) One thinks one is going to die, 2) one is certain that one is going to die, 3) one is afraid one is NOT going to die.

55. See, for instance, "Warships in Replenishment Training," August 9, 2011, available from *www.chnarmy.com/html/2011-08/17389.html*; "Navy Group Conducts Post-Swap Training," *PLA Daily*, available from *english.chinamil.com.cn/english/pladaily/2003/06/10/20030610001011_militarynews.html*; and especially Zhang Yuqing and Zhang Junlong, "Five-dimensional Confrontation in Exercise 'Lianhe-2008' in Bohai Gulf," *Xinhua*, September 22, 2008, in OSC-CPP20080922074019, September 22, 2008, accessed August 10, 2011; and Hu Wei and Dai Zongfeng, "Confrontations in Unfamiliar Sea Area," *Renmin Haijun*, Beijing, August 3, 2010, p. 3, in OSC-CPP20101006090002, October 19, 2010.

56. "PLA Jinan MR Conducts Land-Air-Sea Exercises," *Jiefangjun Bao*, September 12, 2007, in OSC-CPP20070912710003, October 16, 2007; Zhou Yawen, Li Gencheng, and Tang Zhongping, "Letting Warships make a Show of Strength on Future Naval Battlefields," *Jiefangjun Bao*, March 25, 2008, in OSC-CPP20080325710013, March 31, 2008.

57. Author's visits to training centers in Dalian, Qingdao, and Guangzhou; Qian Xiaohu and Wang, *Jiefangjun Bao*, July 20, 2007, in OSC, July 21, 2007.

58. See, for instance, Hsiao Peng, "PLA to Conduct Landing Exercises and Attack Foreign Military Assistance," *Sing Tao Jih Pao*, Hong Kong, November 14, 2001, in OSC-CPP20011114000090, November 14, 2001; Suo Desheng, "Naval Base Trains 'Missile Escorts' to Attack Large Ships," *Jiefangjun Bao*, December28, 2001, p. 1, in OSC-CPP20011228000013, December 28, 2001; Wang Jiasuo, "Aircraft Carriers: Suggest You Keep Out of the Taiwan Strait!," *Junshi Wenzhai*, March 3, 2002, in OSC-CPP20020326000218; Zhou Yi, "Aircraft Carriers Face Five Major Assassins," *Junshi Wenzhai*, Beijing, March 1, 2002, pp. 4-6, in OSC-CPP20020315000200, March 15, 2002; Xin Benjian, "U.S. Concerned Over China's Anticarrier Strategy," *Huanqui Shibao*, Beijing, February 7, 2003, in OSC-CPP20030212000035; Liu Dingping, "Anti-Carrier Methods During a War in the Strait," *Junshi Wenzhai*, July 1, 2004, pp. 19-22, in OSC-CPP20040722000215; "China Accelerates Research in Anti-Carrier Tactics," *Kanwa Defense Review*, Hong Kong, September 1, 2005, pp. 9-13, in OSC-CPP20050912000122, September 1, 2005; Liu Yue-shan, "'Stealth Assassin' Goes Into Action

During Four Troop Training Exercises Within a Month," *Wen Wei Po*, Hong Kong, July 30, 2010, in OSC-CPP20100730788007; and especially Andrew S. Erickson, "Chinese Cruise Missile, Possible ASBM Testing is Part of Combined Arms Anti-Carrier Exercises in East China Sea, June 30-July 5," available from *noreply+feedproxy@google.com* on behalf of Andrew S. Erickson [*Andrew@andrewerickson.com*].

59. Li Jie, "Is the Ballistic Missile a 'Silver Bullet' Against Aircraft Carriers?" *Modern Navy*, Beijing, February 2008, pp. 42-44, translated by Lyle Goldstein, China Military Study Institute, CMSI, Naval War College, Newport, RI, offers discussion of the ASBM by a researcher from China's Naval Operations Research Center.

60. Two recent exercises are reported in "Joint Exercises at Sea Improve the Coordinated Warfare Level of Different Arms of the Military," available from *chn.chinamil.com.cn/jr/2011-08/09/content_4637021.htm*; and an exercise in which *Kunlunshan* participated, "Three Dimensional Landing Operations Started at Dawn," available from *news.mod.gov.cn/headlines/2011-08/09/content_4289161.htm*. These and other articles were translated by Mr. Anton Wishik and associates of NBR, whose assistance I gratefully recognize.

61. Qiu Boxiing and Yin Shengwu, "Eighty-One Experts Come to Seaborne Training Spots [to assist] A Division of Nanjing MR," *Jiefangjun Bao*, September 6, 2001, in OSC-CPP20010906000051, September 6, 2001; "Guangzhou Naval Academy Educating Marines," claims that "90 percent of the marine officers have received education at GNVA," reported in *Duowey News*, May 7, 2002, available from *www4.chinesenewsnet.com/cgi-bin/newsfetch.cgi?unidoc=big5&src=SinoNews/Mainland-Tue_May_7_09_15_49_2002.htm*; "Strengthening Landing Exercises Amid Roaring Waves," *Renmin Ribao*, Guangzhou Supplement, June 6, 2002, p. 3, in OSC-CPP20020606000084; "PLA Marine Brigade Conducted Rapid Response Exercise," *Renmin Haijun*, February 10, 2004, p. 1, in OSC-CPM20040407000198; "Nanjing MR Transport Ship Group Conducts Training," *PLA Daily*, February 8, 2004, available from *www.pladaily.com.cn/gb/pladaily/2004/02/08/20040208001066_zgjs.html*; Li Yanlin and Yin hang, "PLA Navy Conducts Landing Drill to Test Three-Dimen-

sional Force Projection Capability," *PLA Daily*, August 9, 2011, reports participation by *Kunlunshan*, the first operational Type 071 LPD. Also see Ye Wenyong and Jiang Huiyuan, "Marine Brigade Under PLA Navy Organizes Training Program at South China Sea," *Zhongguo Qingnian Bao*, August 12, 2005, available from *zqb. cyol.com/gb/zqb/2005-08/12/content_47856.htm*; Han Haibing and Tao Shelan, "Unraveling the Mysteries of the Chinese Navy's Marine Corps," *Zhongguo Xinwen She*, Beijing, October 9, 2005, in OSC-CPP20051009061004, October 9, 2005; "Take Aim at Actual Combat, Pay Attention to Real Results, Broaden Methods, and Conduct Careful Management," *Renmin Qianxian*, Nanjing, April 12, 2007, p. 2; Li Tang and Yao Zeyong, "Marine Brigade Successfully Conducts Sea Crossing and Island Landing Combat Exercise," *Renmin Haijun*, September 14, 2007, p. 2, in OSC-CPM20040407000198; "SSF Landing Ship Unit, Marine Brigade, Helicopter Unit Training," *Renmin Haijun*, June 13, 2010, p. 1, in OSC-CPP20100921090005, June 13, 2010; and especially two articles by Dennis J. Blasko, "PLA Amphibious Capabilities: Structured for Deterrence," *China Brief*, Vol. 10, issue 17, August 19, 2010, available from *www.jamestown.org/single/?no_cache=1&tx_ ttnews%5Btt_news%5D=36770*, and "China's Marines: Less is More," *China Brief*, Vol. 10, Issue 24, December 23, 2010, available from *www.jamestown.org/single/?no_cache=1&tx_ttnews%5Bsword s%5D=8fd5893941d69d0be3f378576261ae3e&tx_ttnews%5Bany_of_ the_words%5D=blasko&tx_ttnews%5Btt_news%5D=37246&tx_ttne ws%5BbackPid%5D=7&cHash=37c5c7c737aea15c1bbe58ab0e8a3e13*.

62. A recent example is reported in "PLA Navy Landing Ship Group in Collaboration With PLA Navy Aviation Corps Unit Conducts Joint [sic] Operations Training Exercise at Sea," August 9, 2011, available from *chn.chinamil.com.cn/jr/2011-08/09/content_4637021.htm*.

63. By comparison, a German-built conventionally powered submarine sells for less than $400 million, while one equipped with an AIP cell costs approximately $700 million; the world's most advanced boat, a U.S. *Virginia* class SSN, costs more than $2 billion.

64. See, for instance, "Virtual Training Research Center Opens at PLA Navy Submarine Academy," *Ocean News*, October 21, 2003; "China's New Third Generation Submarine Operational

Training Simulator Already in Use," *MilitaryChinaCom*, December 7, 2004; "China's New-Type Submarine Simulator Passes Expert Appraisal," *People's Daily*, March 15, 2004, available from *english. peopledaily.com.cn/200403/15/eng20040315_137548.shtml*; Wang Yang, Wu Dengfeng, and Xu Xingtang, "China's New-Generation Submarine Elites Have Excellent Qualities," *Xinhua*, July 19, 2007, in OSC-CPP20070815436001; and Sun Qinfu and Zhang Jian, "North Sea Fleet Submarine Flotilla Reforms Model for Full Training of Sub Captains," *Renmin Haijun*, April 18, 2008, p. 1, in OSC-CPP20080527436003, both describe efforts to improve officer proficiency.

65. Liu Xinmin and Xu Feng, "Submarine Detachment Intensifies Training As Per the Outline," *Jiefangjun Bao*, August 21, 2002, in OSC-CPP20020821000034; Lin Yongzhi, "NSF Submarines Exercise Tactics of Counterattacking Surface Ships," *Jiefangjun Bao*, April 12 2011, p. 2, in OSC-CPP20020412000064; Huo Weiguo, "When the 'Enemy Situation' is Dangerous, a Concealed Submarine Attacks," *Jiefangjun Bao*, September 19, 2007, p. 2; Liu Gang and Qian Xiaohu, "Great Wall No. 200 Submarine Tops Other PLA Navy Submarines in Sub-Launching of Missiles," *PLA Daily*, Vol. 9, January 29, 20011, available from *www.chnarmy.com/html/2011-01/10551.html*; "Class III Submarine Directly Upgraded to Class I Submarine," *PLA Daily*, November 12, 2007, available from *www.wsichina.org/morningchina/archive/20071113.html*.

66. "PLA NSF Submarine Base Organizes Officers, Men for Submarine Support Operation Training Exercise Focused on Emergency Response Operations," August 15, 2011, available from *chn.chinamil.com.cnjwjj/2011-08/15/content_464078.htm*.

67. Exchanges are discussed in "Build Protective Screen in Ocean and Weave Net of Heaven in Sky," *Jiefangjun Bao*, July 17, 2004, available from *www.pladaily.com.cn/gb/pladaily/2004/07/17/20040717001020.html*; Huo Weiguo, "When the 'Enemy Situation' is Dangerous, A Concealed Submarine Attacks," *Jiefangjun Bao*, September 19, 2007, p. 2; "PLA Navy SSF in Midst of Officer Training Assigns Warship Captains to Aviation Forces, Warplane Pilots to Main Battle Warships," August 11, 2011, available from *chn.chinamil.com.cn/dbtnews/2011-08/11/content_4644024.*

68. "South China Sea Fleet Submarine Chaser Group Trains in Beibu Gulf," *Jiefangjun Bao* , September 5, 2002, in OSC-CPP20020905000071; "Fleet Achieves First Success in Composite Formation, Anti-Sub Attack Exercise," *ChinaComMilitary News*, April 29, 2003, available from *Military.China.Com/Zh_Cn/ News/568/20030429/114661097.Html*; Navy Squadron Explores New Fighting Methods in Antisubmarine Operation," *PLA Daily*, March 10, 2004, available from *english.pladaily.com.cn/english/ pladaily/2004/03/10/20040310001033_ChinaMilitaryNews.html*; "A South China Sea Fleet [sic] Frigate Squadron Trains to Make Weak Areas Strong," *Jiefangjun Bao*, September 11, 2004, in OSC-CPP20040913000122; "NSF Destroyer Flotilla Conducts Anti-Submarine Training," *PLA Daily*, August 9, 2005; "Three PLA Services Conduct Combat Readiness Training," *PLA Daily*, January 27, 2006; Jiang Xiangjie and Mi Jinguo, "Ship-Aircraft Coordinated attack on Submarine," *Renmin Haijun*, May 31, 2006, p. 3, in OSC-CPP20060626318017, reports on several exercises including surface and aviation assets; "ECS Fleet Submarine Chaser Formation on Confrontation Training," Jiefangjun Bao, July 26, 2007, OSC Translation; Tan Jingchun, Yan Runbo, and Li Binfu, "A Group of Eagles Hunt for the Shark," *Renmin Haijun*, November 28, 2007, p. 2, in OSC-CPP20080108318001; "North Sea Fleet Destroyer Flotilla Conducts Confrontational Drill," *Jiefangjun Bao*, January 23, 2008, in OSC-CPP20080123710005; Yu Wenxian, Hu Quanfu, Mi Jinguo, "Frigates and Submarines Carry Out First Joint Training and Achieve 'Beginner's Success'," Zhongguo Wingnian Bao, Beijing, February 18, 2011, in OSC-CPP20110218787011; "Destroyer Flotilla Organizes Air Defense and Anti-submarine Drill," *PLA Daily*, July 8, 2011, available from *eng.chinamil.com.cn/news-channels/china-military-news/2011-07/08/content_4461864.htm*; Li Zhanglong, "PLA Navy's South China Sea Fleet in Ship Supplementary Training and Assessment," available from *www. chnarmy.com/html/2011-02/11396.html*; Zhao Shuanglin, "No. 561 Ship in Training," *Jiefangjun Bao*, August 16, 2011, in OSC-CPP20110816702009, describes a single frigate undergoing ASW training under the direction of the South Sea Fleet "ship training center."

69. Zhong Kuirun, "East Sea Fleet Conducts Drill for Counterattacking Cruise Missiles," *Renmin Wang*, Beijing, September 18, 2001, in OSC-CPP2010918000207; "North China Sea Fleet Detachment of Destroyers Conducts Antiaircraft Firing Prac-

tice and Tests," *Jiefangjun Bao*, February 21, 2001, p. 2, in OSC-CPP20020222000115, February 21, 2002; South and North Sea Fleet AAW exercises were reported—with an emphasis on their joint nature, in *Jiefangjun Bao*, January 8, 2004, available from *www.pladaily.com.cn/gb/pladaily/2004/01/08/20040108001019.html*.

70. An "air capable" ship without a hangar and associated maintenance capability is severely limited in its ability to embark/operate helicopters. "A Certain Shipboard Aircraft Regiment of PLA Navy Cuts Pilot Training Period from 14 to 4 Years," *Jiefangjun Bao*, January 15, 2004, available from *www.p[ladaily.com/gb/pladaily/2004/01/15/20040115001003.html*, *Jane's Fighting Ships, 2011-2012*, London, UK: Jane's Information Group, 2011, estimates 39 helicopters; FAS indicates more than 100; a reliable U.S. researcher gives the number as 54. In any case, the PLAN remains equipped with surprisingly few helicopters, without which a destroyer or frigate is extremely constrained in carrying out several primary mission areas.

71. "PRC Shipborne Helicopters Successfully Conduct Mid-air Refueling Tests," *Jiefangun Bao*, December 11, 2001, in OSC-CPP20011212000088, December 11, 2001; "China's First Maritime Rescue Heliport Goes Into Trial Operation," *Xinhuanet*, March 15, 2003, available from *www.china.org.cn/english/environment/58392.htm*; "Graduate Officers Go to Their Posts," *PLA Daily*, July 22, 2003, available from *chinadaily.com.cn/en/doc/2003-07/22/content_247537.htm*; "Dalian Naval Academy Recruits Pilot Cadets for the First Time," *PLA Daily*, September 5, 2008, available from *english.chinamil.com.cn/site2/news-chanbels/2008-09/05/content_146289*; "China Aviation Industry Corporation Successfully Conducts Aerial Sonar Buoy Ejection Test," *Qianlong Com*, November 17, 2003; a "joint" exercise between a helicopter-equipped destroyer and a shore-based air division is reported in *Jiefangjun Bao*, December 23, 2003, available from *www.pladaily.com.cn/gb/pladaily/2003/12/23/20031223001010_TodayNews.html*; Yan Runbo, Tan Jingchun, and Yang Fengjing, "Firsthand On-Site Witness Reports on the Navy's Continuous Heterotypic [sic] Anti-Submarine Drill," *Zhongguo Qingnian*, June 25, 2005, in OSC-CPP20050627000021; "Training Exercises Test Mettle of Troops, Equipment," *Jiefangjun Bao*, December 6, 2006; "Helicopter Training Over Water," *Qianwei Bao*, Jinan, August 13, 2006, p. 2, in OSC-CPP20061013318004; Christopher Bodeen, "China Military Launches Major Air Exer-

cises," *Seattle Post-Intelligencer*, August 3, 2010, available from *seattletimes.nwsource.com/html/nationworld/2012517069_apaschinaairforce.html*. "PLA ESF Division Upgrades Monitoring Means for Precision Training," *Jiefangjun Bao*, February 22, 2007, discusses the evaluation process.

72. Recent exercises are reported in "PLA Navy's JH-7 Aircraft Practice Sea-Skimming Defense Penetration," May 7, 2011; "China-Built Aircraft of PLA Navy Perform First Minimum-Altitude Live Bombing Exercise at Sea," May 20, 2011; "Training in Aerial Refueling Routinized," May 20, 2011; all in OSC Summary, May 11-28, 2011," FEA20110811020819.

73. "War Games Role for Orbiting Surveillance," *South China Morning Post*, August 13, 2001. China's installation of its own navigational system in space is noted in "China Successfully Launches Fifth Satellite for Its Own Global Navigation Network," *China Daily*, August 2010, available from *www.chinadaily.com.cn/china/2010-08/01/content_11077343.htm*. Also see "China to Build Satellite Navigation System," *Xinhua*, November 2, 2006, available from *chinadaily.com.cn/china/2006-11/02/content_723271.htm*. Gulf of Aden operational support was discussed with the author by a senior PLAN officer in general terms in 2011; Wu is quoted by Andrew Erickson, in Peter J. Brown, "China's Navy Cruises into Pacific Ascendancy," *Asia Times*, April 22, 2010.

74. Reported in Dai Yong and Fang Lihua, "Destroyer Flotilla Has Joint Training With Five Arms," *Jiefangjun Bao*, n.d., in OSC-CPP20080408702007, April 8, 2008, report provided by David Chen.

75. He Yu and Si Yanwen, "A Navy Destroyer Flotilla Realized Information Interconnections in Offshore Maneuver," *Jiefangjun Bao*, n.d., in OSC-CPP2003121800081, December 17, 2003; Chen Wanjun and Cao Jinping, "PLA Navy Develops Combat Software System for Surface Vessels," *Xinhua*, November 14, 2005, in OSC-CPP20051114042057, November 14, 2005; "PLA Air Force, Navy, and Second Artillery Hold Training to Improve Information Operational Capability," *PLA Daily*, March 7, 2006; Mao Jingxiong, "Twice Revised Scientific Research Program," *Jiefangjun Bao*, June 22, 2007, OSC.

76. Analysis of 18 significant PLA exercises by Dennis J. Blasko, December 2009.

77. David Chen, "2011 PLA Military Training: Toward Greater Interoperability," *ChinaBrief*, Vol. XI, issue 2, Washington, DC: Jamestown Foundation, January 28, 2011, pp. 8-12. Chen also translates a phrase in the 2011 training plan as "systems operation" (*tixi zuozhan*) and "systems confrontation (*tixi duikang*), concepts apparently meant to convey the necessity for military units to strive beyond "joint and integrated" warfare, reaching for the "netcentric" paradigm popularized in the U.S. Navy in the early 1990s. This paradigm also involves the U.S. concept of "system of systems" I first heard in 1992 and which is found in a *Jiefangjun Bao* article of August 11, 2011, available from *chn.chinamil.com.cn/gd/2011-08/11/content_4643855.htm*. The 2010 *Defense White Paper* is less effusive in these areas, but see, for instance, "Building of the Army, Navy, Air Force, and Second Artillery Force" for the emphasis on "informationization, . . . digitized units," with the PLAN described as accelerating "the modernization of its integrated combat forces," and emphasizing "combat training in complex electromagnetic environments," available from *news.xinhuanet.com/english2010/china/2011-03/31/c_13806851_8.htm*.

78. An interesting critique of PLA training is offered in Zheng Qin, "Carrying Forward the Causes Pioneered by Our Predecessors and Forging ahead into the Future: Innovations and Development of Army Military Training," *Jiefangjun Bao*, May 13, 2008, p. 6, in OSC-CPP200805123710008.

79. Jiang Yuanliu, "China's Master-Degree Captain Watches US Naval Exercise," *Jiefangjun Bao*, October 22, 2000, p. 5, in FBIS-CHI-98-316, citing Mao Zhenggong and Jia Xiaoguang, both senior captains. Although similar PLA observations are not available in open-source documents, the Guam exercise is reported in *Bai Ruixue*, "Interpreting US Military Exercise in Guam," *Xinhua*, June 21, 2006, in OSC-CPP20060621047001, which focuses on the buildup of U.S. military forces in the western Pacific; and Lin Zhiyuan, a senior official at the PLA's Academy of Military Science, "Positive Signs from Sino-US Military Exchanges," *Renmin Ribao*, Beijing, June 27, 2006, in OSC-CPP200606287. U.S. views are in "China Sends First-Ever Delegation to Observe U.S. Pacific Wargames," AP report (Shanghai) June 20, 2006; other stories available from *www.pacom.mil/exercises/vs2006*.

80. Analysis of18 significant PLA exercises by Dennis J. Blasko, in "Recent Trends in PLA Navy Training and Education." Testimony before the U.S.-China Economic and Security Review Commission, Washington, DC, June 11, 2009, p. 412, available from *www.uscc.gov/hearings/2009hearings/written_testimonies/09_06_11_wrts/09_06_11_vellucci_statement.php.*

81. Author's conversations with senior PLAN officers 2000-2009; Dennis J. Blasko, "China Looks and Finds Its Military Wanting," *Defense News*, Washington, DC, July 21, 2009, citing "Outside View: Know the Enemy and Know Yourself," *China Daily*, July 25, 2008, available from *www.chinadaily.com.cn/cndy/208-07/25/content_6875515.htm.*

82. Liu Nan and Li Yanlin, "Watch Officer, Hold Your Head Up High," *Jiefangjun Bao*, February 27, 2009, p. 5, in OSC-CPP20090227710009; Qi Hongbing, Huang Yuping, and Zhong Kuirun, "Display Skill in the Depths of the Ocean," *Jiefangjun Bao*, May 24, 2009, p. 1, in OSC-CPP20090526702029, reflects this problem for enlisted personnel; officer training challenges are discussed in Li Hongbin and Liang Qingsong, "Composite Captains Need 'Composite' Training," *Renmin Haijun,* Beijing, February 23, 2009, p. 2, in OSC-CPP20090409478014.

83. Comment on the South China Sea exercise is in Ma Liyao and Cui Haipei, "Naval Drills 'Not Linked to Sea Disputes'," *People's Daily,* June 30, 2011, available from *english.peopledaily.com.cn/90001/90776/90883/7424822.html*; those in the Yellow Sea are discussed in "China Launches War Games in Yellow Sea," AFP/wk, September 1, 2010, available from *www.channelnewsasia.com/stories/afp_asiapacific/view/1078415/1/.html*; and in Tini Tran, "China to Conduct Live-Fire Sea Drill This Week," *Seattle Post-Intelligencer,* June 29, 2010, available from *www.seattlepi.com/national/1104ap_as_china_military_exercises.html?source=rss.*

84. Quoted in "We Will Build Larger Ships," *Xinhua,* April 16, 2009, available from *www.china-defense-mashup.com/?p=3279*; and Li Zhihui, Quan Xiaoshu, Zhu Xudong, "Chinese Navy Sees Role Further Afield," *Xinhua,* April 22, 2009, available from *news.xinhuanet.com/english/2009-04/22/content_11233491.htm.*

CHAPTER 3

PLA NAVAL EXERCISES WITH INTERNATIONAL PARTNERS

Michael McDevitt

EXECUTIVE SUMMARY

This chapter addresses the lessons that the People's Liberation Army Navy (PLAN) has learned in its interactions with foreign navies. The main focus is on lessons learned during extended anti-piracy deployments.

MAIN ARGUMENT

Thanks to 3 years of continuous anti-piracy deployments to the Arabian Sea, the PLAN is mastering the operational skills necessary to deploy and sustain surface combatants, amphibious ships, and support ships on distant stations for long periods of time. For the PLAN, these deployments have become a real world "battle-laboratory," thanks to daily interactions with foreign navies. The PLAN has an opportunity to observe the day-to-day operations of most of the world's great navies and absorb best practices for its own use. In short, it is learning the sorts of lessons that are absolutely essential to the effective operation of an expeditionary navy.

POLICY IMPLICATIONS

- Since the Cold War ended, the United States has been unconstrained when deploying naval forces off the coast of another nation to support Western interests and signal determination. A PLAN capable of "distant seas" operations provides Beijing with a new "tool" it can employ to support its friends and buttress its policies. Should the PLAN be employed in this fashion, it could greatly complicate U.S. policy approaches by introducing a new factor into crisis response options.

- The PLAN is becoming "integrated' into the maritime life of the region around the Strait of Hormuz. China already depends upon Gulf oil much more than the United States. Over time it may be desirable to encourage the PLAN to become more of a positive contributor to the overall peace and stability of the region. The military issues that cause tension between the People's Liberation Army (PLA) and the U.S. military are East Asia-specific, whereas there is a very close alignment of interests (but not necessarily policies chosen to advance those interests) between Washington and Beijing in this region.

- The introduction of modern amphibious ships, and shortly, an aircraft carrier force, provides the PLAN with a credible power projection capability that is generating the acquisition of area denial capabilities such as submarines and land-based aircraft with anti-ship cruise missiles by neighboring littoral states. It is also raising the attractiveness of the U.S. naval presence along the long Indo-Pacific littoral. The Barack Obama Administration's rebalance to Asia seems perfectly timed.

INTRODUCTION

Before addressing PLAN interactions with foreign navies, it is useful to review the strategic and political background that provides the context for expanded PLA missions *in addition to* the defense of China and its claimed territories. The expanded mission set is largely driven by the globalization of People's Republic of China (PRC) commercial and security interests, which were outlined in Hu Jintao's "Historic Missions" speech presented at an expanded meeting of the Central Military Commission (CMC) in 2004.[1] Subsequently, the 2008 PLA *Defense White Paper* characterized this mission set as "Military Operations Other Than War" (MOOTW) — in other words, peacetime operations[2]

The combination of China's expanding overseas interests and corresponding need for security created a "demand signal" for a PLAN that could protect PRC interests abroad. This entails supporting United Nations (UN)-sanctioned missions, assisting PRC citizens who are in jeopardy or require evacuation,[3] protecting sea lines of communication, responding to natural disasters, and demonstrating China's resolve in support of embattled friends in Africa and along the South Asia littoral. Over the last half-decade, the PLAN, more so than China's other military services, has been seriously involved in integrating distant, prolonged peacetime operations as part of its core mission set.

As the PLAN has learned, these new missions require a different mix of naval capabilities than its wartime "offshore active defense strategy" (近海积极防御战略).[4] China's military has introduced capabilities over the past 20 years that have expanded the PLA's operational reach further off-shore, beyond the first island chain. In turn, the U.S. Department of Defense (DoD) began to characterize the operational implications of those capabilities as anti-access/area denial. These capabilities are not all resident in the PLA; the PLA Air Force (PLAAF) and Second Artillery Corps play major roles. But for the PLAN, it is the submarine force and land-based naval aviation arm that are the central players in area denial scenarios. The PLAN's surface force plays second fiddle in these scenarios and should a conflict over Taiwan erupt, will probably remain inside the first island chain, conducting anti-submarine warfare (ASW) and air defense roles. This role is reversed during peacetime; it is the surface navy that has pride of place because of its ability to deploy world-wide.

The PLAN is currently mastering the operational skills necessary to deploy and sustain surface combatants, amphibious ships, and support ships on distant stations for long periods of time. In my judgment, they have been a quick study, thanks to 3 years of continuous anti-piracy deployments to the Arabian Sea. These operations are the single most important factor in the growing sophistication and professional competence of the PLAN.

These deployments are a real world "battle-laboratory" for the PLAN, providing an opportunity to observe the day-to-day operations of most of the world's great navies and absorb best practices for its own use — as such, these deployments provide the best area to focus on in order to address the topic of this chapter. I was asked to focus on lessons learned from interactions with foreign navies, which implied to me that the organizers expected a focus on issues related to tactical competence. Frankly, these are difficult to cull out in an open-source environment.

What I have found is that the lessons the PLAN has learned are the more mundane, but crucially important if the PLAN is to operate effectively beyond East Asia: (1) ship design: what sort of capabilities must warships have to operate at sea for sustained periods of time; (2) learning how to manage the logistics that are essential for sustaining forces a long way from home for an extended period; and, (3) development of a growing cadre of relatively junior flag officers, ship commanding officers, junior officers, and sailors who have been exposed on a regular basis to the best navies in the world and who are learning how to operate independently in near-combat operations. In other words, these are the sorts of lessons that are absolutely essential to the effective operation of an expeditionary navy.

THE POLITICAL "GREEN LIGHT"[5]

The political approval for the PLA, especially the Navy, to begin to seriously think about the uses of the PLA in addition to the defense of China proper was given on December 24, 2004, when then-recently-promoted CMC Chairman Hu Jintao announced a new set of Strategic Missions and Objectives for the Chinese armed forces.[6] This speech marks a major turning point in Chinese thinking about the role of the PLA, with major implications for the PLAN. These *New Historic Missions* are:

- The PLA should guarantee the rule of the Party.
- The PLA should safeguard national economic development and territorial sovereignty, ensuring China's sovereignty, territorial integrity, and domestic security during its "strategic opportunity period."[7] This includes responsibility

for dealing with Taiwanese and ethnic separatist issues, nontraditional security issues, territorial land and maritime disputes, and domestic social security problems.[8]

- Safeguarding China's expanding national interests. This mission calls on the armed forces to broaden their view of security to account for China's growing national interests. This refers to resource security, sea lane of communication (SLOC) security, and maritime rights and interests. The mission also calls on the PLA to consider the security of China's overseas investments and presence.

- Helping to ensure world peace. To accomplish this goal, the *Historic Missions* call upon the armed forces to both increase participation in international security activities (such as peacekeeping, search and rescue, and anti-terror operations) as well as to improve their military capabilities to "deal with crises, safeguard peace, contain war, and win a war"[9]

The first mission, defending the rule of the Chinese Communist Party (CCP), had always been a PLA mission. The second mission also was not new — the PLA had always been tasked with defending sovereignty and territorial integrity and had long been tasked with defending economic development. What the *New Historic Missions* changed was the extent to which Chinese leaders saw national economic development and national security as being linked together.

The third and fourth missions were new and very significant. For the first time, the PLA (and therefore the PLAN) was being assigned responsibilities well beyond China and its immediate periphery. This was official recognition that China's national interests were global and that the PLA's missions were to be based on those expanding interests, not just geography. It was also an official announcement that Chinese leaders saw China as a global actor with a role to play in support of global stability through peacekeeping and other missions.

DISTANT SEAS OPERATIONS

Since Jintao's *New Historic Missions* speech, there has been an ongoing discussion in China about developing a new operational concept, termed *yuanhai* (远海) in Chinese and translated as "distant seas," which would extend PLAN operations beyond regional seas.[10] This term is used to differentiate it from "offshore active defense," which is still used to frame doctrinal development and potential operations in regional waters near China.[11] While Chinese military, civilian analysts and policymakers have been discussing the concept of "distant seas," it seems clear that events, especially the beginning of PLAN participation in anti-piracy operations, are creating a new reality that is outpacing discussions surrounding a new operational concept. What the PLAN has demonstrated during its more than 3 years of anti-piracy operations is that it does have the ability to support China's political interests and security concerns "overseas."

In the realm of what might be termed naval diplomacy, the PLAN has recognized the value of deployments intended to show the flag, as the record of overseas deployments indicates. Even before the anti-piracy operation provided the means to do this on a routine basis, it is clear that the Navy was thinking about it at the highest level. As PLAN Political Commissar Hu Yanlin noted in 2006:

The purpose of naval diplomacy has evolved from isolated ship visits to ship visits coordinated with larger political and diplomatic activities. In terms of content, these activities have evolved from working against traditional security threats to working against an expanding number of nontraditional security threats, including piracy and multinational criminal organizations.[12]

PUTTING GUIDANCE INTO ACTION

Although the *New Historic Missions* speech provided an official rationale for distant seas missions as opposed to periodic deployments, it is important to remember that the PLAN has been gradually building the skills necessary to do this for the past 30 years. The first deployment of note beyond the first island chain took place in 1976, when *Romeo* class submarine hull number 252 made a 30-day sortie into the Philippine Sea. This was followed in 1980 by a PLAN task force that was dispatched to the mid-Pacific to support China's intercontinental ballistic missile (ICBM) test.[13]

The PLAN's first interaction with foreign navies took place in November 1985, when a small task force made the PLAN's first foray into the Indian Ocean and visited Pakistan, Sri Lanka, and Bangladesh. That initiated a decade-long pattern that saw an average of one naval interaction with a foreign navy per year. At the time, many Western observers tended to adopt a patronizing attitude toward these fledgling steps.[14] In the late-1980s, a senior active duty naval officer characterized the PLAN to me as a "junk yard" navy that was woefully amateurish. In retrospect, it seems clear that the PLAN was carefully planning each deployment and then absorbing the lessons attendant to long-range deployments—lessons that largely revolve around logistics and communications.

It was these early voyages that started the PLAN down the long learning path associated with learning how to keep the ships refueled, how to deal with equipment breakdowns, how to make certain enough fresh food is available, and so on. In almost all these cases, these problems were manageable because the ships were sailing from point A to point B, and were not conducting multiday operations at sea in between port visits. Meeting logistics demands during transits is far simpler than sustaining ships at sea, because it is possible to provision the ship adequately for relatively short duration transits that require only periodic refueling at sea. Nonetheless, these early excursions were an important start to the learning process. These early deployments are listed below.

PLAN International Voyages: 1985-99[15]

November 1985: Pakistan, Sri Lanka, Bangladesh: *Luda* class (旅大级) DD *Hefei* (合肥舰) and replenishment ship *Fengcang* (丰仓补给舰)

March 1989: United States (Hawaii): *Zheng he* (郑和舰) training ship

March 1990: Thailand: *Zheng he* (郑和舰) training ship

October 1993: Bangladesh, Pakistan, India, Thailand: *Zheng he* (郑和舰) training ship

May 1994: Russia (Vladivostok): A Sub Tender, *Luda II* class (旅大级-II) DD *Zhuhai* (珠海舰), *Jiangwei I* class (江卫级-I) FF *Huainan* (淮南舰)

August 1995: Russia (Vladivostok): *Jiangwei I* class (江卫级-I) FF *Huaibei* (淮北舰)

August 1995: Indonesia: *Luda-II* class (旅大级-II) DD *Zhuhai, Jiangwei I* class (江卫级-I) FF *Huainan* (淮南舰), and one replenishment ship

July 1996: North Korea: *Luhu* class (旅沪级) DDG *Harbin* (哈尔滨舰) and *Luda* class (旅大级) DD *Xining* (西宁舰)

July 1996: Russia (Vladivostok): *Luhu* class (旅沪级) DDG *Harbin* (哈尔滨舰)

February 1997: United States (Hawaii, San Diego), Mexico, Peru, Chile: *Luhu* class (旅沪级) DDG *Harbin* (哈尔滨舰), *Luda-II* class (旅大级-I) DD *Zhuha*i (珠海舰), and replenishment ship *Nancang* (南仓舰)

February 1997: Thailand, Malaysia, Philippines: *Luhu* class (旅沪级) DDG *Qingdao* (青岛舰), *Jiangwei I* class (江卫级-I) FF *Tongling* (铜陵舰)

April 1998: New Zealand, Australia, Philippines: *Luhu* class (旅沪级) DDG *Qingdao* (青岛舰), replenishment ship *Nancang* (南仓舰).

A close examination of this list, and the ships involved, allows some inferences to be drawn. By the 1990s, the *Luda* class destroyers were showing their age. This class is steam propelled, and, at 3,700 tons, is very small to be rated a destroyer; yet, the *Luda* class *Zhuhai* was assigned to the most challenging voyage that the PLAN made during the decade—the voyage to the United States and South America. *Zhuhai* must have been a very well-run and well- maintained ship. However, one important lesson was learned. The ship class was not suitable for long-range (sustained) operations. During the transit to Hawaii, the task force ran into 10 consecutive days of heavy weather, and encountered a great deal of difficulty in getting *Zhuhai* refueled because of high seas. *Zhuhai* has limited fuel storage capacity, she needed to be underway replenished every 3 days, and the weather made that very difficult.[16]

In the mid-1990s, the PLAN simply did not have very many modern, and hence, more reliable, destroyers and frigates. It is important to note that none of the ships that made the overseas deployments listed above are involved in today's ongoing anti-piracy operations. They have been supplanted by larger, helicopter-capable destroyers and frigates better suited for extended operations. A final point worth mentioning is that after the sister ships *Harbin* and *Qingdao* were commissioned, one or the other was always assigned to the longest-range operations. They were the newest and most capable guided missile destroyers (DDG) that the PLAN had at the time. The choice of the newest, most capable ships set the pattern that the PLAN follows to this day—deploying ships for distant deployments relatively soon after their commissioning. As an interesting side note, the *Harbin* was powered by General Electric LM 2500 gas turbine engines, the very same engines used to power modern U.S. Navy (USN) destroyers. These were sold to China in the 1980s, before post-Tiananmen Square sanctions were applied. Subsequently, the ship may have been re-engined with the Ukrainian gas turbines that are in widespread use in the PLAN today, because in the wake of Tiananmen weapons embargo spare parts were hard to come by.

It seems likely that among the more valuable lessons learned during this period of operations, in addition to refining basic seamanship skills associated with crossing large swaths of the Pacific, was the need for ships with better sea-keeping ability (which normally means larger, fin-stabilized vessels), greater fuel and fresh water capacity, and reliable gas-turbine and diesel powered engineering plants. These are the characteristics of the PLAN ships currently conducting anti-piracy patrols—which have all been commissioned since 2004 (one exception is the destroyer *Shenzhen*, which was commissioned in 1999).

INTERNATIONAL NAVAL ENGAGEMENT TAKES OFF—THE PRE-ANTI-PIRACY DEPLOYMENT PERIOD, 2000-08

In terms of international engagement, the first decade of the 21st century should be divided into a pre-anti-piracy operations period and a post-anti-piracy period, because once the PLAN began to conduct anti-piracy operations, the entire nature of its approach to international naval engagement changed appreciably.

The new century marked an increase in the tempo of international deployments, doubling the pattern of annual cruises per year from one to two. Not only did the periodicity increase; the deployments were much more ambitious in terms of the geographic variety of countries visited, which equated to more long-distance voyages. Whereas during the 1990s, four of the PLAN's international voyages were to the Russian Far East or North Korea—both within easy steaming distance inside the first island chain—during the 2000s, the PLAN made its presence felt globally. The PLAN continued to deploy its newest ships as soon as they finished post-commissioning shakedown training. The list below will show that *Qingdao* continued to be kept very active, as was the newly commissioned *Shenzhen* (1999), the first of the *Luhai* class. That the same ships keep showing up during this period is indicative of the fact that just 10 years ago the PLAN had a very small inventory of modern, reliable seagoing destroyers and frigates—a situation that began to change markedly after 2007, when new destroyers and frigates begin to enter the inventory in numbers.

PLAN International Voyages 2000-08.[17]

July 2000: Malaysia, Tanzania, and South Africa: *Luhai* class (旅海级) DDG *Shenzhen** (深圳舰), Replenishment ship *Nancang* (南仓舰)

August 2000: United States (Hawaii, Seattle) and Canada: *Luhu* class (旅沪级) DDG *Qingdao* (青岛舰), replenishment ship *Taicang* (太仓舰)

May 2001: India and Pakistan: *Luhu* class (旅沪级) DDG *Harbin* (哈尔滨舰), replenishment ship *Taicang* (太仓舰)

August 2001: France, Italy, Germany, and Great Britain: *Luhai* class (旅海级) DDG *Shenzhen* (深圳舰), replenishment ship *Fengcang* (丰仓舰)

September 2001: Australia and New Zealand: *Jiangwei II* class (江卫级-II) FF *Yichang** (宜昌舰), replenishment ship *Taicang* (太仓舰)

November 2001: Vietnam: *Jiangwei II* class (江卫级-II) frigate *Yulin** (玉林舰)

May 2002: South Korea: *Jiangwei II* class (江卫级-II) FF's *Jiaxing** (嘉兴舰) and *Lianyungang** (连云港舰)

May 2002: Singapore, Egypt, Turkey, Ukraine, Greece, Portugal, Brazil, Ecuador, and Peru: *Luhu* class (旅沪级) DDG *Qingdao* (青岛舰), replenishment ship *Taicang* (太仓舰 around the world deployment)

October 2003: Brunei, Singapore, and Guam: *Luhai* class (旅海级) DDG *Shenzhen* (深圳舰), replenishment ship *Qinghaihu* (青海湖舰)

November 2003: New Zealand: *Jiangwei* class (江卫级) FF *Yichang* (宜昌舰), replenishment ship *Taicang* (太仓舰)

November 2005: Pakistan, India, and Thailand: *Luhai* class (旅海级) destroyer *Shenzhen* (深圳舰), a new class multi-product replenishment ship *Weishanhu** (微山湖舰)

August 2006: United States, Canada, and the Philippines: *Luhu* class (旅沪级) DDG *Qingdao* (青岛舰), replenishment ship *Hongzehu* (洪泽湖舰)

March 2007: Pakistan: Participate in multi-national exercise *Aman-07*, *Jiangwei II* class (江卫级-II) FF's *Lianyungang* (连云港舰) and *Sanming* (三明舰)

May 2007: Singapore: WPNS Exercise. *Jiangwei II* class (江卫级-II) FF *Xiangfan* (襄樊舰)

August/September 2007: Russia, United Kingdom, Spain, and France: *Luyang* class (旅洋级) DDG *Guangzhou** (广州舰) and replenishment ship *Weishanhu* (微山湖舰)

October 2007: Australia and New Zealand: *Lulu* class (旅沪级) DDG *Harbin* (哈尔滨舰) and replenishment ship *Hongzehu* (洪泽湖舰)

November 2007: Japan: *Luhai* class (旅海级) DDG *Shenzhen* (深圳舰)

October 2008: South Korea and Russia: Training ship *Zheng he* (郑和舰)

November 2008: Cambodia, Thailand, and Vietnam: Training ship *Zheng he* (郑和舰)

March 2009: Pakistan Exercise Peace-09[18]: *Luyang* class (旅洋级) DDG *Guangzhou* (广州舰 diverted from anti-piracy operations to participate.)

September 2010: Australia: Training ship *Zheng He* (郑和舰) and *Jiangwei II* class (江卫级-II) FF *Mianyang* (绵阳舰)

March 2011: Pakistan Exercise Peace-11 *Jiangkai I* class (江凯级-I) FFGs *Ma'anshan* (马鞍山舰) and *Wenzhou* (温州舰)

*Newly commissioned

It is also worth noting that the four Russian-built *Sovremenny* class destroyers in the PLAN order of battle never make an appearance internationally, either on these single ship show-the-flag deployments, or later during the anti-piracy patrols. Not being Chinese designed and built is probably one reason for not employing them to show the flag, but another may be engineering plant unreliability. During the Cold War, there were periodic rumors that the pressure-fired boiler designs that the Soviets adopted for this class were very difficult to maintain and prone to frequent breakdowns. There is a certain irony regarding the fact that these ships are not sent on distant seas deployments, given all the Western press and chattering-class attention they received when first delivered because of their long-range surface to surface cruise missile systems. At this point, it appears to me that the primary value of these four ships may turn out to be exposure to Russian combat systems integration.

Among the notable learning experiences for the PLAN during the decade that arguably gave the PLAN the confidence to undertake the anti-piracy deployments was *Qingdao's* and the oiler *Taicang's* circumnavigation of the world—a PLAN first. This 123-day voyage covered 32,000 nautical miles. However, exercise participation was limited, and simple passing exercises (PASSEX) were only conducted with the French Navy in the South Pacific and the Peruvian Navy. Nonetheless, it was an important milestone in a decade of firsts for the PLAN.

Qingdao made another major out-of-area deployment 4 years later in 2006 to the United States and Canada. During this deployment, the United States and China held a series of unprecedented bilateral exercises. A search and rescue exercise (SAREX) took place off the coast of San Diego on September 20, 2006.[19] This was the first bilateral military exercise ever conducted between the two nations. The two navies stationed observers on each other's ships as they practiced transmitting and receiving international communications signals; they also sent a combined damage control, firefighting, and medical team to the designated ship in distress. Based on news reports, senior U.S. Navy (USN) enlisted sailors stated, "The Chinese sailors did a very good job and were very professional."[20] This was a prelude to a second USN-PLAN exercise in the South China Sea in November 2006. In that exercise, Chinese and American ships and aircraft worked together to "locate and salvage a ship in danger."[21]

The exercises with the USN were not the first time the PLAN had begun to go beyond port-visits and passing exercises. That started 3 years earlier with a modest exercise schedule with foreign navies beginning with Pakistan:

- 2003: The PLAN and Pakistani naval forces conducted a joint search and rescue exercise off the coast of Shanghai in the East China Sea in October. It was the first time Chinese naval forces held a joint exercise with a foreign counterpart since the founding of the PRC.
- 2004: The PLAN and French naval forces held their first joint military exercise off the coast of Qingdao in eastern China.
- 2005: China and Russia held their first joint military exercises, code-named *Peace Mission 2005*. The 1-week maneuvers, which involved 10,000 troops from the two countries, started

in Vladivostok in Russia's Far East and later moved east to China's Shandong Peninsula.

- 2005: The PLAN also held joint military search and rescue exercises with Pakistani, Indian, and Thai naval forces. It was the first time the PLAN took part in a joint military exercise in overseas waters.[22]

What lessons the PLAN learned from these exercises is impossible to say. The exercises themselves were of the most basic kind, oriented around good seamanship and safe practices at sea and studiously avoiding anything that revealed weapons systems capabilities. I have been unsuccessful in trying to obtain specific lessons learned messages and post-exercise reports because they are most likely classified, as they are in the USN, and because they speak candidly about the strengths and weaknesses of both the partner navy as well as one's own navy. It is safe to conclude that the PLAN concluded that it had nothing to be ashamed of in terms of performance in comparison with the navies it had engaged, since, as we shall see, the PLAN kept at it throughout the decade.

2007—AN IMPORTANT YEAR

In terms of international deployments and exercise participation, 2007 was a significant year not only for what the PLAN did, but because in hindsight it seems likely that the successful activities during the year instilled a degree of confidence in the PLAN leadership that the Navy was capable enough to join the ongoing anti-piracy operations in 2008.

In March 2007, the PLAN participated in its first multinational maritime exercise, known as *AMAN*

(Peace)-07. The Pakistani Navy organized this major effort involving 27 countries, including eight that sent ships. The focus was on anti-piracy, terrorism, and illegal uses of the sea in general. Pakistan, with experience gained from a couple of stints in command of the U.S. Fifth Fleet organized Combined Task Force-150 (counterterrorism) operations, took the initiative in hosting a conference and naval exercise in order to display multinational resolve against terrorism; enhance co-operation and interoperability between friendly regional and extra-regional navies; harmonize tactical procedures at sea; and highlight the Pakistani Navy's position as a bridge between regions.[23]

The PLAN dispatched two *Jaingwei II* class frigates to *Aman 07*, not coincidently, the very type that China is building for Pakistan's F22P frigate program. During the 4-day at-sea phase, the highlight for the PLAN was being put in charge of one of the multinational at-sea exercises—a 2-hour search and rescue drill involving 12 ships from eight countries. This meant that the PLAN had to design the exercise scenario, coordinate the positioning of ships, and promulgate a plan that included communications procedures; "It was the first time for the Chinese Navy to lead and coordinate a multinational drill on such a scale," according to Senior Captain Luo Xianlin, the chief of staff of the Chinese force.[24] Subsequently, the PLAN has been a regular participant in this Pakistani biannual exercise series, along with many other regional navies, including the USN.

Singapore held its annual IMDEX maritime exposition 2 months later. This was immediately followed by the Western Pacific Naval Symposium (WPNS), which had an at-sea exercise phase. The PLAN participated in both phases, sending the *Jiangwei II* class

FF *Xiangfan*. Participating in both IMDEX and WPNS was another first for the PLAN.[25] Reportedly, participation enhanced the PLAN's abilities in taking part in multilateral exercises. Showing up and actively participating was an important step for the PLAN, because WPNS, which was launched in 1988 as an Australian Navy-sponsored event that takes place every other year, is intended to promote naval professionalism, maritime understanding, and naval cooperation in the Western Pacific and takes place under the gaze of many other regional navies.[26]

The third important event in 2007 was the August deployment of the recently commissioned *Luyang II* class destroyer *Guangzhou* and an accompanying replenishment ship on an 87-day deployment to the Baltic and Western Europe. The deployment was made because Russia had designated 2007 as "The Year of China." The *Guangzhou* task force's first port of call was St. Petersburg, which marked another PLAN first — its first deployment to the Baltic. Interestingly, the ships went non-stop from China to St Petersburg, a 30-day transit through the Indian Ocean, the Mediterranean, the English Channel, the North Sea, and the Baltic.

After visiting Russia, the PLAN task force conducted a trio of successive bilateral exercises with the Royal Navy off of Portsmouth, the Spanish Navy off of Cadiz, and the French Navy off of Toulon. In each case, the task force conducted a search and rescue exercise. The Royal Navy carrier *Ark Royal* participated in the United Kingdom (UK) bilateral exercise, which marked another PLAN first — an exercise with an aircraft carrier. In each case, the scenarios involved the Chinese replenishment ship simulating a ship in distress. The exercise involved locating the ship, and then coordinating rescue teams to board and deal with whatever mishap was being simulated. Following the major event, there were formation exercises, helicopter landings on one another's ships, and flashing light and semaphore drills.[27]

The final major naval deployment in 2007 was a deployment to Australia and New Zealand in October in which the *Luhu* class destroyer *Harbin* made her first out-of-area deployment since 2001 along with the replenishment ship, *Hongzehu*. The at-sea phase of this deployment was another first — the first multinational search and rescue exercise. It did not go as smoothly as anticipated, because either the Australian ship or New Zealand ship — the press account is not clear — did not get underway on time, and then rough weather in the Tasman Sea resulted in the curtailment of a portion of the exercise program. Nonetheless, this was another example of the PLAN being willing to engage with two well-established navies with a strong sense of professionalism and superb seamanship skills.[28]

Setting aside the fact that the PLAN limited itself to only search and rescue exercises ("one trick pony" comes to mind), 2007 seems to have been a watershed year in terms of building confidence in the senior leadership of the PLAN that it could operate in company with many of the great navies of the world — the United States, British, French, Spanish, and Australian — with self-confidence and without fear of embarrassment. Therefore, it is bit of surprise that after a very busy 2007, no major deployments took place in 2008 until December, when the first anti-piracy flotilla was deployed. In fact, it appears that there were only a couple of cruises by the training ship *Zheng he* prior to this deployment.

It is unknown whether this "pause" was because of maintenance demands on the handful of ships the

PLAN felt comfortable in deploying out of area, or because the operating focus was shifted back to combat preparations and Chinese-only exercises, or the possibility that the PLAN was posturing itself to be ready for a decision to join the anti-piracy effort. Investigating this line of inquiry is beyond the scope of this chapter—suffice it to say the PLAN was not "out and about" for most of 2008 as they had been since the start of the 21st century. This changed dramatically in December 2008, when the recently commissioned *Luyang* class DDG's *Wuhan* and *Haikou,* along with the new multiproduct replenishment ship *Weishanhu,* departed on the first anti-piracy mission.

ANTI-PIRACY PATROLS—A BLUE-WATER NAVY LABORATORY

Whether the leadership of the PLAN saw the anti-piracy patrols as an opportunity or a nuisance when the mission was assigned is unknown. What is clear from the data is the PLAN leadership has embraced the mission, publicized it widely within China, and has recognized that it has been a dramatic "accelerant" in the development of the PLAN into a genuine open-ocean global naval force. To quote a telling observation:

> On a patrol operations in a water area side by side with navies from the European Union, NATO, Russia, India, Japan, the Republic of Korea and other countries, the Chinese naval fleet gained rare opportunities to learn advanced maritime experiences from their foreign counterparts....This has helped the country's navy, which has long been deployed along its own coast, gradually get used to using a variety of modern ways and means to communicate with foreign fleets, creating a new type of cooperation model.[29]

The more than 3 years of continuous operations at the furthest-most reaches of the Indian Ocean from China have provided the PLAN with the opportunity to hone its skills quickly and learn what being a "distant ocean" force really entails. Perhaps most importantly, the PLAN has a growing cadre of relatively junior flag officers, ship commanding officers, junior officers, and sailors who have been exposed on a regular basis to the best navies in the world and who are learning how to operate independently in near-combat operations.

While the "combat" element of anti-piracy patrols has only involved firing warning shots to chase suspected pirate skiffs away, for the PLAN it is the first time that officers and sailors have been in an environment in which lethal force may have to be employed.[30] As early as April 2010, the escort flotilla was sending detachments of PLA special forces to embark on merchant ships they were escorting, foreshadowing the now widespread use of armed private security detachments.[31]

It is clear the PLAN appreciates that it is operating in a different environment. PLAN Commander Admiral Wu Shengli, in an interview on the second anniversary of PLAN involvement in the anti-piracy operations, argued that, "open ocean escorts are actual combat oriented operations that test the Navy's ability to perform missions and tasks." He went on to say that beginning with the fifth rotation, more and more officers and men have made their second deployment to the Gulf of Aden.[32] He is correct that these operations do test the Navy's ability in ways it has never been tested before. See anti-piracy deployments listed below.

Anti-piracy Deployments

1st *Luyang* class (旅洋级) DDG's *Wuhan* (武汉舰) and *Haikou* (海口舰), replenishment ship *Weishanhu* (微山湖舰)

2nd *Luhai* class (旅海级) DDG *Shenzhen* (深圳舰) and *Jiangkai* class (江凯级) FFG *Huangshan* (黄山舰) replenishment ship *Weishanku* (微山湖舰)

3rd *Jiangkai* class (江凯级) FFGs *Zhoushan* (舟山舰) and *Xuzhou* (徐州舰) replenishment ship *Qiandaohu* (千岛湖舰)

4th *Jiangkai* class (江凯级) FFGs *Ma'anshan* (马鞍山舰) and *Wenzhou* (温州舰) and replenishment ship *Qiandaohu* (千岛湖舰)

5th *Luyang* class (旅洋级) DDG Guangzhou (广州舰), *Jiangkai* class (江凯级) FFG Chaohu (巢湖舰), and replenishment ship Weishanhu* (微山湖舰)

6th LPD *Kunlunshan* (昆仑山舰), *Luyang* class (旅洋级) DDG *Lanzhou* (兰州舰), and replenishment ship *Weishanhu* (微山湖舰)

7th *Jiangkai* class (江凯级) FFGs *Zhoushan** (舟山舰) and *Xuzhou** (徐州舰) and replenishment ship *Qiandaohu** (千岛湖舰)

8th *Jiangkai* class (江凯级) FFGs *Ma'anshan** (马鞍山舰) and *Wenzhou** (温州舰) and replenishment ship *Qiandaohu* (千岛湖舰)

9th *Luyang* class (旅洋级) DDG *Wuhan** (武汉舰), *Jiangkai* class (江凯级) FFG *Yulin* (玉林舰), and Oiler *Qinghaihu* (青海湖舰)

10th *Luyang* class (旅洋级) DDG *Haikou** (海口舰), *Jiangkai* class (江凯级) FFG *Yuncheng* (运城舰), and Oiler *Qinghaihu** (青海湖舰)

*Repeat deployers

It seems clear that the PLAN has determined that the *Luyang* class DDGs and *Jiangkai II* class guided missile frigates (FFG) are the preferred anti-piracy deployers. It is not hard to understand why; they are among the newest, and hence most capable, of the PLAN surface combatant force, and they all have decent air defense capability (the *Luyang II* or Type 52C DDGs *Lanzhou* and *Haikou* are known as Chinese *AEGIS* ships, since they carry a phased array radar suite. They are also the first class of PLAN DDGs to go into serial production, with three more in various stages of construction.[33] Both classes are helicopter capable and have the most up-to-date facilities for handling helicopters in all weather conditions. In addition, both classes are relatively large, which makes for good sea-keeping and fuel storage capacity, and both classes have proven propulsion systems. The fact that some of these ships are on their second deployments is indicative of the fact that the PLAN does not yet have many of these classes in commission, although both classes are in serial production, and we should expect to see more of them, especially the FFGs, entering the deployment cycle shortly.

In addition, the multiproduct replenishment ships are being pushed hard, as the list above indicates: the pattern is for them to stay for two rotations (about 8 to 9 months) and then return after less than half a year in China to relieve the other. For example, *Qiandaohu* was featured in a *Renmin Haijun* (人民海军 *People's Navy*) article because in the 6 years it had been in commission it had already made 13 overseas deployments and had operated for over 9 months off Somalia. Regarding this ship, the article goes on to say that:

> They established 10 firsts with regard to things such as distant sea, nighttime replenishment of three vessels abreast, entering the waters of the Red Sea for the first time for escort operations, and carrying out replenishment drills *with foreign military vessels for the first time*, thus filling in numerous blanks for our Navy with regard to carrying out logistical support during non-war military actions overseas. [Emphasis added][34]

The experience the crew of this ship has gathered during these very demanding rotations is invaluable to the PLAN in terms of operations, ship design, training, and, most importantly, logistics support to the fleet.[35] The fact that these two ships have been involved in back-to-back deployments for 3 years does raise the question as to why the PLAN has been so slow to introduce such an essential capability in such limited numbers. Starting with the ninth escort mission, these two ships finally were given some "time off," and the older oiler *Qinghaihu* was dispatched with the ninth escort unit and will remain on station with the tenth escort mission that commenced on November 18, 2011.[36]

An interesting interview with Mr. Zhagwende, the chief designer of the *Fuchi* Class multiproduct replenishment ships (AOE), sheds some light on this question. He suggests that the cost of building ships of this capability was a factor, in addition to the cautious, "build a little, test a little" approach that has marked PLAN surface ship procurement.[37] Another reason, in my judgment, is that until the *New Historic Missions* speech, *sustained* distant seas operations were not a high priority. The PLAN had been able to accomplish 2 decades of single-ship, show-the-flag visits around the world with just an accompanying oiler. A multiproduct ship would have been useful but not essential. However, these ships are essential if one aspires to have an expeditionary navy. Arguably, as the PLAN incorporates more distant seas operations into its normal *modus operandi*, an early indication of intent should be building more multiproduct replenishment ships.

It is also worth noting that the piracy problem in the Arabian Sea is only improving slowly, so it is entirely possible, and may in fact be likely, given the size and continued growth of China's merchant marine, that anti-piracy operations could be a mission that the PLAN will be engaged in for many more years.

ANTI-PIRACY DEPLOYMENTS—THE PLAN LEARNING CURVE

Logistics.

The first anti-piracy deployment provided many lessons for the PLAN—most importantly, it learned that periodic stays in port for fresh food and liberty for its sailors were necessary. The first flotilla made the mistake of sending its replenishment ship in Aden only for water, fuel, and food; the two destroyers never left the station. While that maximized on station escort time, the absence of fresh food become a minor health issue, and the fact that none of the crew could go on liberty had a negative impact on crew morale.[38]

As a *China Daily* article written in the summer of 2009 by a researcher at the PLAN Naval Academy stated:

> China's Navy should make bigger efforts to shorten its material and armament supply cycle to guarantee its success, and if necessary set up some coastal refuel and maintenance stations. Good quality fresh food supplies constitute an indispensable component for a country's naval servicemen to keep up robust and enduring fighting capability . . . fresh vegetables and fruits are still things that are desperately needed . . . on long voyages.[39]

The need for a reliable place for the PLAN port calls for logistics and morale purposes was obvious, and by the second deployment the PLAN began to call routinely at Salalah, Oman, a major transshipment point with good facilities including a secure port area. The commanding officer of *Weishanhu* said the main reason for selecting Salalah "is to further explore and perfect the way of large-batch comprehensive replenishment on a commercialized model, relying on foreign commercial ports so as to accumulate experience for the PLAN in carrying out oceanic logistics during military operations other than war."[40] Djibouti, Djibouti has also been visited for "replenishment and recuperation."

There was a kerfuffle in the China watching community in January 2010, when PLAN RADM Yin Zhou suggested that China needed to establish a permanent base in the Gulf of Aden because resupply and maintaining the fleet off Somalia without such a base was "challenging."[41] Rear Admiral Yin's view was eventually disavowed, and Chinese spokesmen pointed out that there were commercial Chinese shipping companies that could perform the task perfectly well.[42] Formalizing logistic arrangements and procedures that rely on Chinese commercial entities is a different sort of "string of pearls" capability, in the sense that China's commercial footprint along the Indian Ocean littoral provides a functional logistics network that, at least notionally, is under state control.

In any case, there were bugs to be worked out regarding the commercial processes. As one *Renmin Haijun* (人民海军 *People's Navy*) article recounted, every time material needed to be purchased it had to go through four different entities: Navy Headquarters, the Ministry of Transport, the Chinese shipping company in West Asia, and the local distributor. The process normally required more than 20 days[43] (no wonder Admiral Yin wanted a base). The same article goes on to say, that an "emergency foreign purchase plan was instituted allowing the Flotilla commander to directly purchase from a Chinese shipping company in West Asia, cutting the advance time to 2 days." I assume that the Chinese commercial entity that the PLAN is using is COSCO Logistics, which has offices throughout Southeast Asia, South Asia, and the Arabian Peninsula. COSCO Logistics is a subsidiary of COSCO (China Ocean Shipping Company), a very large Chinese state owned enterprise.[44]

Among the other important logistically related issues the PLAN has learned is how to conduct an emergency medical evacuation (MEDEVAC) when a sailor becomes ill and his condition is beyond the capability of the embarked medical team to address. This happened for the first time in December 2010, when an ill sailor wound up being bounced from the hospital in Salalah to one in Muscat until the PLAN finally got around to flying him back to China.[45]

Major Engineering Repair.

In May 2010, the PLAN had another first when the flagship of the Fifth Escort Flotilla had to put into Djibouti because it had a major casualty in its port main engine, which could not be fixed and needed to be changed out. From my personal experience, I can say that replacing a gas turbine main engine overseas is doable, but it takes skilled artificers and a responsive logistics system to do so. The PLAN pulled it off. For the first time, it organized a military air transport resupply, using the Military Transportation Department of the Navy Logistics Department. Once again, the bureaucracy was tortuous, involving the Beijing Military Region, the Main Administration of the Civil Air Fleet, and the general Administration of Customs to facilitate getting the engine through Djibouti customs.[46] This was a big deal, because, as we shall see, the fifth flotilla had a very ambitious port-visit agenda when relieved by the incoming sixth flotilla.

Longer Deployments.

Once the PLAN proved to itself it could logistically support extended distant seas deployments, it began to exploit the presence of three-ship flotillas by dispatching them on show the flag visits around the Indian Ocean littoral and into the Mediterranean Sea. This extended the length of deployments considerably.

The first flotilla deployment lasted a modest 124 days; by the third duration it was up to 158 days, and by the fifth flotilla, to an impressive 192 days (which is a bit longer than the notional 180-day USN standard).[47] This latter group transited the Red Sea and made port calls in Egypt, Italy, and Greece, conducting modest exercises with two Italian frigates in the Gulf of Taranto. The pretext behind the visits was the fact that this flotilla had escorted both Italian and Greek ships, and the visits allowed the governments of Italy and Greece an opportunity to express their appreciation.[48]

Sailors as Diplomats for China.

As these deployments increasingly involve port visits along the Indian Ocean littoral, and frequently into the Mediterranean, PLAN officers have been pressed into service as public representatives and spokesmen for China. A JFJB article captures this with the story of the assistant aviation detachment commander on the frigate *Chaohu*, who was dubbed a "diplomatic star." After visiting eight countries, he was now "an expert on international protocol and talks glibly with his colleagues in foreign militaries. Regardless of whether the topic is complex international law or the customs and sensibilities of other countries, he has a thorough understanding."[49] The PRC Ambassador to Yemen reports that, "The Embassy held a reception at the port. The officers and men of our Navy were able to interact in English, and lead songs and dance with Chinese and foreign friends. They were not constrained, and appeared extremely at ease and self-confident."[50] I can't help but observe that after a social beverage or two, the sailors of many countries act this way.

Realistic Exercises.

After reviewing 3 years of *PLA Daily* articles regarding the anti-piracy patrols, it has become clear that the PLAN learned relatively quickly that specialized and realistic training was necessary to be able to operate in an escort mission environment that might actually involve trying to retake a captured ship or using small arms and helicopters to chase away potential pirates. It was not until several rotations took place that articles began to appear describing how the escort flotilla would practice boarding and "taking down" a captured ship—by using one of its ships as the target vessel. For example, shortly after the tenth escort mission assumed responsibility for the mission, the PLAN conducted an exercise that was widely publicized in China because it was also the third anniversary of the anti-piracy mission.[51]

On January 11, 2012, PLAN Commander Admiral Wu Shengli held what the *PLA Daily* called a symposium that conducted a comprehensive assessment of achievements, lessons learned, and discussions associated with "promoting reform and innovation in escort work."[52] Unfortunately, the proceedings of that event are not available. This, of course, is the basic problem with attempting to assess what the PLAN has learned during its exercises or real world operations. This sort of after-action or lessons learned event inevitably directly or indirectly addresses shortcomings or mistakes, and as a result is sensitive and probably classified.

A month earlier in December 2011, Wu presented a "Commemorative Badge" during a ceremony marking the third anniversary of the anti-piracy missions.[53] According to Wu, 25 different PLAN warships have participated in the 3-year-long effort, during which the PLAN has safely escorted 409 convoys totaling 4,411 ships, and saved 40 ships that were being pursued and attacked by pirates on 29 different occasions.[54]

The accolades are well deserved. The PLAN has capitalized on 3 years of relatively intense operations, which show no signs of abating, and, based on the sketchy information available, has overcome the basic logistics and maintenance challenges associated with maintaining warships at sea on distant stations.

IMPLICATIONS FOR THE FUTURE

Defense of China is Not Sufficient.

The revision of the *Historic Missions* is a clear indicator that a naval strategy built only around the concept of protecting the maritime approaches to China is not sufficient. China's security interests cover a much wider array than can be addressed by the concept of "offshore active defense," which, after all, is essentially a wartime defensive concept and is not particularly relevant for operations beyond the second island chain during either peace or war. What the PLAN has learned in its interactions with foreign navies, largely in the context of anti-piracy operations, is how to operate in "distant seas."

The CMC has adjusted China's national military strategy — the *Military Strategic Guidelines* —twice in the past 10 years.[55] These adjustments have highlighted the value of naval power to China. The PLAN's status has been made a "strategic service," given priority for modernization, and directed to expand its operational focus to include: (1) continuing to improve its offshore active defense capabilities; (2) introducing expanding roles and missions for protecting China's increasingly important maritime and overseas economic interests; and, (3) emphasizing MOOTW, which include fighting terrorism and conducting peacekeeping and humanitarian assistance operations.

China's interests are global and will remain so. The requirement for a navy that can operate globally in peacetime or in situations of limited conflict is central to the interest of the state. Five years ago, then PLAN Political Department Deputy Director Rear Admiral Yao Wenhuai argued that developing new distant seas capabilities is vital, stating that:

> As modern PLAN weapons increase in range and precision and the naval battlefield expands from the offshore to the distant seas, the development of distant seas mobile capabilities will become increasingly important for protecting national security and development.[56]

The interests that are to be defended under the concept of "distant seas" include energy assets in the Persian Gulf, Africa, and Latin America; SLOCs between China and the Middle East; more than 1,800 Chinese fishing vessels operating on the distant seas and off the waters of 40 different nations; ocean resources in international waters; and the security of overseas Chinese.[57] The security of overseas Chinese is a growing problem for Beijing. Starting with the evacuation from Libya in 2011, the evacuation and/or protection of Chinese nationals working abroad has taken greater immediacy. In January 2012, 29 Chinese road construction workers were kidnapped by rebels in the border region of Sudan. According to one article, China now has some 850,000 workers abroad, many of whom are in the violent and potentially volatile regions of Africa and the Middle East.[58]

What this suggests is that the PLAN is increasingly going to be a regular presence on the oceans of the world. Seeing a Chinese warship half a world away from China will no longer be viewed as a novel event.

The PLAN Has Learned Much of What it Needs to Know to Operate on Distant Seas.

While the PLAN had begun to make global transits long before the anti-piracy patrols began, I argue that it is these patrols that will continue to have the most transformative impact on the PLAN. Learning how to operate as an expeditionary force is very significant, as is the experience gained by the commanding officers of the warships involved, and especially by the flag officers, who have learned how to exercise command of an afloat task force in a dynamic tactical real world environment.

These officers have also been on the frontline of Chinese naval diplomacy, which suggests a more "worldly" cohort of officers is being created.[59] The PLAN has learned how to deploy and sustain surface combatants, amphibious ships, and support ships to distant stations for long periods of time. The recently completed hospital ship *Peace Ark* deployment to the Caribbean, which lasted 105 days and covered an estimated 23,500 NM, is yet one more example.[60]

Just 3 years ago, Senior Colonel Chen Zhou, who has played an important role in the drafting of China's *Defense White Papers*, argued that China should be able to project power, especially naval power, in pursuit of peacetime missions in support of China's legitimate overseas interests. Chen notes:

We should expand the sphere of maritime activity, strive to demonstrate our presence in some critical strategic regions, use diplomatic and economic means to establish strategic supporting points, and make use of berthing points to which we legally get access from relevant countries in relevant sea areas.[61]

Chen makes it clear that he is not talking about a permanent global network of bases, but he does lend credence to the "string of pearls" argument by making the case that China should consider the development of some kind of support facilities in more than one region that could be used to support a routine—though not necessarily permanent—presence for the Chinese Navy in the future. Of course, thanks to the requirements to support anti-piracy patrols, capitalizing on China's global network of state-owned trading companies has now made this development a reality.[62]

The Growing Importance of the PLAN's Surface Force.

When it comes to off-shore defense—the PLAN's wartime strategy—it is the submarine force and fixed-wing naval air force that play the most significant role. When not at war, which is to say virtually all of the time, it is surface combatants—including, in the near future, the PLAN aircraft carrier—are most useful to the country. While continuing to maintain a defensive strategy to protect China and its possessions, the PLAN will also deploy surface warships, whose primary utility will be to provide a peacetime presence, sea-lane monitoring, and crisis response.[63]

Because the PLAN is embarked on this new operational vector that is very different from offshore active defense, it will, in my judgment, continue to acquire different sorts of capabilities, such as more logistics support ships, amphibious helicopter capable ships, and more destroyers with better endurance and air defenses (this usually means bigger, because increased range demands more storage capacity).[64] Although it has not used its sophisticated air defense systems in combat, the PLAN has undoubtedly learned important lessons regarding reliability, detection capabilities, problems with mutual electronic interference with sister ships, and sustained intership data linking.

The anti-piracy operations have permitted the PLAN to learn what mix of propulsion, size, and combat suite for its surface warships is best for distant deployed operations. Such missions have reinforced the basic rationale behind the PLAN's decision to build a modestly sized aircraft carrier force.[65] Operating alone in waters where the air space is dominated by either the United States or India must have emphasized the importance of air cover for distant operations that could someday involve combat.

Looking into the future, it is not hard to imagine how the emphasis on distant seas operations could result in a PLAN that becomes a more balanced force in terms of its mix of ships and range of capabilities, and begins to resemble the United States or French Navy.

Policy Implications for the United States.

Since the Cold War ended, the United States and its friends and allies, which constitute the vast majority of naval power in the world, have been unconstrained when deploying naval forces off the coast of another power to support Western interests and signal determination. China has frequently not seen eye to eye with the West when it comes to policies involved with African or Middle Eastern powers. A PLAN capable of distant seas operations provides Beijing with a new tool it can employ to support its friends and buttress its policies. Should the PLAN be employed in this fashion, it could greatly complicate U.S. policy approaches by introducing a new factor into crisis response options.

The longer the PLAN is involved in anti-piracy patrols, the more it becomes integrated into the maritime life of the region around the Strait of Hormuz. China already depends much more upon Gulf oil than does the United States. Over time it may be possible and desirable to have the PLAN become more of a positive contributor to the overall peace and stability of the region. The military issues that cause tension between the PLA and the U.S. military are East Asia-specific, whereas there is a very close alignment of interests (but not necessarily policies chosen to advance those interests) between Washington and Beijing in this region.[66]

Finally, as the PLAN demonstrates genuine competence and professionalism on distant seas operations, despite being oriented on peacetime missions, this is, ironically, raising concerns among the littoral states of the Indo-Pacific over the security implications of a PLAN that is becoming more expeditionary. Clearly, the introduction of modern amphibious ships, and shortly, an aircraft carrier force, provides the PLAN with a credible power projection capability. This emerging capability is, in turn, creating a demand by the littoral states for area denial capabilities such as submarines and land-based aircraft with antiship cruise missiles. This capability is also enhancing the desirability of a U.S. naval presence along this long littoral. The Obama administration's rebalance to Asia seems perfectly timed.

ENDNOTES - CHAPTER 3

1. For the full text, see Hu Jintao, "Understand the New Historic Missions of our Military in the New Period of the New Century," available from the National Defense Education website of Jiangxi Province, *gfjy.jiangxi.gov.cn/yl.asp?did+11349.htm.*

2. Information Office of the State Council of the People's Republic of China, *China's National Defense in 2008,* January 2009, p. 12.

3. There is no official indication that this is a mission that has been assigned to the Navy. Although the diversion of a frigate from anti-piracy patrols to "protect" the commercial ship that China had chartered to evacuate Chinese workers from Libya is an example of how deployed surface combatants can contribute to a rapidly developing emergency or crisis.

4. Alexander Chien Cheng Huang, "Chinese Maritime Modernization and its Security Implications: The Deng Xiaoping Era and Beyond," unpublished Ph.D. dissertation, George Washington University, 1994, pp. 225-240. Huang argues that the PLAN strategy has long been identified as active defense, offshore operations (积极防御, 近海作战), or the formulation I have used above. He cites senior PLAN leaders as indicating that "offshore" represents the Navy's operational radius, while "defense" spells out the nature of the strategy. He also goes on to discuss that over the years the definition of how far offshore "offshore" represents was determined by a combination of desired capabilities based on threat perceptions and of extant capabilities.

5. The following six paragraphs are drawn from Michael McDevitt and Fredrick Vellucci, "The Evolution of the People's Liberation Army Navy: The Twin Missions of Area-Denial and Peacetime Operations," in Geoffrey Till and Patrick C. Bratten, eds., *Sea Power and Asia-Pacific: The Triumph of Neptune,* London, UK, and New York: Routledge, 2012, pp. 75-92.

6. Hu Jintao, "Understand the New Historic Missions of our Military in the New Period of the New Century."

7. The phrase "strategic opportunity period" is a standard term that refers to a period when various international and domestic factors create a positive environment for a nation's economic and social development. Jiang Zemin first used this term during his report to the 16th Party Congress (November 8, 2002) in reference to the first 20 years of the 21st century.

8. Sun Kejia, Liu Feng, Liu Yang, and Lin Peisong, eds., *Faithfully Implementing Our Military's Historic Missions in the New Period of the New Century*, Beijing, China: Ocean Tide Press, 2006, pp. 102-126.

9. Wang Zhaohai, "Honestly Undertake the Historic Missions of Our Armed Forces in the New Period of the New Century," in *Seeking Truth*, No. 23, 2005, p. 25.

10. The term *yuanhai* can also be translated as "open seas" or "distant oceans." Some English sources translate the term as "blue water." However, current usage of the term indicates that the Chinese are not using it to describe what the U.S. Navy would consider a blue-water navy, so "distant seas" is the most commonly used translation.

11. The 2008 *Defense White Paper* states that China continues to develop its ability to conduct "offshore" operations while gradually building its ability to conduct operations in distant seas. *China's National Defense in 2008*, Beijing, China: Information Office of the State Council, 2009.

12. Zhang Yongyi, ed., *The Science of Naval Training*, Beijing, China: Academy of Military Science Press, 2006, p. 250.

13. Christopher D. Yung *et al.*, *China's Out of Area Naval Operations: Case Studies, Trajectories, Obstacles and Potential Solutions*, INSS China Strategic Perspectives, Washington, DC: National Defense University (NDU) Press, December 2010, p. 9.

14. *Ibid.*, pp. 10-11.

15. Office of Naval Intelligence, *China's Navy 2007*, p. 114.

16. Huang Li, *Sword Pointed at the Gulf of Aden: The PLAN's Far Seas Shining Sword*, Guangzhou, China: Sun Yet-sen University Press, 2009.

17. ONI, *China's Navy 2007*, p. 114; and Information Office of the State Council of the People's Republic of China, *China's National Defense in 2008*, Beijing, China, January 2009, available from *www.fas.org/programs/ssp/nukes/2008DefenseWhitePaper_Jan 2009.pdf*.

18. According to Foreign Ministry spokesman Huang Xueping, "The purpose for attending the operation is to allow the Chinese navy to gain useful experience from foreign counterparts, strengthen its communication capacity, learn how to cooperate with foreign navies in handling new threats and challenges at sea, and maintaining regional peace and stability." Available from *www.defense.pkforum/pakistan.html*.

19. "Chinese Fleet Visits San Diego," *People's Liberation Army Daily*, September 18, 2006, in English, available from *pladaily.com. cn/site2/special-reports/2006-09/19/content_591087.htm*. Recently, I spoke to a USN officer who participated in this exercise; he recalled them as being very rudimentary.

20. As recently as 2008, Hong Kong was the site for in-port search and rescue exercises, but the ships did maneuver together at sea. "U.S.-Chinese Navies Complete SAREX Together," *Navy Newsstand*, September 21, 2006, available from *www.navy.mil/ search/display.asp?story_id=25702*.

21. "U.S., China Complete 2nd Phase SAREX Off Southern China," available from *navy.mil/search/display.asp?story_id=26734*.

22. Available from *www.marinebuzz.com/2009/04/23/China-pla-navy-celebrates-60th-anniversary/*.

23. A blog by Defense News Correspondent Usamn Ansrai, available from *usmanansari.com/id.25.html*.

24. Available from *news.xinhuanet.com.englich/2007-03/10/ content_5825249.htm*.

25. "Xiangfan Returns from 'Western Pacific Naval Symposium' Maritime Exercise,"*Jiefanguin Bao* WWW-text in English, May 24, 2007, OSC CPP20070525715007.

26. Andrew Forbes, "Western Pacific Naval Symposium," Papers in Australian Marcitime Affairs, No 19, 2006, p. 183, available from *www.navy.gov.au/w/images/PIAMA19.pdf*.

27. Beijing Xinhua in English 1500 GMT, September 6, 2007, Xinhua in English, 1357 GMT September 18, 2007, Xinhua in English 1549 GMT, September 25, 2007. See also *www.military-quotes. com/forum/358530-post.html*.

28. Available from *www.china.org.cn/english?China/223960.htm*; *www.minister.defense.gov.au/n...0928/index.htm*; and *www,defense. gov.au/news/navynews/editions/5019/5019.pdf*.

29. "China's Navy Still has Far to Go," available from *www. chinadaily.com.cn/opinion/2009-08/14/content_8568918.htm*.

30. "PLA Navy Repels Pirates with Grenades, Bullets," *South China Morning Post Online* in English, September 4, 2010, OSC CPP20100904722002. For an interesting discussion of PLAN rules of engagement, circa 2009, see Richard Weitz, "Priorities and Challenges in China's Naval Deployment in the Horn of Africa," " *China Brief,* Vol. 9, Issue 24, December 3, 2009, available from *www.jamestown.org/single/?no_cache=1&tx_ttnews*.

31. " PLA Navy Commander Expounds on Anti-piracy Campaign in Gulf of Aden," *Zhongguo Qingnian Bao Online* in Chinese, April 16, 2010, p. 4. OSC CPP201000416710006.

32. JFJB Marks 2nd Anniversary of Start of PRC Navy Escorts off Somalia," *Jiefangjun Bao* Online, December 24, 2010, OSC CPP20110105088005.

33. Throughout the research for this chapter, I have come across a number of references to the accidental bombing of the Chinese embassy of Belgrade as the reason why it is important that PLAN ships operating in the vicinity of U.S. air power require an adequate air defense capability.

34. Jiao Pufeng (焦蒲峰), "'Qiandaohu' Far-Ocean Comprehensive Replenishment Ship: Moves About the World Freely, Shows Strength in All Directions" ("千岛湖" 远洋综合补给舰：综合四海，扬威八方), *Renmin Haijun* (人民海军 *People's Navy*), June 21, 2010.

35. The *Qiandaohu* and her sister ship, *Weishanhu*, form what is called the *Fuchi* class. They were commissioned in 2004 and are the first PRC-built multiproduct replenishment ships (AOE) capable of resupplying fuel, water, stores, and ammunition, while previous indigenous replenishment ships were actually fleet oilers (AO). Importantly, the ship is aviation-capable and has a hanger large enough for two multipurpose helicopters.

36. "9th and 10th Chinese naval escort task forces conduct mission handover," *PLA Daily*, November 21, 2011, available from *eng.mod.gov.cn/DefenseNews/2011-11/21content_4317916.htm*.

37. "Chief Designer Talks about PLA Navy Replenishment Ship," *China Navy*, Featured Articles, February 12, 2009, available from *www.china-defense-mashup.com*.

38. Salalah was used as a liberty port as well, "The officers and men on board ship who have been at sea for a long period of time will take rest in turns and go ashore for exercise," see, "PLAN Navy Berths in Port Salalah for First Replenishment," *Chinese Military News*, cited from *chinamil.com*, available from *www.china-defense-mashup.com/?tag=pirates*.

39. "China's Navy Still has Far to Go," available from *www.chinadaily.com.cn/opinion/2009-08/14/content_8568918.htm*.

40. "PLAN Navy Berths in Port Salalah for First Replenishment."

41. "China to Establish a Naval Base Around Somalia," available from *www.newstimeafrica.com/archives/9895*.

42. For example, "Navy has no plans for overseas bases," available from *www.chinadaily.com.cn/china/2010-03/11/content_9570126.htm*.

43. Yu Yonghua (余永华), "Lifting Warships Towards the Deep Blue: A Record of a Detachment's Shore Logistics Unit Exploring a Far-Ocean Logistics Guarantee Model" (托举战舰向深蓝：某支队岸勤部探索远洋后勤保障模式纪事), *Renmin Haijun* (人民海军 *People's Navy*), September 30, 2010.

44. See *en.wikipedia.org/wiki/COSCO* and *www.cosco.com/en/global_offices/staff.jsp?catId=299.*

45. Yu Yonghua (余永华), "Lifting Warships Towards the Deep Blue."

46. *Ibid.*

47. JFJB Marks 2nd Anniversary of Start of PRC Navy Escorts off Somalia.

48. "Italy, China Conduct Joint Naval Exercise off Taranto," Turin, Italy: *La Stampa*, August 3, 2010, EUP20100803058002; Xinhua Feature: "Chinese Naval Flotilla Visits Greece After Anti-Piracy Mission," *Xinhua*, August 9, 2010.

49. JFJB Article on PLA Navy's Efforts to Push Forward its Transformation, *Jiefangjun Bao Online* in Chinese, December 5, 2011, p. 9, OSC CPP20111205787016.

50. *Ibid.*

51. Zhang Qingbao (张庆宝), "Writing a New Chapter on the Escort Missions from a New Starting Point" (在新的起点上谱写护航行动新篇章), *Renmin Haijun* (人民海军 *People's Navy*), December 21, 2010. For the exercise conducted by the 10th escort mission, see *www.china.org.cn/video/2011-12/27/content_24257074.htm.*

52. "Symposium on third anniversary of Chinese naval escort held," *PLA Daily* January, 13, 2012, available from *eng.chinamil.com.cn/news-channels/china-military-news/2012-01/13/content_4768273.htm.*

53. "PLA Navy awards commemorative badge for major mission performance," *PLA Daily*, December 29, 2011, available from *eng.mod.gov.cn/DefenseNews?2011-12/29/content_4332515.htm.*

54. "Symposium on third anniversary of Chinese naval escort held."

55. Daniel Hartnett's unpublished paper, "Towards a Globally Focused Chinese Military: The Historic Missions of the Chinese Armed Forces," Summer 2008.

56. Yao Wenhuai, "Build a Powerful Navy, Defend China's Maritime Strategic Interests," *Guofang*, No. 7, 2007, pp. 1-2. RADM Yao was Deputy Director of the PLA Navy's Political Department at the time the article was published.

57. Lu Xue, "Views on Improving the Armed Forces' Ability to Execute the Historic Missions," *Zhongguo Junshi Kexue*, No. 5, 2007, p. 107.

58. David Pilling, "The trials of a reluctant superpower," *Financial Times*, February 1, 2012.

59. It would be an interesting research project for an analyst to document by name the flag officers who have commanded the escort missions, so their future careers can be tracked to determine if unique operational experience has any impact on professional advancement.

60. Chen Zuyi (陈祖怡), "'Peace Ark' Goes to 4 Latin American Countries to Visit and Develop Medical Services" ("和平方舟" 赴拉美4国访问并开展医疗服务), *Renmin Haijun* (人民海军 *People's Navy*), September 16, 2011.

61. Chen Zhou, "On Development of China's Defensive National Defense Policy under New Situation," *Zhongguo Junshi Kexue*, No. 6, 2009, pp. 63-71.

62. *Ibid*. See also "Jiefangjun Bao Article on Building PLA Strategic Power Projection Capability," *Jiefangjun Bao* OSC Translation, August 26, 2010, OSC CPP20100826702001.

63. Michael McDevitt and Fredrick Vellucci, "The Evolution of the People's Liberation Army Navy: The Twin Missions of Area-Denial and Peacetime Operations," in Geoffrey Till and Patrick

C. Bratten, eds., *Sea Power and Asia-Pacific: The Triumph of Neptune,* London, UK, and New York: Routledge, 2012.

64. An article by the East Sea Fleet Commander makes the point that, "China is a maritime power, and its Navy must have both off-shore comprehensive combat capabilities as well as the ability to conduct mobile combat operations far out at sea." Du Jingchen (杜景臣), "Use Distant Seas and Oceans as Troop Training Grounds" (把远海大洋当作练兵场), *Renmin Haijun* (人民海军 *People's Navy*), May 18, 2010.

65. Nan Li and Christopher Weuve, "China's Aircraft Carrier Ambitions: An Update," *Naval War College Review,* Winter 2010, p. 15, available from *www.usnwc.edu/publications/Naval-War-College-Review/2010---Winter.aspx.*

66. India worries about the PLAN's success in integration itself into the region. See, for example, Rahul Prakash , "For Chinese Navy, piracy a blessing in disguise?" Observer Research Foundation (ORF *China Weekly*), Vol. 22, Issue 4, January 23, 2012, available from *www.observerindia.com/ems/sites/orfonline/modules/chinaweekly/ChinaWeeklyListAll.htm.*

CHAPTER 4

"CONTROLLING THE FOUR QUARTERS": CHINA TRAINS, EQUIPS, AND DEPLOYS A MODERN, MOBILE PEOPLE'S ARMED POLICE FORCE[1]

Cortez A. Cooper III

The author wishes to express thanks to Sam Berkowitz and Lyle Morris for their research assistance.

EXECUTIVE SUMMARY

This chapter focuses primarily on Chinese People's Armed Police (PAP) capabilities development for counterterrorist and anti-riot missions and, specifically, on lessons learned from training, exercises, and deployments. The application of these lessons has resulted in a better trained, equipped, and ready PAP than had been the case at any previous period in the force's history.

MAIN ARGUMENT

The author proposes that a pivotal transition for the PAP occurred in response to a series of events in early-2008 to late-2010. The outcome is manifest in both the manner of PAP deployments and in mission capabilities. This chapter summarizes five areas of PAP capabilities development, in the form of administrative adjustments, joint integration, "informatization" (信息化), equipment modernization, and logistics and infrastructure enhancement. The chapter then examines the PAP's capacity to handle diverse missions, as evidenced in exercises and emergency deployments. PAP training and deployments provide a picture of increased and sustained readiness across the force, and indicate the adoption of new operational concepts to meet expanding mission requirements.

POLICY IMPLICATIONS

- For U.S. and partner policy and decisionmakers, the implications of a highly ready, mobile, and increasingly capable PAP fall into three general issue areas: advantages and disadvantages of bilateral exchanges on policing, disaster relief, and counterterrorism initiatives; advantages and disadvantages of multilateral engagement for peacekeeping and humanitarian assistance/disaster relief (HADR) operations; and promotion of People's Republic of China (PRC) transparency regarding PAP wartime roles and missions.
- As China's leaders seek more measured approaches to handling domestic unrest, exchanges with U.S. and partner police forces can provide concepts of operation and techniques that may facilitate de-escalation of domestic crises and improve responses to terrorist activity. These same exchanges, however, potentially provide training for the PAP to quell nonviolent public demonstrations more effectively.
- Despite the inherent problems, a cautious approach to exchanges, focusing on small-unit, nonescalatory crowd control and techniques for specific counterterror operations such as hostage rescues, likely shifts the balance in favor of engagement.

- On the multilateral front, the advantages further outweigh the risks. A variety of PAP forces, to include medical units, provide a wide range of policing and security force options for United Nations (UN) peacekeeping and multilateral HADR missions.
- Engagement with the PAP also provides a potential window into wartime missions for the force. Promoting transparency regarding PAP conflict roles and missions could provide a better understanding of PRC mobilization and escalation control.

INTRODUCTION

> Without stability, nothing could be done, and even the achievements already made could be lost. This is a lesson that all the comrades in the Party should keep in mind, and we should make all the people keep this lesson in mind.
>
> Hu Jintao, July 1, 2011[2]

Preservation of domestic stability and maintenance of Chinese Communist Party (CCP) control throughout the country is the top priority for China's leadership. Most, if not all, major Chinese policy issues, foreign and domestic, are evaluated with internal security implications in mind. In the 2 decades since the military crackdown in Tiananmen Square, CCP and security bureaucracy leaders have modernized and reorganized a multilayered internal security structure to provide more rapid, measured responses to internal emergencies. PAP modernization, current training, and recent deployments indicate that the lessons learned over these years have been applied to posture the force at a historically high state of readiness.

The CCP's evaluation of threats to domestic stability, and the context for upgrading domestic emergency response capabilities, is anything but straightforward. Party leaders often conflate a number of political, economic, and ethnic issues into a general "threat" rubric, and the anxieties facing the Party since Tiananmen have reinforced for elite leaders the need for more decisive but flexible control over developing internal crises.[3] Threats to PRC domestic stability and central Party control are lumped together under the rubric of the "three evils" ("三股势力"): international terrorism, national separatism, and religious extremism. While perturbations due to economic reforms and angry calls for social policy built on rule of law do not appear on the surface to be categorically "evil," the three groupings provide a big tent. Instability in the Tibet and Xinjiang Autonomous Regions is viewed as a manifestation of all three "evils."

China's central and local leaders turn to three multitiered organizations to meet the threat: the PAP, the Ministry of Public Security (MPS), and the People's Liberation Army (PLA). As the Party's "backbone and shock force in handling public emergencies," the PAP is a paramilitary force run jointly by the State Council and the Central Military Commission (CMC).[4] China's 2008 *Defense White Paper* puts PAP strength at 660,000, but other reports have put the PAP at as high as one million troops.[5] The MPS has approximately 1.7 million police officers assigned to provincial and municipal Public Security Bureaus (PSB) responsible for first-line local law and order. In 2005, the MPS developed special police forces similar to Western SWAT teams to conduct counterterror and antiriot operations. These forces have trained with foreign police forces for these missions. The PLA remains the final arbiter of CCP control throughout the country, and in instances of unrest in Tibet and Xinjiang in 2008 and 2009, respectively, PLA forces were involved in response to deteriorating security conditions in the face of PAP failures to enforce control.

The antecedents for security force developments, whether active service PLA forces, PAP, reserves, or militia, are tied to CCP strategic guidance traced to threat perceptions, and linked to budgetary priorities outlined in 5-year program directives. Developments during the 10th and recently completed 11th 5-year plan resulted in improved capabilities but mixed success in emergency response activities in 2008-09, particularly in instances of major tension in Tibet and Xinjiang and disaster relief operations following the Wenchuan earthquake.[6] The State Council reacted to shortcomings by increasing the internal security budget, initiating significant legislative initiatives, and stressing priorities through high-level pronouncements.[7]

This chapter focuses primarily on PAP capabilities development for counterterrorist operations, and specifically on lessons learned from training, exercises, and deployments. The application of these lessons, forged on the anvil of real world responses to multiple and varied domestic crises over the past 2 decades, has resulted in a significantly better trained, equipped, and ready PAP than had been the case at any previous period in the force's history. PAP crisis response actions as late as 2009 indicate that the force still falls short of CCP expectations in some critical capabilities, but there is evidence that changes implemented for and since the 2008 Olympics have shored up these gaps considerably.

ACHIEVING RAPID, NATIONAL-LEVEL RESPONSE CAPABILITIES: THE ROAD TO HISTORICALLY HIGH READINESS

The PAP was established in 1982. The first pivotal event in the evolution of the PAP came less than a decade later with the Tiananmen crackdown in June of 1989. PAP failures to control the Tiananmen demonstrations are well-documented, and the subsequent deployment of PLA forces to quell the protests marked a turning point for Chinese internal security forces in general, and the PAP in particular.[8] After Tiananmen, the PAP focused on developing a rapid national-level response capability. As part of a major ground force reduction in the mid-1990s, 14 PLA divisions were reassigned to the PAP as "strategic mobile units," and in 2002, special counterterror response units were created.[9] The objective of this period of the PAP's evolution is to a great extent summed up in CCP General Secretary Hu Jintao's call in 2004 for security forces to be prepared to apply developing capabilities to "diverse missions" across the national security spectrum.[10]

I propose that a second pivotal transition period for the PAP occurred not in the face of a single event, but in response to a series of events—some planned, some not—in the early-2008 to late-2010 period. The outcome of this evolutionary phase is manifest in both the manner of PAP deployments and in mission capabilities. Between early-2008 and the Shanghai Expo in April 2010, the PAP was tasked with spearheading internal security and emergency response operations in a sensitive period of economic downturn, complicating responses to major riots in Tibet and Xinjiang, extreme weather and earthquake disasters, Olympic security requirements, and a number of politically sensitive anniversaries—including the 50th anniversary of the Dalai Lama's flight, the 20th anniversary of the Tiananmen crackdown, and the 60th anniversary of the founding of the PRC. China's public security bureaucrats learned a number of lessons from these exigencies, and have implemented training programs, systems upgrades, and new concepts of operation to achieve the flexibility, mobility, and interoperability required by Hu's "diverse missions" directive.[11]

This chapter summarizes five areas of PAP capabilities development in the form of administrative adjustments, joint integration, "informatization" ("信息化"), equipment modernization, and logistics and infrastructure enhancement; the chapter then examines two specific venues where the PAP's capacity to handle "diverse missions" are tested—namely, exercises and emergency deployments. Reports on PAP training and deployments provide a picture of increased and sustained readiness across the force, and indicate the adoption of new operational concepts to meet expanding mission requirements.

Focusing on actual deployments as well as training inherently bears the assumption that the PAP is, in fact, frequently responding to real world crises or security requirements and that these responses either build on or detract from PAP efforts to improve readiness. Assessing PAP capabilities development and implementation of new operational concepts is different from observing similar phenomena in the PLA in one very significant area—the PAP regularly deploys to conduct its primary mission. As a result, the PAP is forced to juggle the need for a continuous ready response capability with the requirement to modernize concepts, equipment, and training regimens and facilities. While the jury is still out regarding the level of success in this pursuit, available reports indicate that at the very least resource prioritization and national-level leadership support provide a foundation for both improved capabilities and increased deployment.

Over the past 2 decades, training and equipment modernization for redundant security forces have greatly improved capabilities and readiness; including the ability to measure responses to minimize escalating violence. While this is not readily apparent from responses to ethnic unrest in 2008 and 2009, there is nonetheless marked evidence of incremental progress from Tiananmen to the present. Protests in Tibet in March 2008 resulted in a "political mobilization order" to the PAP to prepare the force for the period leading up to and encompassing the Olympics. For the 2008 Games, the PAP played a role in the inter-ministry Olympics Security Leading Small Group (国家奥运安保协调小组); reportedly formed a PAP Leading Small Group on Olympic Security Work; and managed the Games without any apparent lapse in normal regime protection capacity.[12]

Lessons learned from the slow and ineffective response, particularly by local PAP, to the 2008 Tibet riots were applied to Xinjiang unrest in 2009, but with mixed results. For the Xinjiang response, the PAP reportedly drew about 5,000 police from several strategic divisions within 2 weeks and deployed them by PLA Air Force aircraft. While mobilization and deployment of national-level PAP forces had improved, local units still failed to provide warning of the impending violence and collapsed to some extent in the face of its ferocity. This likely indicates a significant shortfall in intelligence warning support to domestic stability operations, as evidenced by the subsequent resource priority placed on intelligence, surveillance, and reconnaissance (ISR) capabilities development.

Exacerbating concerns of increasingly explosive unrest in western China and ongoing Middle East unrest have driven China's leaders to revamp the security posture in the region. The resulting strategy of tight social control and a strong security presence in minority regions and around key infrastructure means that increased readiness levels are now *de rigeur* for PAP forces. Beijing-based national-response PAP forces deployed rapidly from forward bases to Kashgar in August 2011 to augment already beefed-up local security forces.[13] Elements of national-level forces from Beijing's Snow Leopard (进驻) PAP commando unit have been forward-based in Xinjiang since the 2009 unrest. This level of readiness is not likely to diminish any time soon, with a national-level leadership transition set to culminate in less than a year at the 18th Party Congress.

ADMINISTRATIVE ADJUSTMENTS

Legal and Regulatory Frameworks.

The Law on the PAP (中华人民共和国人民武装警察法) was passed shortly after the 2009 Xinjiang riots, following criticism of the PAP's slow response and in anticipation of security requirements for celebrations surrounding the 60th anniversary of the founding of the PRC. The legislation reportedly removes the authority of county-level officials to call out the force, providing provincial and national level authorities a better chance to limit escalation of small-scale local disturbances into larger uprisings.[14] The law spells out eight main security and defense tasks. In major cities, Xinjiang, and Tibet, specialized PAP units have primary responsibility for counterterror and emergency

135

response. In other urban areas and townships, PSB special units figure more prominently.[15]

In late-October 2011, the National People's Congress (NPC) enacted a new antiterrorist law to clarify China's definition of "terrorism" and outline responsibilities for counterterror actions.[16] A stated objective of the law is to facilitate Chinese cooperation in international anti-terrorism efforts, though it also potentially provides codification for martial responses and detentions in cases of civil dissent.[17]

According to China's 2010 *Defense White Paper*, the CMC approved and promulgated "Regulations on Emergency Command in Handling Emergencies by the Armed Forces" ("军队处置突发事件应急指挥规定") governing social stability and emergency response operations. The white paper gives few details on specific implications for the PAP, but indicates that the document provides guidelines for organizing, commanding, and integrating security and military forces for response to sudden incidents. Integrated command and control (C2) of combined PLA, PAP, and PSB forces for counterterror exercises and drills is a high priority.

PAP Structure.

The PAP is under the dual leadership of the State Council and the CMC. The State Council assigns routine tasks and is responsible for administrative and financial management. The CMC is responsible for determining PAP organizational structure, managing officers, and establishing guidelines for training and political work.[18] The PAP comprises approximately 660,000 paramilitary police. According to China's 2008 *Defense White Paper*, the missions of the PAP in peacetime are to "perform guard duties, handle emergencies, combat terrorism, and participate in and support national economic development," and, in wartime, to assist the PLA "in defensive operations."[19]

The PAP has four general force groupings. The first and largest group is comprised of the internal defense or guard corps units, under the direct control of PAP headquarters. The second group consists of the security guard, fire-fighting, and border defense units managed primarily by provincial-level and county-level departments and MPS bureaus. The final grouping includes hydropower, gold mine, transportation, and forestry security and construction units. These are managed jointly by the PAP headquarters and corresponding ministries (Land and Resources, Forestry, Transportation, etc.) under the State Council.[20] Unlike the 2008 version, China's 2010 *Defense White Paper* does not have a separate section devoted to PAP modernization or force building, and it is difficult to determine from limited available sources the extent to which the PAP may reorganize, if at all, under the new PAP and antiterror laws.

While sources vary in delineating the exact unit structure of the PAP from top to bottom, five levels of command are noted throughout the literature: the General Headquarters in Beijing (总部); General Corps/Contingents (总队) at the provincial or centrally controlled city level; detachments (支队) at the prefecture or municipality level; brigades/battalions/groups (大队) at the county level; and companies/squadrons (中队) at the township level.[21] According to one *Xinhua* report, the PAP has 30 border security contingents; 110 prefecture level detachments; 20 prefecture-level marine police detachments; 310 county-level groups; 1,691 border police substations; 207 border inspection stations; 46 frontier inspection stations; and 113 mobile groups deployed along the various sections of the border.[22] According to the 2010 *Defense White Paper*: "The State Commission of Border and Coastal Defense, under the dual leadership of the State Council and the CMC, coordinates China's border and coastal defenses. All military area commands, as well as border and coastal provinces, cities and counties, have commissions to coordinate border and coastal defenses within their respective jurisdictions."[23]

Probably the most important structural adjustment to internal security forces in recent years is the modernization and deployment of national-level rapid response forces. Both MPS and PAP have special police in every province and most major cities, with counterterrorism and antiriot mission responsibilities. Contingency antihijacking squads align under provincial armed police corps; other internal defense forces, border defense units, and fire brigade units undergo counterterror training.[24]

Special units are trained at the PAP Special Police School (武警特种警察学院), which features sniper instruction, riot control, hostage rescue, and related training. The school dates to the early 1980s, when several hijacking incidents in China led to the establishment of a special anti-hijacking squad—a regimental-sized unit formed from elements transferred from the PLA Air Force's (PLAAF) 15th Airborne Corps and the Air Force Reserve School. When the PAP was established shortly thereafter, the special police group was subordinated to the PAP as "the special police school," responsible for both operational and training missions. In 2000, the school was renamed the PAP Special Police School, commanded by a division or deputy army command-level officer.[25]

Each provincial PAP Corps reportedly has at least one special combat group or squadron trained and equipped for counterterrorism operations. One source notes that the first of these was the Cheetah Commando unit subordinate to the 9th Detachment of the Shanghai armed police.[26] Shenyang's Tiger Commando Unit reportedly recently conducted an exercise focused on anti-hijacking operations related to a mass transit target in Harbin. The most visible of these units, however, is the Beijing 13th Detachment Snow Leopard Commando Unit. Established in 2002, the Snow Leopard unit is a national-level counterterror force headquartered in Beijing, and is considered China's premier hostage rescue and counterterrorist assault unit.

The Snow Leopards participated in a hostage rescue exercise during the Sino-Russian "COOPERATION 2007" exercise near Moscow, and elements have provided protection for Chinese diplomats in Iraq and Afghanistan.[27] The unit served a central role in the 2008 Olympic security operations, and deployed in August 2011 to Xinjiang to secure the town of Aksu in the aftermath of violence that the Chinese media blamed on "religious extremists" trained in Pakistan. Elements of the Snow Leopards remained in Xinjiang to provide security for the China-Eurasia Expo held in Urumqi in early-September 2011.[28] A CCTV documentary on the Snow Leopards indicates that the group comprises assault, reconnaissance, engineer, explosive ordinance disposal, and sniper squadrons, and claims that 90 percent of new commando recruits are eliminated during an 8-month initial training program.[29]

A PAP helicopter group is subordinate to the Xinjiang General Corps, focused on counterterrorism response and assault missions. This is reportedly the

PAP's only aviation unit, and it has participated in numerous major exercises and "frontline anti-terrorism operations."[30]

Responsibility for maritime domestic security operations in China is somewhat ambiguous. The China Coast Guard (CCG) transitioned from PAP control to the Ministry of State Security's Border Control department in mid-2006. With 11 regional units and 28 detachments, the CCG aspires to move from strictly riverine/coastal missions to open water operations, but faces stiff competition for these missions from forces serving under the Bureau of Fisheries and State Oceanic Administration.[31] The PAP retains marine police detachments, but their roles and responsibilities in counterterror operations are unclear.

PAP Funding.

There are traditionally three main sources of funding for the PAP. The first is a distinct budget line in the PRC state budget, reflected in the Minister of Finance's Budgetary Report and Premier's Government Work Report. This source includes funds from the central budget and the departments or ministries that maintain specialized PAP units. These specialized units include gold mine, forestry, hydroelectric facility, and transportation security units. There is no evidence that the PAP receives funds from the PLA budget, although the PAP falls under the operational control of the PLA General Staff Department during wartime, and likely would receive some operational PLA funding subsequent to a mobilization order.

The second major source of funding is provided by provincial, municipal/prefecture, or county governments. The money spent on paramilitary units as a percentage of provincial budgets is again relatively low, ranging from 0.03 percent to 0.36 percent of total provincial expenditure. Border and coastal provinces generally have the highest per capita expenses on PAP. While still small in absolute terms, local expenditures on the PAP have grown significantly in relative terms since the mid-1990s, rising from as low as 2.5 percent of total PAP funding to as high as 15 percent in the decade from 1996 to 2006. Stressing the increasing importance of local investment in PAP modernization, the Political Commissar of the Guangdong provincial PAP General Unit noted that the stability of local Party government requires grassroots funding for PAP facility construction, "informatization" initiatives, and counterterrorist equipment.[32]

The final category is extra budgetary funds from PAP businesses, fines, and security fees from government units and enterprises. The latter category largely includes fees paid by ministries in Beijing for PAP protection of their facilities and housing.[33] According to official statistics, China's public security spending almost doubled from 2007 to 2010, in line with the wide array of perceived threats discussed earlier and CCP focus on security force flexibility and readiness. The 2009 PAP Law, however, does not address funding issues or provide any evidence of shifting budget priorities or increased control over the PAP budget by central authorities. The law ostensibly prevents officials at county level and below from ordering PAP unit deployment, but rising local PAP funding potentially complicates national-level control of deployment decisions. Investigations into various Chongqing municipality organs in the aftermath of the Bo Xilai purge may drive a new look at local PAP unit posture, funding, and allegiances, but writings by senior provincial-level PAP leaders indicate a desire to improve links between local governments and PAP units, rather than weaken them. These same sources also link the development of civil-military emergency response plans to close relationships between PAP units and local officials and committees.[34]

JOINT INTEGRATION AND MULTI-LATERAL COORDINATION

A national counterterrorism coordination center reportedly governs PLA, PAP, and PSB integration for counterterror and antiriot response operations, addressing a key gap in coordination between central and local authorities that reportedly was to blame for poor performance in the face of terrorist attacks in Xinjiang in the early-1990s.[35] The center is subordinate to the State Council, but located in the MPS. It is responsible for coordinating counterterrorism actions across bureaus, departments, and regions.[36] Li Wei, the Director of the Anti-terrorism Studies Center at the China Institute of Contemporary International Relations (CICIR), is quoted as saying that all provincial and municipal governments have established counterterrorism offices under the control of the local governments and Party committees, but also answerable to higher-level counterterrorism offices.[37]

PRC border defense missions are split between the PLA and the PAP, with PSB, militia, and reserve units also involved in various aspects of border security. For the PLA, border defense regiments subordinate to military sub-districts provide the backbone for securing the border. The PAP and PSB run customs facilities, and PAP border defense troops provide border inspections, immigration control, maritime port security, counterintelligence and counterterrorism response forces.[38]

Coordination in counterterrorism is one of the cornerstones of China's approach to achieving national objectives in the multi-lateral context of the Shanghai Cooperation Organization (SCO). Cooperative security regimes involving the member states (China, Russia, Kazakhstan, Kyrgystan, Tajikstan, and Uzbekistan) provide a mechanism for China to exercise a modest level of influence over developments in Muslim areas beyond China's western border and approaches to stability maintenance in the region. The "regional ant-terrorist structure" (RATS) under the SCO was established in 2004, and a series of antiterrorism agreements signed in 2009 further strengthened the expansion of China's "three evils" construct into a general framework for addressing regional security issues.[39] Threats on the Northwest frontier offer opportunities for joint counterterrorism coordination and training under these constructs.

"INFORMATIZATION" ("信息化")

In a 2006 article, then-director of the PAP Engineering College, Major General Yang Zhengwu, noted that the "East Turkestan" terrorist threat provided the opportunity for the PAP to develop as an "informatized" force and put new high-technology capabilities to use in actual counterterror crackdown operations.[40] The subsequent fielding of a video teleconference-capable integrated command system appears to confirm that the PAP is following the PLA's suit in building a modern command information and data transmission backbone. Reports are unclear as to whether or not the PAP command system integrates with or is modeled on the PLA's similarly touted integrated command platform.[41] One recent source refers to a multifunctional, "informatized" command platform deployed by the Hainan PAP General Unit to provide security for the Boao Forum annual conference. This platform reportedly has many of the same capabilities ascribed to the PLA system, with interfaces for communications, logistics, ISR, positional and navigational data, and other automated command tools.[42]

A similar system reportedly provided a platform for a recent exercise in the Guangxi Military District. Sixteen PSB, PAP and PLA border defense units reportedly interfaced with each other and civilian authorities via a joint network with eight functional sub-systems. These sub-systems included C2, ISR, positional, meteorological, and hydrological capabilities; and facilitated the intelligence sharing that previous sources noted was conspicuously absent in emergency responses in the 2008-09 period.[43]

According to one source, the Xinjiang PAP HQ has invested tens of millions of *renminbi* (RMB; currently about 7 RMB to the U.S. dollar) to build a four-tiered command training network connected by the PAP's integrated command system—comprising a headquarters command training center, detachment and group training nodes, and company or squadron terminals. The system reportedly incorporates satellite links and provides communication, location, and automated decisionmaking aids.[44] According to another report, PAP command decisionmaking tools include state-of-the-art geo-locational equipment—during the *Guardian 08* counterterrorism exercise in April 2008, the PAP unit commander used a three-dimensional simulator system to pinpoint terrorist locations.[45]

A number of Chinese television and print media sources have highlighted over the past year the proliferation of advanced ISR technologies to PAP units. One report focuses on a reconnaissance team from the Shandong PAP General Unit, which used a small, rotary-wing unmanned aerial vehicle and other optical devices to provide locational data during a hostage-rescue exercise.[46] As with the PLA, PAP resource prioritization clearly focuses to a great extent on fielding automated command and intelligence decision tools, and these systems figure prominently in PAP training at various levels.

EQUIPMENT MODERNIZATION

While reporting is spotty regarding specifics relating to PAP modernization across the board, most of the 14 national-level response divisions transferred in the 1990s from the PLA to the PAP underwent equipment modernization and facility renovation over the past 5 years. This includes fielding new WZ-551 armored personnel carriers (APC) equipped for counterterrorism operations. Six- and four-wheeled APC variants have been featured in CCTV video clips and reportedly include versions designed for counterterrorist assault, riot control, and psychological operations (broadcast vehicles). These vehicles are illustrative of increased specialization and sophistication in dealing with diverse internal security tasks.

As seen in several CCTV clips, some posted to YouTube, the Snow Leopards unveiled a new, modified armored personnel carrier at the National Day Parade in October 2009—18 of these vehicles participated in the parade, manned by commandos in anti-riot gear. A 2008 media report focused on other items in the Snow

Leopards' arsenal, including 5.8 mm assault rifles, silenced submachine guns, sniper rifles, protective gear, bomb-detecting and disposal gear and robots, and a counterterrorism assault vehicle equipped with various boarding and assault ladders. Interestingly, the report noted that as a result of the Western arms embargo against China, China's light arms are not quite up to state-of-the-art standards.[47]

The Engineering College of the Armed Police Force is reportedly the research and manufacturing base for special commando equipment for the PAP. Since 2005, the Engineering College has managed 64 projects related to the development of communication, reconnaissance, night vision, and life detection systems.[48] Commando equipment includes fire-resistant black combat uniforms, bullet-proof helmets, night vision goggles, and holographic scopes. There is also evidence from *Xinhua* photos that the PAP has fielded jamming equipment—possibly devoted to jamming Voice of America and other foreign-generated transmissions during periods of unrest.

LOGISTICS AND INFRASTRUCTURE ENHANCEMENTS

Perhaps the primary lesson learned from the Wenchuan earthquake relief operations in 2008 concerned logistics support under international scrutiny. The Joint Logistics Department in the Lanzhou MR reportedly relied on a campaign reserve system to support a variety of PLA, PAP, PSB and civil organizations involved in noncombat operations such as disaster relief, counterterrorism, and stability operations. One report noted that multitiered, multidomain training has been implemented to enhance responses to emergencies that involve joint domestic forces, international organizations, and mass media.[49]

The earthquake response is also held up as an example of the success of joint C2 and command training systems and programs. One report applies the lessons of joint military, police, and militia C2 during the earthquake to the challenges faced by joint border defense forces in their duties. The author notes that transportation and communication infrastructure problems in border and frontier areas potentially hamper both wartime and peacetime emergency response operations, and posits that joint civil-military construction projects and training systems are required.[50]

The events of 2008 and 2009 provided ample impetus for the construction of new training facilities, which also provide improved response capabilities and logistic bases. Reports of a new counterterrorism training base at the Xinjiang PAP Headquarters reveal bomb disposal, anti-hijacking, and reconnaissance training aided by bomb disposal robots, life detection equipment, and satellite communications and positioning systems.[51] According to a CCTV documentary, the Snow Leopard Commando training facility has a live-fire target simulation system that collects data on trainee performance and allows for interactive scenarios, and a laser engagement simulation system for commando assault and hostage rescue training.[52]

A more permanent PAP footprint in unstable areas following the 2008-09 difficulties has accompanied major upgrades to or new construction of training facilities. These facilities also serve as bases to support more rapid responses by national-level units when required. Since 2008, an increased permanent security presence in Tibet has enabled the PAP to respond more quickly to destabilizing events and allows the

PLA to maintain a lower profile. Recent events, such as the multiple incidents involving self-immolation by Tibetan monks over the past year, indicate that local forces are perhaps more capable of managing incidents and are less reliant on immediate PLA or strategic PAP support. A recent *China Daily* report indicated that a new special police force had been established in Urumqi with 5,000 elite forces, though the source was unclear on mission specifics.[53]

Some evidence of the focus on developing infrastructure in support of operations in western China can be found in the 2008 *Defense White Paper*. The chapter posits that between 2006 and 2008, "the PLA and PAP . . . have contributed more than 16 million workdays and utilized 1.3 million motor vehicles and machines, and participated in construction of more than 600 major infrastructure projects relating to transportation, hydropower, communications and energy."[54] While these projects are linked to improving quality of life for local residents, they also support improved mobility, logistics support, and communications for security forces throughout western China, and particularly along the northwestern border.

ACHIEVING HISTORICALLY HIGH READINESS: LESSONS LEARNED FROM TRAINING AND MOBILIZATION

In July of 2011, President Hu gave a speech during a meeting of PAP Delegates to the CCP Party Congress, stressing that despite improvements in readiness over the past two years, more emphasis should be placed by the PAP on training.[55] Training and real world mission deployments are focused primarily but not entirely on western China, and involve both domestic and international exercises. Local and national-level PAP units regularly train to integrate with other public security organs on riot control, civil disturbance policing, counterterror, border control and disaster response tasks, and mobilize routinely to meet threats to domestic stability across a broad range of mission areas.

Mobilizing to Police the Homeland.

The readiness and responsiveness of China's internal security forces have been a particular focus of elite leadership attention in the wake of proliferating calls from across China's demographic landscape for greater government accountability and social justice. Popular resentment over official corruption, land appropriation, religious intolerance, food safety issues, and related social grievances have intersected with ethnic unrest in Tibet, Xinjiang, and Inner Mongolia to convey an increasingly virulent threat to CCP leadership. The perception of the existential nature of the threat is compounded by a belief among the senior leadership that a variety of foreign actors seek to exacerbate challenges to CCP control. As a result, any number of domestic crises can be categorized as "separatist" or "terrorist" in nature. Events over the past 2 years, however, potentially indicate that national and provincial Party leaders have learned from past protest escalations to consider the potential advantages of more nuanced approaches to defining and responding to varying types of internal unrest.

The links between counterterrorism, ethnic unrest, and emergency response in the minds of China's leaders are key drivers behind PRC domestic and international policy decisions. The response to the domestic threat is all-encompassing—propaganda, media, legal, political, military, and police organs and bureaucracies are all involved in mobilization against internal challenges to Party order and control. As threats to control evolve in form and function, however, so do Chinese official responses to them. Last year's reactions to Internet calls for a "Jasmine Revolution," creating fears of "Arab Spring"-like protests, were greeted throughout China by immediate PSB, PAP, and other security force deployments—largely preempting the ability of protests to materialize.[56] Concerns of organized social unrest on a large scale resulted in martial deployments, much like those generated by iterations of "separatist" unrest in Tibet and Xinjiang, but with authorities reaping a mobilization advantage from the interception and exploitation of the very social media tools used by activists to rally public gatherings (the mission statement of provincial and local PSB units now includes a requirement to "take charge in security monitoring of public information networks").[57]

Protests in Guangdong Province in late-2011, however, engendered a different response. When protesters in the seaside village of Wukan scattered local police and took control of the town in response to illegal land grabs by local Party officials, a heavy-handed paramilitary response never materialized. Security forces cordoned off the village, but provincial Party Deputy Secretary Zhu Minguo negotiated with protest leaders and agreed to meet several key demands in exchange for a return of the village to a degree of normalcy. This sufficiently defused tension to the point that protesters could believe, albeit with little precedent, that the higher levels of the CCP could be trusted to listen to local grievances. This, in turn, rendered the environment less interesting to the international media spotlight.[58]

Senior Party leaders increasingly recognize that certain situations demand a more delicate touch when applying force in order to de-escalate tension and undermine the coherency of a given domestic threat. For situations in a predominantly rural area such as Wukan, where venal local leaders are both guilty and conveniently expendable, negotiations serve the cause of social calm. In urban areas, where the populace is less likely to trust senior officials, and local leaders are more likely to be rising in the Party ranks, negotiations might be underpinned by additional force. Threats and rumors of threats in areas of ethnic unrest, or escalating tension along with potential terrorist activity at major events or sensitive venues, will most likely continue to evoke martial responses. Evidence of increased interest in variegated approaches is also found in reports of training visits by Chinese police to the United States and England. One source notes that these visits may indicate "that a shift is underway (in China) toward a more fluid style of policing, at the same time as maintaining the military option in areas of particular unrest."[59]

While a more detailed study is needed on policing patterns and CCP reactions to geographically and topically disparate incidents of social conflict, it is evident that Party leaders and bureaucrats have learned to seek scalable options to keep the peace without appreciably improving the lot of the common citizen to influence social policy. This superficial solution guarantees that Party leadership will continue to prioritize a mobile, well-trained paramilitary force to augment local police and rapidly bring domestic emergencies under control.

Counterterrorism and Riot Control Training.

From mid-2006 through mid-2011, Chinese media sources identified approximately 55 major PAP counterterrorism exercises. The frequency of these exercises is increasing, from nine in 2007 to 15 in 2010. Four of these exercises were international exercises, three of which were conducted under the auspices of the SCO. All of these involved the Snow Leopard Commando unit. The 2008 *Defense White Paper* notes that PAP units participated in *Great Wall 2003* and *Great Wall II* counterterrorism exercises; deployed for the SCO-sponsored *Joint 2003* exercise; and hosted *Guard 04* and *Guard 06* exercises focused on large-scale emergency response operations. The 2008 *Defense White Paper* claimed that as of the writing of that document, the PAP had sent contingents to over 30 countries for counterterrorism exchanges and had hosted delegations from 17 countries in such exchanges.

The joint counterterrorism exercises within the SCO framework have received a great deal of attention in the international press and have provided consistent venues for China both to influence regional approaches to regional security issues and to train its security forces on the northwest frontier. In 2002, China's joint counterterrorism military exercise with Kyrgyzstan was the first ever with a foreign country, and a 2003 SCO joint counterterrorism exercise represented a first for training in a multilateral context.[60] A series of Sino-Russian *Peace Mission* exercises in 2005, 2007, 2009, and 2010 also included other SCO country forces, and were primarily focused on counterterror operations.

Preparatory training for the 2008 Olympics also provides a window into PAP training and readiness regimes. This training progressed over the course of 14 months from basic skills training through simulated event responses and live exercises.[61] Simulated and live field training activities focused on counterterrorism and emergency response while providing security at pre-Olympic events, creating a realistic training environment corresponding to ethnic unrest deployments. This training environment also provided significant joint training opportunities for the PAP, as they participated in emergency response scenarios with PSB, militia, People's Air Defense, and other PLA units.[62] Anti-hijacking exercises also featured prominently in Olympic preparatory joint training—involving not only PAP and PSB, but China's Civil Aviation Administration and civil health departments as well.[63] These training opportunities provided a basis for a wider distribution of realistically trained and experienced PAP personnel in both local and national mobile response units following the games.

As is the case with the PLA, the PAP has also sought to increase training realism by introducing opposing forces into counterterrorism exercise scenarios. One report cites a 2007 hostage response exercise, *Great Wall No. 4*, as the first PAP opposition force exercise (对抗演习). In this exercise, a Beijing PAP unit conducted hostage rescue operations against a PSB contingent acting as a terrorist group.[64]

It is difficult and ultimately misleading to divorce PAP preparations for counterterrorism operations from those of disaster relief and anti-riot operations. These are all stability operations in the eyes of CCP leadership; and counterterror and antiriot operations are particularly wedded in the eyes of CCP elites because of the fear of violence and political opposition from ethnic "separatist" organizations. A good example can be seen in the Party's frequent conflation of ethnic political reform organizations, such as the World Uyghur Congress (WUC) headed by Rabiyah Kadeer, with internal "separatist" groups.[65] While fear of outside forces exacerbating domestic tensions is and likely will remain a driver of CCP responses to domestic unrest, even in this area, the Party has learned lessons that correspond to more modulated approaches.

In incidents prior to the 2009 Xinjiang uprisings, CCP fears of outside forces aiding and abetting domestic "separatists" led Chinese media and propaganda organs to immediately draw highly suspect connections between the WUC and local violence. These actions served to increase the stature and credibility of the WUC outside China, and potentially may have heightened threats of retaliation from international terrorist groups. In 2009, while propaganda outlets immediately blamed outside forces and media controls were tightened, less emphasis was placed on attacking the WUC. Instead, China sought to reach out to Muslim countries and appeal to the inherent fears of destabilizing extremism within the leadership of these nations.

Border Control Training and Operations.

Peripheral state instability has a significant impact on the domestic security equation as it pertains to PAP capabilities development. The PAP and PLA both have roles in border control operations, and concerns over an increased flow of extremists trained in Central Asian training camps is reflected both in Chinese foreign policy—particularly in Chinese objectives for the SCO—and in security force training and deployment.

China blames the Xinjiang-based East Turkestan Islamic Movement (ETIM) for carrying out at least 200 bombing attacks between 1990 and 2001, including attacks on armed police officers who were not appropriately trained to deal with terrorist elements mingling with "religious believers."[66] While evidence is at best sketchy, information obtained from Uighurs captured in Afghanistan and held at Guantanamo indicates that some ETIM personnel received training in Afghanistan and crossed back into China to conduct attacks.[67] The ETIM was listed as a terrorist organization by the United States in 2002.

In the decade since, both the PAP and PLA have made marked improvements in border control operations on China's immense western frontier. Despite this, the Turkestan Islamic Party (TIP), believed to be based in Pakistan, has taken responsibility for attacks that left dozens dead in Hotan and Kashgar in July 2011. Reports backed by video clips indicate that "core members" of TIP have been trained by al-Qaeda in Pakistani camps.[68] TIP also claims responsibility for a bus attack in Shanghai in 2008, but these claims remain unverified, and even Chinese experts are cautious in drawing connections between TIP and ETIM.[69] In any case, legitimate concerns regarding international and home-grown terrorist activity in western China are muddied by the frequent use of "counterterror" language, laws, and responses to address clear cases of peaceful civil dissent.

Joint training for border control and stability has been a priority for China's security forces over the past decade. As noted previously, border control and stability operations include peace, domestic crisis, and wartime missions, and involve PLA border defense units, reserve and militia forces, PAP, and PSB personnel. In an attempt to break down administrative barriers and improve coordination, the Chengdu Military Region (MR) and its sub-districts have instituted joint training and exercise programs focused on civil-military integration under leadership groups composed of prefecture and county-level border defense committees. The training program focuses on three mission areas: defensive operations, counterterrorism, and disaster response. According to a Chengdu media report, the command of two actual emergency response operations in the border region in 2008 followed a model developed through the joint training and exercise program.[70]

This report also indicated that in the Wenshan sub-district of the Chengdu MR, all prefectural and township military and police units were required to form "one unit" for joint training for at least 20 days each year. Within this structure, personnel and units from across organizations were integrated into joint training units by specialty areas—to include command and control, intelligence, communications, emergency rescue, and counterterrorism.[71] The extent to which this approach has taken root across the vast expanse of China's border regions is unclear, but MR and sub-district leaders have exercised processes for integrating PAP units with PLA and PSB units across a range of peacetime, emergency response, and combat operations scenarios.

Humanitarian Assistance and Disaster Response (HADR).

According to the 2010 *Defense White Paper*, "in January 2009 . . . China formed eight State-level emergency response professional units, boasting a total of 50,000 personnel, specializing in flood control and emergency rescue, earthquake rescue, nuclear, biological and chemical emergency rescue, urgent air transportation, rapid road repair, maritime emergency search and rescue, emergency mobile communication support, and medical aid and epidemic prevention."[72] The paper also indicates that in 2009, PAP forces responsible for protecting water and electricity infrastructure were integrated into the "national emergency rescue system." Between 2008 and 2010, the PAP and PLA reportedly combined in "1.845 million troop deployments and 790,000 deployments of vehicles or machines of various types . . . organized 6.43 million militiamen and reservists . . . [and] rescued or evacuated a total of 1.742 million people."[73]

The 2010 *Defense White Paper* and several media reports also indicate that PAP medical personnel affiliated with the PAP General Hospital in Beijing serve on the China International Search and Rescue (CISAR) team. According to the paper, the team has participated in eight international rescue operations, including in Haiti and Pakistan following the earthquake and flood disasters in those two countries. Civil-military joint emergency rescue teams have been established over the past year at provincial-level PAP units, with new emergency care vehicles deployed to improve HADR medical response capability.

While disaster relief support on the scale described in the most recent defense white paper conceivably detracts from overall PAP readiness to respond to counterterrorist and riot control operations, these deployments also provide exceptional training opportunities for the development of rapid reaction and sustainment procedures. These deployments are clearly associated with the priority placed by Hu Jintao's military guidelines on diverse, non-war missions, and likely will remain a core function for the PAP.

UN Peacekeeping Operations.

The first Chinese police unit deployed to a peace operation joined the United Nations Stabilization Mission in Haiti (MINUSTAH) in 2004. While the MPS managed the unit and its deployment, PAP forces likely participated. In subsequent deployments, PAP provincial-level border police forces (公安边防) appear to have formed the core of deployed units. [74] Deployments require close coordination between the PAP and the Office of Peacekeeping Affairs at the Ministry of Public Security, which is responsible for the selection, training, and deployment of police units for UN peacekeeping operations.

CCP elites recognize both the theoretical importance and practical advantage of dispatching police to help with UN peacekeeping. One 2008 source states that "dispatching riot police to participate in UN peacekeeping activities helps embody our proactive attitude towards UN peacekeeping activities, establish our image as a great nation, and satisfy the requirement of our foreign relations work; it has great significance."[75] To accompany a rising need for trained police and paramilitary forces in peacekeeping operations, and to reinforce the value Beijing places on support for these missions, in 2002, Chinese officials announced the establishment of Asia's largest peacekeeping civil police training center in Langfang City, near Beijing. The facility reportedly has the capacity to train 250 police officers at a time.

An annual snapshot of Chinese police participation in UN peacekeeping missions from 2008 to the present indicates that anywhere from 70 to 200 Chinese police are deployed at any given time. It is difficult from the sources, however, to ascertain how many of these are from PAP units and how many are from PSB units.[76]

POLICY IMPLICATIONS

For U.S. and partner policy and decisionmakers, the implications of a highly ready, mobile, and increasingly capable PAP fall into three general issue areas: advantages and disadvantages of bilateral exchange on policing, disaster relief operations, and counterterrorism initiatives; advantages and disadvantages of multilateral engagement for peacekeeping, HADR, and other operations; and the importance of promoting PRC transparency regarding PAP wartime roles and missions.

Chinese security forces generally, and the PAP specifically, pose a conundrum for U.S. policymakers considering engagement with Chinese police forces. As China's leaders seek more measured approaches to handling domestic unrest, exchanges with U.S. and partner police forces can provide concepts of operation and techniques that may facilitate de-escalation of domestic crises and improve responses to terrorist activity. These same exchanges, however, potentially provide training for the PAP as a paramilitary force to quell nonviolent public demonstrations more effectively.

Cooperation on counterterror initiatives continues to provide a foundation for building exchanges, but the problem of clear classification and differentiation of terms remains when coordinating with China on counterterrorism issues. The recent PRC Anti-terror Law provides ample maneuver space for the classification of various forms of public dissent as terrorist activity, and does not protect China's citizens from arbitrary detention. Despite the inherent problems, a cautious approach to exchanges, focusing on small-unit, nonescalatory crowd control, and techniques for specific counterterror operations such as hostage rescues, likely shifts the balance in favor of engagement.

On the multilateral front, the advantages further outweigh the risks. A variety of PAP units have benefited from modernization and increased resources, providing a wide range of policing and security force options for UN peacekeeping and multilateral HADR missions. PAP medical units are experienced and increasingly well-equipped to meet UN mission requirements, and could provide particularly beneficial visibility for China in international emergency response scenarios. China's clear prioritization of peacekeeping involvement and development of Asia's largest police training center for peacekeeping operations, provide excellent but underappreciated avenues for promoting international policing norms.

Engagement with the PAP on bi- and multilateral fronts also provides a potential window into wartime missions for the force. While PAP concepts and capabilities for potential regional conflict are understandably not high on the radar of most U.S. security analysts, they are critical components of Chinese mobilization for war. Chinese concerns of internal chaos arising in the face of an escalating external crisis underpin political education and training for the PAP, and likely translate to missions essential to CCP war control operations. As such, promoting transparency regarding PAP conflict roles and missions could provide a better understanding of PRC mobilization and escalation control.

CONCLUSION

While fully engaged in providing the paramilitary component of China's increasingly complex emergency response strategy, over the past few years local and national PAP forces have responded vigorously to CCP calls for modernization of equipment and facilities, improvements in training aids and concepts, and adjustments to basing and infrastructure. A confluence of significant planned events and exigencies between 2008 and 2010 marked a transition period for the PAP, during which a high operational tempo combined with force modernization efforts to place the force at what appears to be a historically high state of readiness.

At the same time, CCP leaders seem to be searching for strategic and operational concepts that provide a wider array of policing options to ensure control while minimizing escalation. The implications of this for the PAP remain to be seen, but in the context of conducting counterterrorist and riot control operations, the PAP is expected to respond rapidly to apply decisive, measured force with specially trained units in coordination with PLA, PSB, and certain civil organizations. Exchanges with foreign police forces, international and domestic exercises, and real world deployments over the past 2 to 3 years indicate that the PAP is pursuing this on all fronts of capability development. The application of resulting capabilities will, as always, depend on CCP definitions of "counterterror" and "antiriot."

Legal guidelines lack specificity in terms of missions and rules of engagement regarding the potential transition of the PAP to wartime footing. However, current border security missions and counterterrorism training activities provide some insight. National-level PAP training, basing, and capabilities are well-suited to support the PLA in border control, key infrastructure defense, and rapid response operations; local forces, while still experiencing problems with measured crowd control, likely will constitute a critical defense against antiregime opportunism the Party fears would arise during an external crisis.

It remains to be seen if the rising rate of civil unrest in China will whittle away at PAP capabilities across peacetime and wartime mission areas. For the present, force readiness appears higher than ever, and resources and leadership emphasis for further capabilities improvements are not on the wane. Several potential avenues are open for U.S., partner, and UN engagement with these increasingly capable PAP forces on counterterror, HADR, and peacekeeping fronts, albeit with the risks inherent in engaging a paramilitary force that provides security for a regime at odds with several international human rights norms.

ENDNOTES - CHAPTER 4

1. "Control the four quarters" is an admonition taken from "T'ai Kung's Six Secret Teachings," purportedly written to provide advice to Kings Wen and Wu of the Chou Dynasty in the 11th Century B.C., in Ralph Sawyer, trans., *The Seven Military Classics*, Boulder, CO: Westview Press, 1993, p. 46.

2. From a speech by Hu Jintao at the 90th Anniversary of the Chinese Communist Party, *Xinhua*, July 1, 2011, available from *www.chinadaily.com.cn/china/cpc2011/2011-07/01/content_12818048_15.htm*.

3. For a general discussion of the internal challenges of building and maintaining CCP legitimacy and the implications for policy, see Susan Shirk, *China: Fragile Superpower*, New York: Oxford University Press, 2008.

4. *China's National Defense in 2010*, Beijing, China: The Information Office of China's State Council, March 31, 2011, available from *www.china.org.cn/government/whitepaper/node_7114675.htm*.

5. *China's National Defense in 2008*, Beijing, China: The Information Office of China's State Council, January, 2009, available from *www.china.org.cn/government/central_government/2009-01/20/content_17155577.htm*.

6. For an excellent discussion of PAP and PLA responses to 2008 and 2009 emergency response exigencies, see Harold M. Tanner, "The People's Liberation Army and China's Internal Security Challenges," in Roy Kamphausen, David Lai, and Andrew Scobell, eds., *The PLA at Home and Abroad: Assessing the Operational Capabilities of China's Military*, Carlisle, PA: Strategic Studies Institute, U.S. Army War College, June, 2010.

7. Unattributed, "Social Governance Debuts in Five-Year Plan," *South China Morning Post Online*, March 6, 2011, available from *www.archive.scmp.com*. China's internal state security budget has surpassed the official defense budget. See Chris Buckley, "China Internal security Spending Jumps Past Army Budget," *Reuters*, March 5, 2011, available from *www.reuters.com/article/2011/03/05/china-unrest-idUSTOE72400920110305*.

8. For an overview of PAP historical antecedents, structural and organizational developments, and missions, see: Tai Ming Cheung, "The People's Armed Police: First Line of Defence," in David Shambaugh and Richard H. Yang, eds., *China's Military in Transition*, Oxford, UK: Clarendon Press, 1997; and Murray Scot Tanner, "The Institutional Lessons of Disaster: Reorganizing the People's Armed Police After Tiananmen," in James Mulvenon and Andrew N.D. Yang, eds., *The People's Liberation Army as Organization, Reference Volume v 1.0*, Santa Monica, CA: RAND Corporation, 2002.

9. Dennis J. Blasko, "PLA Ground Forces Moving Toward a Smaller, More Rapidly Deployable, Modern Combined Arms Force," in James Mulvenon and Andrew N. D. Yang, eds., *The People's Liberation Army as Organization, Reference Volume v 1.0,* Santa Monica, CA: RAND Corporation, 2002.

10. Hu Jintao, "Report to the 17th Party Congress," Beijing, China, October 25, 2007, available from *www.china.org.cn/english/ congress/229611.htm.*

11. Harold M. Tanner, "The People's Liberation Army and China's Internal Security Challenges," in Roy Kamphausen, David Lai, and Andrew Scobell, eds., *The PLA at Home and Abroad: Assessing the Operational Capabilities of China's Military,* Carlisle, PA: Strategic Studies Institute, U.S. Army War College, June, 2010; Dennis Blasko, " People's Liberation Army and People's Armed Police Ground Exercises with Foreign Forces, 2002-2009," in Roy Kamphausen, David Lai, and Andrew Scobell, eds., *The PLA at Home and Abroad: Assessing the Operational Capabilities of China's Military,* Carlisle, PA: Strategic Studies Institute, U.S. Army War College, June, 2010; and Murray Scot Tanner, "How China Manages Internal Security Challenges and Its Impact on PLA Missions," in Roy Kamphausen, David Lai, and Andrew Scobell, eds., *Beyond the Strait: PLA Missions Other Than Taiwan,* Carlisle, PA: Strategic Studies Institute, U.S. Army War College, April, 2009.

12. Howard French, "Rattled, Chinese Make Security for Olympics Top Priority," *The New York Times,* April 1, 2008, available from *www.iht.com/articles/2008/04/01/asia/tibet.php.*

13. Unattributed, "China sends anti-terrorist unit to restive west," *Associated Press* wire report, August 14, 2011, available from *www.dawn.com/2011/08/14/china-sends-anti-terrorism-unit-to-restive-west.html.*

14. Michael Wines, "China Approves Law Governing Armed Police Force," *The New York Times,* August 27, 2009, available from *www.nytimes.com/2009/08/28/world/asia/28china.html.*

15. *Ibid.*

16. Chen Liping (陈丽平), "全国人大常委会作出决定加强反恐怖工作" ("The NPC Made a Decision to Strengthen Anti-terrorist Work"), 法制日报 (*Legal Daily*), October 29, 2011, available from *www.legaldaily.com.cn/index_article/content/2011-10/29/content_3066938.htm?node=5955*.

17. Martha Mendoza, "Nations turned to ant-terrorism laws as shield—and sword—after 9/11," *The Seattle Times*, September 4, 2011, available from *seattletimes.nwsource.com/html/nationworld/2016104402_sept11convicted04.html*.

18. *China's National Defense in 2008*.

19. *China's National Defense in 2010*.

20. Yuning Wu, Ivan Sun and Aaron Fichtelberg, "Formalizing China's Armed Police," in *Crime, Law and Social Change*, Vol. 56, No. 3, November 2011, available from *www.citeulike.org/group/11075/article/8820036*.

21. For more detail on PAP structure and command, see David Shambaugh, *Modernizing China's Military: Progress, Problems, and Prospects*," Berkeley, CA: University of California Press, April 2004.

22. Unattributed, "White Paper: China Has 260,000 Armed Police on Guard Every Day," *Xinhua*, January 20, 2009, available from *www.news.xinhuanet.com/english/2009-01/20/content_10688124.htm*.

23. *China's National Defense in 2010*.

24. Mi Aini, "详解中国反恐布局" ("Detailed Explanation of China's Anti-terrorism Disposition"), 瞭望东方周刊 (*Oriental Outlook*), No. 28, July 15, 2010, pp. 18-20.

25. *Ibid.*, p. 19.

26. *Ibid.*, p. 20.

27.王作葵和赵嘉麟 (Wang Zuokui and Zhao Jialin), "中俄'合作—2007'联合反恐演习圆满结束" ("Sino-Russian 'Cooperation 2007' Joint Anti-terrorism Drill Brought to Successful Conclusion"), 新华 (*Xinhua*), September 6, 2007; and Zhang Dongbo (张东波), "中国武警'雪豹突击队'初步具备反恐制胜作战能力" ("China's Terrorist Crack Troops, the 'Snow Leopards,'" Display Their Ability to Win"), *Xinhua*, November 12, 2007.

28. Unattributed, "Unit Sent to Xinjiang to Smooth Way for Expo," *China Daily*, August 13, 2011, available from *www.china.org.cn/china/2011-08/13/content_23202225.htm*.

29. From August 4-7, 2008, CCTV-7 aired a four-part documentary on the Snow Leopards as part of its weekly 军事纪事 (*Military Documentary*) series.

30. Zhu Jianjun (朱建军), "反恐处突的空中利剑"("A Sharp Sword in the Sky for Combatting Terrorism and Emergency Response"), 解放军画报 (*PLA Pictorial*), December 1, 2008, pp. 54-55.

31. Unattributed, "China Coast Guard," *SinoDefence.com*, March 21, 2009, available from *www.sinodefence.com/navy/coast-guard/default.asp*.

32. Zhu Fengyun (朱凤云), "在继续解放思想中推进武警部队建设又好又快发展" ("Liberate thought to improve and accelerate the development of the People's Armed Police"), 国防大学学报 (*Journal of the National Defense University*), No. 12, 2007, pp. 98-99.

33. For discussions of PAP funding, see Roger Cliff, Evan Medeiros, James Mulvenon, and William Overholt, *Modernizing China's Military*, Santa Monica, CA: Rand Corporation, 2005; John Lee, "PAP: The Rise of the Party's Army," *Jamestown China Brief*, June 19, 2008, available from *www.jamestown.org/programs/chinabrief/single/?tx_ttnews%5Btt_news%5D=4999&tx_ttnews%5BbackPid%5D=168&no_cache=1*; and Shaoguang Wang, "China's Expenditure for the People's Armed Police and Militia," in *Chinese Civil-Military Relations: The Transformation of the People's Liberation Army*, Hong Kong: Asian Security Studies, 2006, available from *www.cuhk.edu.hk/gpa/wang_files/MilitiasPAP.doc*.

34. See for example Zhu Fengyun, p. 99; and Liu Dongsheng (刘东升), "要重视对武警部队处突战略的研究" ("We must emphasize research on emergency response strategies for People's Armed Police units"), 新世纪新阶段国防和军队建设 (Construc-

tion of National Defense and the Military in the New Century and the New Phase) 上册 (Vol. 1), 2008, pp. 236-238. Originally published in军事学术 (*Military Review*).

35. Mi Aini, p. 19.

36. *Ibid.*

37. *Ibid.*

38. M. Taylor Fravel, *Strong Borders, Secure Nation*, Princeton, NJ: Princeton University Press, 2008.

39. Unattributed, "SCO to deepen pragmatic cooperation," *China Daily*, May 20, 2011, available from *www.chinadaily.com.cn/opinion/2011-05/20/content_12550033.htm*.

40. 杨正武 (Yang Zhengwu), "武警院校要成为反恐人才库" ("Academies of Armed Police Should Become Repositories for Anti-terrorist Talent"), 光明日报 (*Guangming Daily*), August 23, 2006, available from *www.gmw.cn*.

41. For further information on the PLA's "integrated command platform," see Cortez A. Cooper III, "Joint Anti-Access Operations: China's 'System of Systems' Approach," Testimony presented before the U.S.-China Economic and Security Review Commission, January 27, 2011.

42. From a CCTV-7, 军事报道 (*Military Report*) on April 3, 2012.

43. From a CCTV-7, 军事报道 (*Military Report*) on January 5, 2012.

44. 张建军，张怀敏和王国银 (Zhang Jianjun, Zhang Huaimin and Wang Guoyin), "武警新疆总队遥控排爆机器人5分钟解体爆炸物" ("Xinjiang Armed Police Unit's Remote Controlled Bomb Defusing Robot Dismantles Explosive in 5 Minutes"), 解放军报 (*PLA Daily*), November 21, 2007.

45. Mi Aini, p. 19.

46. From a CCTV-7, 军事报道 (*Military Report*) on November 18, 2011.

47. Unattributed,"'雪豹突击队'和奥运反恐精英" ("The 'Snow Leopard Commando Unit' and the Olympic Anti-Terror Elite"), 三联生活周刊 (*Life Week*), August 11, 2008, pp. 66-73.

48. 邹永星, 田西柱和程清志 (Zou Yongxing, Tian Xizhu and Cheng Qingzhi), "新型警用装备显威特殊战场" ("New-Model Police Equipment Demonstrates Power on a Special Battlefield"), 解放军报 （*PLA Daily Online*), November 27, 2008, available from *www.chinamil.com.cn*.

49. Zhang Wansong (张万松), "打造应对非战争军事行动后勤保障新格局" ("Create a New Logistic Support Pattern for Coping With Non-combat Military Actions"), 人民军队 (*PLA Activities Report*), July 22, 2008.

50. Wang Lanjun (王兰军), "着眼维护边境稳定增强军警民联合指挥能" ("Enhance the Military, Police, Militia Joint Command Capability for Safeguarding Frontier Stability"), 人民军队 (*PLA Activities Report*), July 22, 2008.

51. Zhang Jianjun, Zhang Huaimin, and Wang Guoyin, p. 3.

52. From August 4-7, 2008, CCTV-7 aired a four-part documentary on the Snow Leopards as part of its weekly 军事纪事 (*Military Documentary*) series.

53. Unattributed, "600 Million More Yuan for Xinjiang Armed Police," *China Daily Online*, March 6, 2010, available from *www.chinamil.com.cn*.

54. *China's National Defense in 2008*.

55. Unattributed, "Chinese President Urges Comprehensive Efforts to Build Modern Armed Police Force," *Xinhua*, July 11, 2011, available from *english.gov.cn/2011-07/11/content_1903815.htm*.

56. See multiple reports from the Hong Kong press in the January to March 2011 timeframe.

57. See, for example, the mission statement of the Beijing Municipal Public Security Bureau, available from *www.bjgaj.gov.cn/eng/gajjjAction.do?methodname=gajjjIndex&cateCode=GAJJJ*.

58. Professional and amateur media coverage of Wukan abounds, but for concise analysis of Wukan and its implications, see Russell Leigh Moses, "Will Wukan be the New Normal," *The Wall Street Journal Real Time Report*, December 28, 2011, available from *blogs.wsj.com/chinarealtime/2011/12/28/will-wukan-be-the-new-normal/*; and Elizabeth Economy, "Wukan's Struggle Is Not Over," *The Atlantic*, January 12, 2012, available from *www.theatlantic.com/international/archive/2012/01/wukans-struggle-is-not-over/251314/*.

59. Tim Parsons, "Police State: China's Community-based Policing," *Jane's Intelligence Review*, January 5, 2012.

60. *China's National Defense in 2010*.

61. Unattributed, "武警部队奥运保安训练全面启动" ("PAP Olympic Security Training Comprehensively Kicks Off"), *Xinhua*, May 17, 2007, available from *news3.xinhuanet.com/sports/2007-05/17/content_6111315.htm*.

62. Meng Xiaodong, "Promoting the Launch of Olympic Security Work," *Qinhuangdao Ribao*, July 5, 2007, p. A01.

63. Li Jing (李静), "武警军队反劫机演练备战奥运，重点防范三种威胁" ("Armed Police, Military Anti-Hijacking Exercise to Prepare for the Olympics, Focus on Preventing Three Types of Threats"), 世界新闻报 (*World News Journal*), August 26, 2007, available from *2008.sohu.com/20070826/n251782660.shtml*.

64. Shen Xiaohong, "PAP Special Police Units Participate in Great Wall No. 4," 人民武警报 (*PAP News*), June 20, 2007, p. 1.

65. Ben Mah, "The July 5 Riots in Xinjiang," *The New Legalist*, July 18, 2009, available from *ninfajia.net/content/review/6484.page*; and Uyghur American Association, "Exile Brings Voice to Uighur Movement," July 27, 2009, available from *www.uyghuramerican.org//articles/3363/1/exile-brings-voice-to-movement.html*.

66. *Ibid.*

67. Holly Fletcher and Jayshree Bahoria, "East Turkestan Islamic Movement," Council on Foreign Relations Backgrounder, July 31, 2008, available from *www.cfr.org/china/east-turkestan-islamic-movement-etim/p9179.*

68. Unattributed, "Turkestan Islamic Party claims western China attacks," *Associated Press* wire report, 8 September, 2011, available from *www.dawn.com/2011/09/08/turkistan-islamic-party-claims-western-china-attacks.html.*

69. Michael Wines, "Militant band Claims Role in Western China Attacks," *The New York Times,* September 8, 2011, available from *www.nytimes.com/2011/09/09/world/asia/09china.html.*

70. Zhang Xudong (张旭东), Bian Fubin (边富斌), and Zhou Fengwu (周风武), "军地互动探新路：文山军分区组织边境地区军警民联训联演纪" ("Exploring New Ways of Military-Local Interaction: Wenshan Military Sub-district Organizes Military-Police-Civilian Joint Training and Exercises in Border Areas"), 战旗报 (*Zhanqi Bao*), August 12, 2008, p. 3.

71. *Ibid.*

72. *China's National Defense in 2010.*

73. *Ibid.*

74. Bates Gill and Chin-Hao Huang, "China's Expanding Role in Peacekeeping," SIPRI Policy paper 25, November 2009, available from *books.sipri.org/files/PP/SIPRIP25.pdf.*

75. 赵会领 (Zhao Huiling), "提高维和警察防暴队培训质量的实践与思考" ("Thoughts on the Enhancement of FPU Training Quality"), 武警学院学报 (*Journal of the Chinese People's Armed Police Force Academy*), No. 5, 2008.

76. See the UN Peacekeeping website available from www.un.org/en/peacekeeping/resources/statistics/contributors.shtml.

CHAPTER 5

CLARITY OF INTENTIONS: PEOPLE'S LIBERATION ARMY TRANSREGIONAL EXERCISES TO DEFEND CHINA'S BORDERS

Dennis J. Blasko

EXECUTIVE SUMMARY

This chapter examines People's Liberation Army (PLA) Army and Airborne transregional exercises conducted from 2006 to 2011.

MAIN ARGUMENT

Since 2006, official Chinese sources have identified transregional mobility as among the major training objectives for PLA ground forces. Several exercises have focused on moving large units (brigades and divisions) from one Military Region (MR) to another, incorporating into these exercises other experimental training topics such as command and control for joint operations, operations in a complex electromagnetic environment, formation of combined arms battalion task forces, and logistics support. Chinese media reports have documented many of these exercises in considerable detail.

POLICY IMPLICATIONS

None of the transregional exercises to date have been designed to intimidate Taiwan, but rather have focused on reinforcing operations in distant regions within China after a conflict has broken out. Cross-border operations outside China would require different logistics support than has been demonstrated in these exercises.

Within the context of the PLA's entire training program, transregional exercises are exploring many operational concepts that other advanced militaries have implemented for decades. Based on their own comments and observations, Chinese military leaders are aware that PLA experimentation in modern tactics and techniques probably will take much longer for them to achieve proficiency than many foreign observers imagine. If deemed successful, transregional exercises could provide the rationale for future cuts in ground units and allow personnel slots and funding to be applied to transportation assets necessary for long-distance movements, a recognized shortfall in PLA capabilities.

Contrary to perceptions about a lack of transparency in PLA intentions, transregional exercises have been clearly identified as a training objective, and the exercises themselves have been covered by the Chinese media, enabling foreign analysis. In short, the PLA told us what it was going to do, then did it so we could see it.

INTRODUCTION

Since 2006, official Chinese sources have clearly identified transregional exercises among the major training objectives for the PLA ground forces. For the PLA, transregion mobility (全域机动型or 跨区机动) means movement across MR boundaries within China, not beyond China's borders. Official media reports (print, electronic, and television) have documented in some detail several such exercises conducted from 2006 to today. These reports reveal an Army training according to its published doctrine and experimenting with new organizational and tactical concepts.

In most cases, Army units, frequently supported by the other services and civilian assets in joint operations, are the main maneuver units in transregional exercises, though the PLA Air Force (PLAAF) 15th Airborne Army (or Corps) also has conducted a high-profile exercise of this nature. Over time, transregional exercises have become larger and more complex as they test new command and control procedures. Units from all over the country have participated, except for combat units from the Nanjing MR. If judged successful by the Chinese military leadership, these exercises may provide insight into future developments for the entire PLA, such as further cuts in ground forces and increases in the transportation assets necessary for force projection.

In prior decades, units conducted nearly all PLA ground force training within their own MRs. With a massive Army, limited budgets, multiple potential opponents, and vastly differing geography around China's periphery (ranging from jungles and forests to plains, mountains, and deserts), localized training was a rational response to conditions at the time. However, as defense budgets increased, new equipment was introduced into the force, doctrine was updated, and the ground forces were restructured to become smaller, more mobile, and more informationized (better equipped with modern communications, computers, and other electronics). These new conditions and technologies permitted new operational concepts to be tested, one of which was transregional operations.

Prior to 2006, a few exercises had included the deployment of small units across MR boundaries, but not as the main focus of the exercise. For example, the first reported trans-MR movement reportedly occurred during the large 2001 Dongshan amphibious exercise (东山登陆演习), which in total included over 100,000 personnel. At that time, PLAAF Il-76 transport aircraft moved a rapid reaction unit (of unspecified size) subordinate to a group army from Beijing MR to the exercise area.[1] Long before that, however, during the period of border clashes between China and Vietnam in the mid-1980s, a number of divisions rotated from distant MRs to the conflict area in order to expose PLA troops to combat. Entire units moved administratively, i.e., not subject to harassment by the enemy, from their garrison locations to training areas behind the lines where they acclimatized and prepared for up to 5 months before moving to the front. There they spent 6 months conducting infantry and artillery operations against the Vietnamese before moving back to their home bases.[2] These previous examples of transregional deployments differ from the exercises starting in 2006 in that they were adjuncts to larger operations, not the main focus of the exercises as seen recently.

Recent transregional operations focus on tactical movements across MR boundaries by large units (brigades and divisions), often while subjected to simulated enemy reconnaissance, harassment, and attack, followed by a period of training in areas of operations unfamiliar to the units involved. This training includes force-on-force maneuvers, usually with units stationed in the region acting as the "enemy," and often incorporating live fire and evaluations of unit capabilities.

Most major large-scale ground force training occurs at the seven MR Combined Arms Tactical Training Bases (CATTB), with preparatory lower-level training taking place in garrison and at local unit training areas prior to deployment to a CATTB. Brigades and divisions within the MR (sometimes acting as parts of a group army) travel to their respective CATTBs, according to schedules defined by MR headquarters. Due to limited time and training space, each CATTB can accommodate only a portion of an MR's ground forces each year, and MR headquarters must prioritize which units have access to their own CATTB. Since they involve more than one MR, transregional exercises must be ordered by the General Staff Department (GSD). Joint training is also conducted in coordination zones that include large swaths of terrain beyond the boundaries of military bases in the various MRs.[3] Most long-distance travel is conducted by road or rail; movement by PLAAF transport aircraft and/or civilian airlines is also practiced, but is limited mostly to personnel with some accompanying equipment. PLAAF aircraft may also provide ground attack support and combat air patrol cover for ground force operations. So far, PLA Navy (PLAN) or civilian maritime participation has been minimal (seen in only one exercise).

The PLA still is at the beginning of a process of experimentation and learning that integrates its new doctrine, equipment, and logistics with better educated personnel. To date, the new transregional capabilities exercised have been demonstrated by only a portion of the ground force and, as in other training, shortfalls are uncovered in each exercise. Though transregional exercises may have demonstrated "proof of concept," it is still too early to credit the entire army with the capability to move routinely outside of its own MR, much less to be able to project significant ground forces (say a division or more) outside the country's borders to any great distance. Such objectives clearly are on the PLA's agenda, but many long-term problems remain, mostly with long-range transport, logistics, and command and control.

This chapter will first illustrate the official Chinese declarations on training to achieve transregional proficiency and then summarize Chinese media reports of the various transregional exercises and training events. Implications for the future are addressed in the conclusion.

STATEMENTS OF CHINESE INTENTIONS

China's 2006 *Defense White Paper* on national defense outlined the following intentions for PLA ground force training: "The Army aims at moving from regional defense to *trans-regional mobility*, and improving its capabilities in air-ground integrated operations, long-distance maneuvers, rapid assaults and special operations."[4] The same white paper included the PLAAF role in transregional mobility among the goals of "speeding up [the PLAAF] transition from territorial air defense to both offensive and defensive operations, and increasing its capabilities in the areas of air strike, air and missile defense, early warning and reconnaissance, and *strategic projection* [emphasis added]." Contemporary media reports illustrated that many of the individual operational objectives listed in the white paper were simultaneously being practiced in transregional and other joint training from 2006 forward.

China's 2008 *Defense White Paper* repeated the transregional training objective and added more detail about other aspects of joint training for its warfighting missions: "The PLA is intensifying strategic- and operational-level command post training and troop training in conditions of informationization, holding transregional evaluation exercises with opposing players, conducting whole-unit night training and carrying out integrated exercises for logistical and equipment support." A separate paragraph highlighted training in complex electromagnetic environments, a major component of nearly all exercises in the last half of the decade. Later, another important organizational experiment — the creation of modular, multifunctional units, focused on the temporary formation of combined arms battalions within brigades and divisions (through a process similar to what the U.S. Army calls "task organization") — was linked with transregional capabilities:

> In recent years, in line with the strategic requirements of mobile operations and three-dimensional offense and defense, the Army has been moving from regional defense to trans-regional mobility. It is gradually making its units small, modular and multi-functional in organization through appropriate downsizing and structural reform.

As will be seen, several transregional exercises highlighted operations of modularized, combined arms battalions. Transregional and other exercises further require participating units to form various temporary "tactical groups" (战术群) made up of elements of different units — sometimes from more than one service — to accomplish specific tasks, such as assault, firepower, air defense, or logistics.

Once again, many of the same training themes were included in the 2010 *Defense White Paper*:

> Based on and supported by command information systems, the PLA organizes combined training of different combat components, assembly training of various combat elements, and joint training of all systems and all components. It intensifies joint training of task formations and confrontational training, and places emphasis on training in complex electromagnetic environments, unfamiliar terrain, and complex weather conditions. The PLA holds trans-regional exercises for organic divisions (brigades) led by campaign-level command organs, raises training evaluation standards, and organizes training based on the needs, formations and procedures of actual combat.

The mention of "campaign-level command organs" (also called the *juntuan* [军团] level of operations, i.e., group army headquarters and above) for transregional exercises reflects the fact that most joint operations for the PLA have traditionally been organized at the army level or higher. The *Defense White Paper* does not mention experimentation in joint command relationships that extend down to division and brigade levels, called the *bingtuan* (兵团) level. Contemporaneous reporting about a few transregional exercises shows them to emphasize control at the *bingtuan* level, thus pushing responsibility for command and control for joint operations down to field grade officers (majors to senior colonels) instead of generals.

In short, PLA training seeks to integrate all new capabilities of the active duty forces, reserves, militia, and civilian support into joint operations under conditions of informationization, thus creating "information system-based 'system of systems' operations capabilities" (信息系统的体系作战能力), or the slightly differently stated 信息化条件下体系作战能力, 'system of systems' operations capabilities under informationized conditions). These terms, both of which are formed around the words "体系作战能力" ("system of systems operations capabilities"), appear to be the PLA's latest formula (replacing "integrated joint operations") to describe its concept of joint operations, which takes advantage of all the new capabilities entering the force.

The internal Chinese military and civilian media have documented nearly 20 transregional exercises and described many training tasks consistent with the objectives outlined in the white papers. Some of these capabilities also have been tested in real world transregional deployments for domestic disaster relief operations, such as the 2008 Wenchuan (汶川) earthquake relief effort. As a result of both exercises and real world operations, the PLA has learned lessons and identified shortcomings that need to be addressed in personnel and doctrine development, future training, and force structure changes (particularly in long-distance transport capabilities and command and control structures).

THE EARLY EXERCISES

In 2006, the Chinese media first reported on PLA exercises specifically designed to test the operational capabilities of large ground force units (brigade and above) in exercises that started in one MR and moved into another. Transregional exercises usually begin with assembly and deployment, using multiple modes of transportation. Scenarios reflect an attack on China, which then presents multiple high-tech threats to PLA forces during movement. These threats include satellite reconnaissance, electronic warfare and cyber attacks, and precision strikes by long-range enemy weapons. By crossing MR boundaries, leaders and troops are confronted with terrain they have not operated in before and local conditions that may differ significantly from their home region. A variety of civilian logistics support often is rendered while en route to another MR's CATTB. Once at the training base, the out-of-area units conduct preliminary training, organize for combat, and engage in force-on-force confrontational exercises. Unit evaluations and live-fire exercises are often included. After the exercises, the units return to their home garrison locations.

In early-September 2006, the 190th Mechanized Infantry Brigade left its garrison in Benxi, Liaoning (辽宁本溪) in the Shenyang MR for the Zhurihe (朱日和训练基地) CATTB in the Beijing MR in what was called "the first-ever transregional long-distance maneuvers to test and evaluate the results of military training and further explore new training methods and war tactics under high-tech conditions."[5] The entire brigade of approximately 3,000 personnel participated, using both rail and road transport. No PLAAF or army aviation assets were reported in support.[6] En route, the brigade encountered snowstorms along with simulated enemy satellite reconnaissance, electronic jamming, and biochemical and air attacks. After arriving at the training base, the brigade entered into a force-on-force exercise with an armored brigade from the Beijing MR. Photos of the exercise show both units equipped with Type 59-series tanks using laser engagement simulation equipment. In addition, more than "50 experts from the Shijiazhuang Army Command College, the Bengbu Tank Institute, and the Shijiazhuang Mechanized Infantry Academy" made up an exercise directorate to evaluate the execution of the exercise.[7] Though no name was given to the exercise, the Chinese media covered it extensively.[8] The exercise lasted approximately 10 days, not including the redeployment period to return to the Shenyang MR.

At about the same time, a motorized infantry brigade from the Beijing MR also engaged in a 20-day exercise that included land and (unspecified) water movement of 3,000 kilometers through unfamiliar territory: "This long-distance movement exercise involved a long way to go, both land and water movement, and entirely new training topics. Nothing was pre-planned for any juncture in the exercise. The brigade did not survey the terrain in advance." This exercise was *not* called a "transregional exercise," but the distance traveled suggests the unit *may* have left its home MR. Apparently, the brigade did not enter a CATTB in the Beijing MR or any other MR. No PLAAF or army aviation participation was reported. This exercise did not receive as much press attention as the 190th Mechanized Infantry's transregional event, but was said to be "a first in the history of the brigade's training."[9]

Sometime in mid-autumn 2006, the Beijing MR conducted a "transregional online confrontation exercise" involving personnel from Beijing MR Headquarters (located at a training base), the Shijiazhuang Mechanized Infantry Academy (石家庄机械化步兵学院), and a unit stationed in Hohhot (呼和浩特). Beijing MR Headquarters personnel directed the exercise as the Shijiazhuang Academy and Hohhot unit fought against each other as reinforced motorized infantry divisions of a "Red Army" and "Blue Army." The unnamed exercise included functions of satellite, radar, and Unmanned Aerial Vehicle (UAV) reconnaissance;

electronic warfare; airborne and army aviation operations; and logistics command.[10]

These three exercises were publicized months before the 2006 *Defense White Paper*'s release in late December. Nonetheless, they foreshadowed the emphasis on transregional mobility identified in the white paper. In 2007, no major transregional exercises were publicized, though it appears to have been a topic of study within the force. In 2008, transregional exercises became more complex as PLAN and PLAAF units became involved. Moreover, the Jinan MR became the focus of experimentation for transregional mobility.

JINAN MR TAKES THE LEAD IN 2008

Due to its location (devoid of any international land borders) and the extensive transportation networks within its boundaries, the Jinan MR is positioned as the PLA's strategic reserve force. This mission was demonstrated in the response to the May 2008 earthquake in Wenchuan, when numerous MR ground force units were deployed across several provincial boundaries to support disaster relief efforts. Furthermore, as illustrated in the two transregional exercises emanating from the region in 2008, Army forces can be used to reinforce military operations in other parts of the country.

Beginning in late August, 砺兵-2008 (*Sharpening Troops-2008*) was the first transregional exercise of the season. Only a month after the 58th Light Mechanized Brigade of the 20th Group Army in Jinan MR returned from the Wenchuan disaster relief mission, it moved by rail and road to the Zhurihe CATTB.[11] Once there, the brigade acted as the "Red Army" against a "Blue Army" comprised of an armored regiment from the

Beijing MR. The brigade was reinforced with an electronic countermeasures unit, more than 10 helicopters from the Jinan MR 1st Army Aviation Regiment (subordinate to the 54th Group Army), and PLAAF assets, including both an airborne mechanized infantry unit (probably company-size) and fighter support. The month-long exercise included over 5,200 personnel from both MRs and the PLAAF. Fuel for the brigade was provided through coordination by the group army and Jinan MR staffs with the Beijing MR Joint Logistics Department, which then tasked local units to provide support. Reportedly, over the course of the exercise the brigade consumed up to "400 tons of gasoline and diesel fuel of various grades, which represent[ed] 60% of all the war materiel . . . supplied in the exercise."[12] The force-on-force maneuver element of the exercise was unscripted and included parachute delivery of airborne infantry combat vehicles and personnel. Over 100 military leaders, representatives, and observers from 36 countries were invited to attend the final day of the exercise at Zhurihe.[13] In summarizing *Sharpening Troops-2008* (砺兵-2008), the exercise deputy director noted the experimental nature of this training: "the multi-service and multi-arm joint training implies the transition from the research-centric stage to the normal test-oriented stage."[14]

In September, during 联合-2008 (*Joint-2008*), the 138th Motorized Infantry Brigade of the 26th Group Army in the Jinan MR moved from Yantai (烟台) in the Weifang (潍坊) Coordination Zone in Shandong to a landing area near Dalian, Liaoning (辽宁大连). The amphibious lift for the exercise was provided by some 10 PLAN amphibious ships with PLAAF air cover.[15] In total, more than 5,000 troops from all three services participated in the 5-day exercise.[16] During the phase in which vehicles were loaded onto ships, and while en route to the beachhead, the "Red" force was harassed by "Blue Army" naval and air units using surface vessels, attack aircraft, and electronic warfare. These attacks resulted in the execution of joint defensive actions by "Red" ground, naval, and air forces. The exercise culminated with an amphibious landing and inland assault supported by army aviation and special operations elements. Integrated joint logistics, including civilian food, vehicle repair, and medical support, was emphasized at all stages of the exercise.

During this exercise, the 26th Group Army commander was the overall exercise director in charge of a "joint campaign formation" (联合战役军团) with a subordinate "joint tactical formation" (联合战术兵团), sometimes translated as "joint tactical corps," formed by the 138th Brigade headquarters.[17] Under this sort of command relationship, Navy and Air Force officers were present in the group army and brigade tactical operations centers *to command* their services' support through "distributed embedded"-style (分布嵌入式) command, and were not there simply to perform liaison functions. The PLA newspaper, *Jiefangjun Bao*, highlighted the experimental nature of this type of command relationship and the need for further work to solve problems discovered in practice:

> This kind of joint command model was attempted in the "联合-2006" ["*Joint Operations-2006*"] and "联合-2007" ["*Joint Operations-2007*"] live troop exercises that followed, and although it reduced the conflicts with the existing command systems, and it had a definite jointness, the one flaw was that *the three-service arm tactical formations had relatively lax coordination with each other, which weakened the degree of integration of the joint operations. . . .* After several years of actual practice, the Weifang Military Training Coordination Zone's

three-service arm commanders recognize more and more clearly that *the PLA's joint training effort is still in its "initial stage"*, and whether in ideological concepts and formation systems or in command methods, *there are a lot of issues that still need to be resolved*, and he who is anxious to be successful will, on the contrary, only have more haste and less speed.[18] [emphasis added]

As can be seen from the transregional exercises in 2006 and 2008, the first examples of these new-style, joint operations were relatively small (up to about 5,000 personnel at most), but over time the operations became increasingly complex. The transregional aspect was a new wrinkle added to the other operational methods (command and control, coordination of multiple service actions, joint logistics support, etc.), which were under experimentation in other PLA ground force exercises. In the following years, transregional exercises became much larger and longer in duration.

LARGER, MORE COMPLEX EXERCISES IN 2009 AND 2010

跨越-2009 (*Stride-2009*) was the largest transregional exercise to date, involving approximately 50,000 troops from four divisions in four different MRs crisscrossing the country over a 2-month period. While there was some PLAAF support to transport a few small units and provide air cover, the exercise was primarily a ground operation. Though the General Staff Department was in overall command of the exercise, Stride 2009 focused on the *bingtuan* level of joint operations by emphasizing the joint actions of divisions.

During deployment periods of approximately 5 days, small reconnaissance, headquarters, and communications units (less than 20 percent of total force levels) were flown on both PLAAF and chartered civilian aircraft while larger formations of personnel (over 80 percent of the force) traveled over highways, and heavy equipment was transported via rail. Reportedly, each division deployed with 80 to 97 percent of its roughly 10,000 total personnel strength along with over 90 percent of their organic "artillery, engineering machinery, and other large weapons," but *only about 50 percent of armored vehicles*. During deployment, units were resupplied with fuel and provisions by military and civilian logistics teams. The divisions were reinforced with army aviation, special operations, reconnaissance, UAV, and electronic countermeasures units.[19]

In mid-August 2009, the 61st ("Red Army") Division moved from the Lanzhou MR to Taonan in the Shenyang MR. In mid-to late-August, the 162nd Motorized Infantry Division ("Ferocious Tigers") traveled from the Jinan MR to Luzhai in the Guangzhou MR. In early-September, the 115th Mechanized Infantry Division from the Shenyang MR moved to Qingtongxia (青铜峡) in the Lanzhou MR. In mid-to late-September, the Guangzhou MR's 121st Motorized Infantry Division moved to Queshan (确山) in the Jinan MR.[20] Some of the troops traveling to the Jinan MR rode on "China Railway High-speed trains traveling at speeds of up to 350 km per hour."[21] As can be seen, deployments occurred sequentially (not simultaneously) over a month's time with units from the Lanzhou and Shenyang MRs and the Jinan and Guangzhou MRs switching locations.

Upon reaching its out-of-area CATTB, each division took part in force-on-force engagements in complex electromagnetic environments against local "Blue" forces.[22] Reporting indicated that at least two divisions formed combined arms battalion task forces. The 61st Division formed a combined arms battalion based upon an armored infantry (mechanized) battalion of a regiment. The division commander implied the experimental nature of this form of task organization by stating that, "Judging by the data collected, we can see that the integrated combat index of the new-type combined arms battalion has a clear advantage. In some sense, *the new-type combined arms battalion is a main component and important force in future joint operations*"[23] [emphasis added]. In addition, the 162nd Motorized Infantry Division formed two modularized groups based on battalions during an attack mission:

> The 1st *Motorized Combat Group* of the Red Force, which was the main attack unit, commanded its engineer, armor, tactical missile, and EM jamming modules to deliver a combination of hard destruction and soft kill against the enemy with different tactical means. . . . As the battle process gathered pace, the joint command and control center ordered the *armored assault group* to take over. The armored assault group consisted of army aviation, engineer, chemical defense, communications, artillery, and infantry modules, centering around an armored battalion.[24] [emphasis added]

The report then summarized the organizational principles of modularization:

> Modular grouping typically centers around a motorized or armored battalion, bringing together communications, artillery, engineer, chemical defense, army aviation, and aerial electronic countermeasure as fixed combat modules. They are variously grouped according to the mission, the environment, and the target, to form a combined-arms group capable of independent performance of tasks.[25]

Though divisions specifically practiced this method of organization for combat in Stride 2009, the same principles also are applied by brigades during other training.[26]

A few months later, a *Xinhua* report summarized PLA training lessons from 2009. Three areas requiring attention were highlighted: 1) the command system; 2) long-distance delivery capability, "especially the strategic delivery capability in the air"; and, 3) "transformation of operational and training types [combat methods] and operational thoughts [doctrine] caused by the change of equipment and techniques."[27] In other words, new equipment is changing the way the PLA plans to fight (or "technology determines tactics"[28]). The article provided a realistic assessment of problems at hand, while demonstrating the PLA is working to overcome its deficiencies:

> There is no need for reticence that many problems in the military training of the PLA are still waiting to be settled. In 2009, not every difficulty can be rapidly and effectively settled. However, the PLA did not avoid these difficulties in military exercises; they still carried out exploration and research.[29]

The observation that "not every difficulty can be rapidly and effectively settled" is a nuance that often is misunderstood or glossed over by many foreign analysts of PLA modernization. Building combat capabilities requires more than new equipment—the PLA understands that just as important as acquiring new equipment is preparing personnel to operate and maintain it and employ it in a joint doctrine that has never been tested in battle by the Chinese. In addition to its discussion of Stride 2009, the *Xinhua* article also addressed the PLAAF's transregional exercise, *Airborne Maneuver-2009.*

In mid-October 2009, 空降机动-2009 (*Airborne Maneuver-2009* or Airborne Movement) was called "the largest trans-theater comprehensive campaign maneuver exercise in the history of the Chinese airborne force."[30] Elements of all three divisions of the 15th Airborne Army participated, totaling some 13,000 personnel, 1,500 vehicles, and 7,000 pieces of equipment. Based on the analysis of the media coverage, elements of the 43rd Airborne Division in Kaifeng (开封 in the Jinan MR) probably acted as enemy forces facing elements of the 44th and 45th Divisions from the Wuhan area (武汉 in the Guangzhou MR). Although some parachute jumps and heavy equipment drops were conducted, the majority of the forces moved by road or rail or marched on foot for most of the exercise. ZBD03 airborne combat vehicles that had taken part in the October 1 parade in Beijing were moved by rail to Henan to join the exercise. During the first week of training, regiments fought force-on-force battles and conducted annual unit evaluations. Individual skills were also tested.[31] Later, the units conducted a 3-day ground movement over multiple routes through Hubei and Anhui to Jiangsu (湖北, 安徽, 江苏 in the Nanjing MR), during which they continued to fight a simulated "Blue" force. The participation of other services was not reported during the 20-day exercise.

The following year, 使命行动-2010 (*Mission Action-2010*) involved a series of multi-region, joint air-land exercises that were smaller in scale than those for Stride 2009.[32] However, *Mission Action-2010* was more complex, involving ground force units from three MRs, which deployed by road, rail, and air across MR boundaries, and were supported by PLAAF and Second Artillery units in addition to reserve, People's Armed Police (PAP), militia, and civilian forces. In total, approximately 30,000 personnel took part. Three group army headquarters controlled the movements of a division and two brigades along with elements of army aviation, special operations, communications, engineer, and logistics units. While Stride 2009 focused on the *bingtuan* level of command, *Mission Action-2010* focused at the *juntuan* (group army) level, emphasizing informationized joint operations — especially command, control, communications, computers, intelligence, surveillance, and reconnaissance (C4ISR).

In *Mission Action-2010A*, the 188th Mechanized Infantry Brigade of the 27th Group Army deployed from the Zhurihe CATTB in the Beijing MR to the Taonan CATTB in the Shenyang MR. In *Mission Action-2010B*, the 139th Mechanized Infantry Brigade of the 47th Group Army deployed from Qingtongxia CATTB in the Lanzhou MR to Xichang CATTB in the Chengdu MR. In *Mission Action-2010C*, the 149th Mechanized Infantry Division of the 13th Group Army deployed from the Chengdu MR to Qingtongxia. Of note is that the movement directions and pairing of MRs in *Mission Action-2010* were different from those of *Stride-2009*, with Beijing and Chengdu MR units participating. Thus, in 2 years' time, units from all MRs except Nanjing took part in transregional exercises. Moreover, two parts of the exercise took place simultaneously, not sequentially, as in the year before. Also, adding to the degree of difficulty, in Mission Action, units reportedly deployed with *all* required equipment and ammunition.

After an alert and planning phase, load-out and deployment for both *Mission Action-2010A* and *C* began around October 12.[33] *Mission Action-2010B* began deployment around October 21, after several days of preparation.[34] Both offensive and defensive information operations and electronic countermeasures were employed throughout the exercise during live fire and confrontational drills. Each of the exercise's three increments practiced many of the same tasks, but each also had its own special feature.

In *Mission Action-2010A*, the 188th Mechanized Infantry Brigade deployed first from its home base at Xinzhou, Shanxi, to the Zhurihe CATTB. Chinese television showed the brigade's Type 55 tanks, Type 63 armored personnel carriers, and other equipment being loaded onto railcars as personnel and light vehicles were loaded onto PLAAF transports (one Il-76 and one Y-8 were shown) and at least one China Air Boeing 737 passenger jet. The aircraft flew to the Wulanhaote (Ulan Hot) Airfield, from which the troops then moved to the Taonan CATTB. Two other columns of troops drove to the exercise area.[35] During the 4-day movement phase to the exercise area, in which an early snowstorm complicated the effort, PLAAF aircraft also performed reconnaissance and simulated strike missions as part of the "Blue" force. The brigade was supported by a local militia unit as it used a mobile bridge to cross a river after the enemy force had destroyed the existing bridge.[36] At Taonan, the brigade was reinforced by army aviation, special operations, and PLAAF fighter support during the force-on-force and live-fire phase of the exercise.[37] The deputy chief of staff of the Beijing MR summed up *Mission Action-2010A* as:

the first large-scale trans-region long-range mobile exercise of whole units carried out by the Beijing Military Region. . . . integrated command platform, information countermeasure, air-ground joint actions, and comprehensive assessment and test methods were adopted in the whole course of the exercise. In a complex and unfamiliar environment, the exercise tested the joint tactical corps' information offense and defense, command and control, joint strike, multi-dimensional protection, and comprehensive support capabilities, and enhanced the forces' "system of systems" operations capability based on information systems.[38]

In *Mission Action-2010B*, the 139th Mechanized Infantry Brigade first moved from its home in Weinan, Shaanxi, to Qingtongxia in Ningxia. There it began a multi-mode deployment to Xichang CATTB, similar to that conducted in *Mission Action-2010A*, including many of the same tasks en route. The distinguishing feature of this exercise, however, was a joint anti-terrorist drill performed with PAP forces.[39] The confrontational phase of the exercise at Xichang included many of the same elements as seen in Taonan:

> Reconnaissance and anti-reconnaissance, jamming and anti-jamming, suppression and anti-suppression. . . . While facing the sudden attacks, the group army commanders responded calmly and confidently. . . . Before the struggle in the invisible battlefield calmed down, joint fire strikes and the battle of sabotaging the "enemy" operation system started. All at once, howitzers, tank guns, aircraft guns, and vehicle-based missiles demonstrated their great power. Being guided by the informatized reconnaissance means, all sorts of firepower roared toward the "enemy" command posts, airports, radar positions, communications hubs, and other targets in a form of three-dimensional assaults. At the same time, multiple special operations detachments secretly sneaked into the rear positions of the "enemy" force through helicopter landing, and carried out special sabotage against the "enemy" command hubs. Under the joint strikes by the integrated air, ground, space, and electromagnetic forces, the "enemy" operation structure was destroyed before

long, and the "enemy" defensive line was broken in multiple places.[40]

Once again, the role of the group army headquarters was emphasized in conducting joint operations.

Mission Action-2010C included many of the same elements of the other *Mission Action* exercises during its multimode deployment phase, which moved the 149th Mechanized Infantry Division from the Chengdu MR to Qingtongxia. Notably, the exercise began with the deployment of an MR-level general communication station to provide communication support.[41] The highlight of the movement to Ningxia was the crossing of the Yellow River using a pontoon bridge erected by a group army engineer regiment with air cover provided by PLAAF and army aviation aircraft.[42] Perhaps most important, *Mission Action-2010C* is the only transregional exercise to date reported to have had Second Artillery participation. During the final live-fire phase at Qingtongxia CATTB, a Second Artillery missile unit temporarily assigned to the 13th Group Army launched "long-range precision missile strikes on the 'enemy' targets in the depth of the rear area." PLAAF fighters and army aviation helicopters provided additional support. After a "fire strike assessment," (also known as battle damage assessment), the group army "joint fire center" ordered a second round of firepower attacks by armed helicopters and conventional artillery.[43] The group army commander summarized the exercise:

> During this exercise, we gave full play to the advantages of the integrated command platform. Through the information system, we networked various combat forces and operational platforms into an organic whole. This way, all the elements in the combat system

are grouped scientifically and integrated coherently. The weapons, equipment, and combat elements that are far removed from one another can preliminarily form a systemic combat capacity. We have explored ways to, and laid a foundation for, making training in the context of systemic operations more standardized, systematic, and scientific.[44]

This statement once again reflects the exploratory nature of these exercises and how the PLA intends to build upon the lessons learned from the field. PLA combat leaders understand they still have work to do before advanced joint operations are standardized throughout the force.

As the *Mission Action*-series of exercises was winding down, *Jiefangjun Bao* carried a short article about the 127th Light Mechanized Infantry Division of the 54th Group Army in the Jinan MR, which traveled more than 1,000 kilometers across four provinces along the Qingdao-Yinchuan Expressway (青岛银川高速公路). Since there are only two provinces in the MR, this would appear to have been an unannounced transregional mobility exercise. The focus of this event apparently was military-civilian logistics support:

> They did not repair vehicles nor cook meals by themselves, and completely relied on the support forces of friendly military units and local civilian institutions along the route of movement. As a result, the support time was shortened by half. . . . The division sorted out six categories of 38 mobile support nodes, arranged collaboration with the friendly units and the local civilian support resources, and established a network of precise and efficient support along the route of movement. They also arranged reserved services with main repair and maintenance factories along the route of

movement, shaping an emergency repair support system for more than 30 types of vehicles in the whole division.[45]

As seen in 2006, some transregional events did not get the massive media exposure as did the exercises that took place from 2008 to 2010. The 127th Mechanized Division's logistics exercise is a good example of a less publicized exercise that might not be as well known as the bigger exercises. In 2011, no transregional exercises of the scale of *Stride* or *Mission Action* were reported. Nonetheless, several small transregional events were mentioned in the PLA media.

OTHER RELATED TRANSREGIONAL TRAINING EVENTS

In late-March 2011, a PLAAF airborne unit organized a transregional, long-distance movement of more than 2,000 kilometers through six provinces. An unidentified unit used road, railroad, and water movement during this event. Details are sketchy for this first-of-its-kind force projection exercise, but its primary emphasis appeared to be working out the logistics of a multi-mode, long-distance movement.[46]

In June 2011, the Engineer Command Academy located in Xuzhou, Jiangsu (江苏徐州), in the Nanjing MR, organized a cross-regional exercise named 先锋-2011 (*Vanguard-2011*), which took some 2,000 personnel to the Queshan CATTB in Jinan MR. Participants included graduating cadets from the academy, a GSD camouflage regiment, a group army engineer regiment from the Nanjing MR, a GSD engineer research institute, and reserve personnel. Movement to Queshan was conducted by train, followed by a 40 kilometer road march. More than 600 pieces of engineering equipment were involved in a confrontational exercise that portrayed a "joint mountain attack operation under information-based conditions." Tactical situations included "road and bridge rush repair, field command post and helicopter landing field construction, artillery and air defense position camouflage, field water supply station creation, and sabotage of important objectives in [the] enemy's rear."[47] Also included were measures to assist local governments in disaster relief, counter-terrorism, and explosive removal in military operations other than war (MOOTW).[48]

In addition, a 1-day "force projection drill" called 腾飞-2011 (*Soaring-2011*) was conducted in Harbin involving a 130-man unit and an A320 from China Southern Airlines on July 16, 2011. The exercise was described as "the first standardized real-troop and real-equipment transport drill jointly organized by the PLA's Shenyang Military Area Command (MAC) and the civilian aviation sector."[49] To transport the unit, which included medical personnel, to a location "thousands of kilometers away," eight military and civilian units — including the Air Traffic Management Bureau, the airline, an airport management agency, a fuel company, an element of the Shenyang MR headquarters, an aviation military representative office, and the unit being transported — "set up a joint military-civilian command office, held a joint conference, coordinated transportation plans, devised action plans, and implemented integrated commands."[50] This joint command structure demonstrates how complex even a small-scale, long-distance movement can be. One of the exercise directors commented that these exercises are relatively new for the PLA:

China has, relatively, a small number of experiences in this area and has no past experiences for reference in organizing transportation drills of air emergency transport and combat units—it has to fumble its way through—and such issues as how to coordinate the entire action and what is the specific task of every unit have troubled leaders of various units at the drill headquarters . . . during the preliminary preparatory stage of the drill, there was no clear division of individual responsibilities for various participating units, and it was like flies flying around without heads and bumping into things and the results can be imagined.[51]

Less than 2 weeks earlier, Chinese television carried a report on the PAP 8720 unit (based on the location provided), which was seen conducting the first ever aviation loading and transportation exercise for an inter-regional mission.[52] Approximately seven truckloads of PAP troops with riot gear and accompanying supplies were shown loading and boarding at least one Shenzhen Airlines aircraft. It is unclear if the unit actually left the airport or whether this was just a preliminary loading drill.

Also on July 16, the G224 high-speed train from Qingdao took nearly 1,000 personnel from the Jinan MR over 1,300 kilometers to Shanghai in about 6 1/2 hours—4 hours faster "than the ordinary bullet trains." This movement was organized by the Jinan Rail and Waterways Military Representative Office.[53]

CONCLUSIONS

Most transregional exercises seem structured to represent PLA forces moving to border areas to repel attacks on China. As such, they would involve second-echelon forces dispatched with the intention of reinforcing main force and local force PLA units in the region. This mission is particularly applicable to Jinan MR forces, which have, in fact, been involved in several transregional exercises. Jinan MR units indeed have participated in four such exercises, more than any other MR—a situation consistent with the Jinan MR's role as a strategic reserve.

The emphasis on civilian support in many of these exercises also suggests that cross-border operations outside of China are not the specific intention of the exercises. It is unlikely that PLA forces invading another country will have the opportunity to avail themselves of gas stations and maintenance facilities in the foreign country they are attacking. Likewise, the extensive use of rail movement may be appropriate to move forces toward China's borders, but it is unlikely that rail movement would extend too far into another country's territory. If cross-border operations were the intent of these transregional exercises, there likely would have been more emphasis on reinforcing combat troops with additional fuel trucks and pipeline units that could provide fuel to advanced positions.

It is worth noting that none of the transregional exercises to date have had the intimidation of Taiwan as one of their direct objectives. The two large transregional exercises in 2009 and 2010 (*Stride* and *Mission Action*) appear to have been specifically designed *not* to intimidate Taiwan. Neither exercise included units moving into the Nanjing MR nor into amphibious training areas as might be expected if the scenario were to depict follow-on forces moving into the region to conduct second wave amphibious assaults as part of a larger campaign. Had the PLA and Chinese Communist Party wanted to, they easily could have modified these exercises so that forces could have flowed into amphibious training areas in the Nanjing or Guangzhou MRs. The one exercise that did include amphibious operations, *Joint 2008,* had PLA troops moving as far away from Taiwan as possible, from the Jinan to Shenyang MR. Again, had intimidation of Taiwan been an objective, the direction of that movement could easily have been changed.

To be sure, it can be argued that *any* large-scale military exercise contains tasks and operations that *could* be applied in some form to a Taiwan scenario. But when Beijing feels compelled to remind Taiwan of the military potential deployed opposite its shores, it has shown no hesitation to do so directly. However, such military shows of force, as seen in exercises in 1995, 1996, 2001, and 2004, generally have not resulted in behavior by Taiwan in line with Beijing's preferences. If anything, overt intimidation usually produces counterproductive reactions in Taiwan and much of the rest of the world. Especially following the change of administration in Taiwan in 2008, even the hard-headed leaders in Beijing appear to have gotten this message.

Instead, transregional exercises appear to be experimenting with defense of China's land borders, however improbable an invasion scenario currently seems. If it is deemed operationally feasible for out-of-region forces to be deployed to assist in relatively time-sensitive operations, it is possible that China's senior military leadership may decide that fewer standing, active duty forces are needed in every corner of the country. Smaller, more technologically advanced units (like brigades and battalions) can be moved more quickly than larger, old-style infantry and armored divisions and still have considerable combat power due to new weapons and communications systems.

Success in transregional exercises could provide the rationale for future cuts in main force ground units. At the same time, reserve units and militia units could be strengthened to support the movement of main force units into and out of their areas. Reducing the number and size of combat units could free up personnel slots and, more importantly, money to be applied to transportation assets necessary for long-distance movements—whether they be long-range transport aircraft, helicopters (including heavy-lift aircraft), heavy trucks and trailers for transporting armored vehicles over roads, amphibious ships, or railroad rolling stock. Improvements in command and control, informationization, and the country's transportation infrastructure make transregional movement more viable than in previous decades.

For movements within China, some resources may be saved by the PLA's doctrinal reliance on reserve forces and civilian support. Logistics support provided by reserves and civilians makes sense when using China's interior lines of communications, but less so for force projection missions using exterior lines outside of China. Reserve and civilian support could be helpful to some degree outside of China, particularly for long-distance transportation, but is not likely to provide the wide array of support activities (food, supply, maintenance, etc.) practiced during exercises within the country itself.

The comments of operational commanders about the experimental nature of the transregional exercises performed in recent years could also be applied to many forms of doctrinal and training development currently underway in the PLA. Chinese military leaders are well aware that they are still exploring concepts other advanced militaries have implemented for decades. Their timeline for experimentation in this and other operational tactics and techniques, not the least of which involves improving joint command and control systems, probably extends much further into the future than many foreign observers imagine. Given more time, PLA leaders will be able to train their forces better for the new missions and joint operations that they have never conducted against a thinking, adaptive enemy. The forces' experiences in noncombat missions both inside and outside of China will be some help, but are no substitute for actual combat.

The longer the PLA has to practice, the more likely its forces will be prepared for modern combat and its leaders confident in the PLA's new capabilities. As the PLA trains more frequently and openly than in previous decades, Chinese leaders probably see these efforts adding to China's deterrence posture. Accordingly, the Chinese and PLA propaganda machines are likely to publicize many more exercises in the future and report many "first-time" accomplishments. We should treat many such reports with the degree of skepticism they deserve, but we should also be open to new information that, when combined with other data, helps us assess the state of Chinese military modernization in an objective and comprehensive manner.

One final lesson from the PLA's transregional exercises of relevance to larger policy issues is the actual transparency of intentions found in official Chinese documents. The *Defense White Papers* clearly identified transregional exercises as a training focus in 2006 and 2008. Subsequently, many details of exercises from 2006 to 2010 were published in the official Chinese media confirming the intentions identified by the white papers. These details were consistent with many of the training themes identified in other PLA literature.

In short, the PLA told us what they were going to do; then they did it so we could see it.

Chinese leaders understand that increased defense budgets and new equipment will not by themselves modernize the PLA. They also have a realistic view of the progress the PLA has made in modernization and the gaps between current PLA capabilities and those of other advanced militaries. Accordingly, within the PLA itself attention is focused on personnel development, command and control, doctrine, training, and logistics issues as well as integrating new equipment into the force. We can expect to see additional, new areas of emphasis in training and doctrine as long-standing problems and shortcomings are overcome gradually.

Summary of PLA and PAP Transregion Exercises and Events.

Military Region/ PLAAF Airborne/PAP	Date, Unit, Transregion Exercise, and Events
Shenyang MR (沈阳军区)	• Sept 2006, 190th Mechanized Infantry Brigade, Unnamed Exercise • Sept 2009, 115th Mechanized Infantry Division, *Stride-2009* (跨越-2009) • Jul 2011, 130-man company, *Soaring-2011* (腾飞-2011)
Beijing MR (北京军区)	• Sept 2006, Motorized Infantry Brigade, Unnamed Exercise • Oct 2006, Online Confrontation Exercise • Oct 2010, 188th Mechanized Infantry Brigade, *Mission Action-2010A* (使命行动-2010A)

Lanzhou MR (兰州军区)	• Aug 2009, 61st ("Red Army") Division, *Stride-2009* (跨越-2009) • Oct 2010, 139th Mechanized Infantry Brigade, *Mission Action-2010B* (使命行动-2010B)
Jinan MR (济南军区)	• Aug 2008, 58th Light Mechanized Brigade, *Sharpening Troops-2008* (砺兵-2008) • Sept 2008, 138th Motorized Infantry Brigade, *Joint Operations-2008* (联合-2008) • Aug 2009, 162nd Motorized Infantry Division, *Stride-2009* (跨越-2009) • Oct 2010, 127th Light Mechanized Infantry Division, Unnamed Transregional Logistics Exercise
Nanjing MR (南京军区)	• Jun 2011, Engineer Command College, Group Army Engineer Regiment, GSD Camouflage Regiment, *Vanguard-2011* (先锋-2011)
Guangzhou MR (广州军区)	• Sept 2009, 121st Motorized Infantry Division, *Stride-2009* (跨越-2009)
Chengdu MR (成都军区)	• Oct 2010, 149th Mechanized Infantry Division, *Mission Action- 2010C* (使命行动-2001C)
PLAAF Airborne	• Oct 2009, 15th Airborne Army, *Airborne Maneuver- 2009* (空降机动-2009)
PAP	• Jul 2011, 8720 Unit, Unnamed Exercise

ENDNOTES - CHAPTER 5

1. "China's Dongshan Island Military Exercises to Aim at Air Superiority Over Taiwan" (东山岛军事演习), CPP20040703000045, Beijing, China, Renmin Wang WWW-Text in Chinese, July 3, 2004, translated by the Open Source Center (OSC).

2. Edward C. O'Dowd, *Chinese Military Strategy in the Third Indochina War: The Last Maoist War,* London, UK: Routledge, 2007, p. 101.

3. Kevin McCauley, "PLA Developing Joint Operations Capability (Part Two): Military Training Coordination Zones," in *China Brief,* Vol. 11, Issue: 10, June 3, 2011, available from *www.jamestown.org/single/?no_cache=1&tx_ttnews[tt_news]=38016.* Additionally, large-unit amphibious training (organized by regiments, brigades, divisions, and group armies) takes place in several amphibious training areas along the coast, including the Dongshan training area on the southern border of the Nanjing MR and the eastern edge of the Guangzhou MR. Dongshan is accessible to units stationed in both MRs. However, to date, no training specifically identified as transregional has been conducted at a large amphibious training area.

4. Links to all Chinese government white papers are available from *english.gov.cn/official/2005-08/17/content_24165.htm.*

5. "Chinese Army's land forces launch exercise," September 6, 2006, available from *www.gov.cn/english/2006-09/06/content_378991.htm.* JFJB: "Shenyang MR, Beijing MR Brigades Stage Transregional Maneuvers," CPP20060906718002, Beijing, China, *Jiefangjun Bao* (Internet Version-WWW) in Chinese, September 6, 2006, translated by OSC, identifies the mechanized infantry brigade as stationed in Liaoning, which makes it the 190th.

6. "XNA Reporters Witness Logistics Support During PLA Long-Range Maneuvers," CPP20060910004006, Beijing, China, *Xinhua Domestic Service* in Chinese 1044 GMT, September 20, 2006, translated by OSC.

7. China: "Exercise Directorate in PLA Long-Range Maneuvers Represents a 'First'," CPP20060913708002, Beijing, China, *Xinhua Domestic Service* in Chinese 0325 GMT, September 13, 2006; and "PLA's 10-day First Long-range Mobility Combat Exercise Ends," CPP20060914708001, *Beijing Xinhua Domestic Service* in Chinese 0221 GMT, September 14, 2006, translated by OSC.

8. The Open Source Center published roughly 20 translations and English-language reports from the Chinese media on this one exercise.

9. "PRC Motorized Brigade Stages 20-day Long-range Mobile Exercise," CPP20060907710006, Beijing, China, *Jiefangjun Bao (Internet Version-WWW)* in Chinese, September 7, 2006, translated by OSC.

10. "Beijing MAC organizes trans-regional online exercise," October 12, 2006, available from *english.chinamil.com.cn/site2/militarydatabase/2006-10/13/content_614237.htm*. According to the Directory of PRC Military Personalities, October 2006, an active duty motorized infantry brigade and a reserve army infantry division are located in Hohhot. It is not clear which of these two units participated in the online exercise.

11. *Sharpening Troops-2008* received a lot of press and television attention. For a few examples, see PRC Jinan, "Beijing Military Region Units Hold Joint Military Exercise," CPP20080826074008, Beijing, China, *Xinhua Domestic Service* in Chinese 1151 GMT, August 26, 2008; "PRC Military Exercise 'Libing-2008' Long-Range Movement Begins," CPP20080828074009, Beijing, China, *Zhongguo Xinwen She* in Chinese 0834 GMT, August 28, 2008; DVD/Web Product of *Joint-2008*, Video Report: "Profiles of Red Force Units Taking Part in *Sharpening Troops-2008*," CPM20081015035008, Beijing, China, CCTV-7 in Mandarin, September 17, 2008; "*Sharpening Troops-2008* Military Exercises," FEA20081016789275-OSC Feature- China—OSC Multimedia, August 25, 2008-September 25, 2008, translated by OSC.

12. PRC: "Jinan MR Brigade's Cross-region Fuel Support in '*Sharpening Troops-2008*'," CPP20080918705010, Beijing, China, *Zhongguo Xinwen She* in Chinese 0247 GMT, September 18, 2008, translated by OSC.

13. *Xinhua*: "China Invites Foreign Leaders To Observe '*Sharpening Troops-2008*' Exercise," CPP20081016424001, Beijing, China, *Xinhua Domestic Service* in Chinese 1251 GMT, September 24, 2008, translated by OSC. Foreigners included personnel from Nepal, Brunei, Thailand, Pakistan, South Africa, Mongolia, Bangladesh, India, Sri Lanka, the United States, Germany, Argentina, and Russia. According to *Xinhua*, "Military Exercise in North China to Invite Foreign Observers," September 23, 2008, available from *www.highbeam.com/doc/1P2-19549575.html*, the portion of the exercise open to foreigners was called "Warrior 2008."

14. "'*Sharpening-2008*' exercise stretched to cover tactics," *PLA Daily*, September 18, 2008, available from *english.chinamil.com.cn/site2/special-reports/2008-09/18/content_1483028.htm*.

15. "Three-service joint logistics support in '*Joint Operations-2008*' exercise," *PLA Daily*, September 22, 2008, available from *english.chinamil.com.cn/site2/news-channels/2008-09/22/content_1486636.htm*; "PLA Holds Joint Military Drill Spanning Shandong, Liaodong Peninsulas," CPP20080920163011, Beijing, China, *Zhongguo Xinwen She* in Chinese 1125 GMT, September 20, 2008; PRC: "Joint Cross-sea Transportation Drill '*Lianhe-2008*' Off Dalian," CPP20080921163009, Beijing China, *Zhongguo Xinwen She* in Chinese 1127 GMT, September 21, 2008; "PRC Daily Details Jinan Military Region '*Lianhe-2008*' Exercise," CPP20080926710017, Beijing, China, *Zhongguo Qingnian Bao* Online in Chinese, September 26, 2008, translated by OSC. The "Blue" commander was Zhang Quan, apparently another brigade commander in the 26th Group Army. According to PRC: "First Trans-Regional Joint Combat Exercise '*Joint Operations-2008*' Ends," CPP20080924710003, Beijing, China, *Jiefangjun Bao* Online in Chinese, September 24, 2008 p 1, translated by OSC, "navy and air force troops from other theaters of operations also directly participated in the exercise" — these forces probably were part of the "Blue Army."

16. "Jinan Military Region Conducts 5-Day '*Joint Operations-2008*' Research Exercise," CPP20080919172017, Beijing, China, *Xinhua Domestic Service* in Chinese 1442 GMT, September 19, 2008, translated by OSC.

17. "China Conducts '*Joint Operations-2008*' Military Exercise in Bohai Gulf" (渤海湾), CPP20080922074019, Beijing, China,

Xinhua Domestic Service in Chinese 1217 GMT, September 22, 2008, translated by OSC.

18. "JFJB Reviews PLA's "*Lianhe-2008*" Exercises, Joint Training Base, Related Issues," CPP20081111702024, Beijing, China, Jiefangjun Bao Online in Chinese, November 11, 2008, p. 3; and CCTV-7 "'*Junshi Jishi*': Amphibious Assault Exercise in '*Lianhe-2008*'," CPP20081224138001, Beijing, China, CCTV-7 in Mandarin 1203 GMT, November 28, 2008, translated by OSC. See also Kevin McCauley, "PLA Developing Joint Operations Capability (Part One): Joint Task Force Experimentation," in *China Brief*, Vol. 11, Issue: 9, May 20, 2011 available from *www.jamestown.org/single/?no_cache=1&tx_ttnews[tt_news]=37958*.

19. "Largest-ever mobilization of troops sees 50,000 move across nation," *China Daily*, August 12, 2009, available from *eng. mod.gov.cn/MilitaryExercises/2009-08/12/content_4024379.htm*; and "Attractive sidelights of '*Stride-2009*' series exercise," *PLA Daily*, August 12, 2009, available from *eng.chinamil.com.cn/news-channels/china-military-news/2009-08/12/content_4021540.htm*.

20. *PLA Daily* has a series of reports, available from *tp.chinamil. com.cn/manoeuvre/kuayue2009.htm*; unit identifications can be derived from information available from *news.xinhuanet.com/mil/2009-08/10/content_11858323.htm*.

21. "Largest-ever mobilization of troops sees 50,000 move across nation."

22. PRC, "JFJB Details Confrontation Training in '*Stride-2009*' Queshan Exercise," CPP20091208702002, Beijing, China, *Jiefangjun Bao* Online in Chinese, December 8, 2009, p. 11, translated by OSC, identifies the 3rd Battalion of the 60th Brigade (which would be a Motorized Infantry Brigade of the 20th Group Army), "equipped with low light night vision devices, infrared monitors, thermal imaging monitors, and ultra long-wave eavesdropping systems," acting as the "Blue" force against Guangzhou MR's 121st Motorized Infantry Division.

23. Video, "Lanzhou MR Division in '*Stride-2009*' Presents New-Type Combined Arms Battalion," CPM20091015017010, Beijing, China, *CCTV-7* in Mandarin 1130 GMT, August 18, 2009, translated by OSC.

24. Video, "Jinan MR Motorized Division Holds Drill With Modular Combat, Tactical Units," CPM20091015013024, Beijing, China, *CCTV-7* in Mandarin 1130 GMT, August 28, 2009, translated by OSC.

25. *Ibid.*

26. For example, see Video, "Beijing MR Mechanized Infantry Brigade Holds Confrontation Exercise," CPM20091015013006, Beijing, China, *CCTV-7* in Mandarin 1130 GMT, August 5, 2009; and Clip, "Jinan MR Motorized Infantry Brigade Conducts Exercise in Mountain Area," CPM20091015017003, Beijing, China, *CCTV-7* in Mandarin 1130 GMT, September 18, 2009, translated by OSC.

27. PRC, "Article Reviews PLA Training Reforms Through Military Exercises in 2009," CPP20091210004012, Beijing, China, *Xinhua Domestic Service* in Chinese 1040 GMT, December 10, 2009, translated by OSC. The *Xinhua* report was based on a *PLA Daily* report found at JFJB: "Analysis of PLA's Training Reform from Military Exercises in 2009 (II)," CPP20091214702013, Beijing, China, *Jiefangjun Bao* Online in English, December 14, 2009.

28. See Dennis J. Blasko, "'Technology Determines Tactics': The Relationship between Technology and Doctrine in Chinese Military Thinking," *Journal of Strategic Studies*, Vol. 34 Issue 3, pp. 355-381.

29. PRC, "Article Reviews PLA Training Reforms Through Military Exercises in 2009," CPP20091210004012, Beijing, China, *Xinhua Domestic Service* in Chinese 1040 GMT, December 10, 2009, translated by OSC.

30. PRC, "Large Scale Paratroop Military Exercise *'Kong Jiang Ji Dong 2009'* Begins," CPP20091018074006, Beijing, China, *Xinhua Domestic Service* in Chinese 1405 GMT, October 18, 2009, translated by OSC; "*'Airborne Maneuver 2009'* exercise enters battle implementation stage," *Xinhua*, October 21, 2009, available from *eng.mod.gov.cn/MilitaryExercises/2009-10/21/content_4096853. htm;* "Combat vehicles for *'Airborne Maneuver 2009'* exercise arrive at destination," *Xinhua*, October 20, 2009, available from *eng.mod.gov.cn/MilitaryExercises/2009-10/20/content_4096565.htm;*

"'*Airborne Maneuver 2009*' enters second stage," *PLA Daily*, November 2, 2009, available from *eng.mod.gov.cn/Photos/2009-11/02/content_4100134.htm*.

31. "'*Airborne Maneuver 2009*' trans-theater exercise kicks off," *PLA Daily*, October 26, 2009, available from *eng.mod.gov.cn/Photos/2009-10/26/content_4097961.htm*.

32. This section is based upon information found at Dennis J. Blasko, "Mission Action 2010: Three Complex, Transregional, Integrated Joint Operations," *China Brief*, November 5, 2010, available from *www.jamestown.org/single/?no_cache=1&tx_ttnews%5Btt_news%5D=37142*.

33. "Exercise participating troops of Beijing MAC unfolds three-dimensional transportation," *PLA Daily*, October 15, 2010, available from *eng.chinamil.com.cn/special-reports/2010-10/15/content_4314651.htm*; and "'*Mission Action 2010*' exercise unfolds combat readiness level transition," *PLA Daily*, October 13, 2010, available from *eng.chinamil.com.cn/special-reports/2010-10/13/content_4313825.htm*. *PLA Daily* has an English-language webpage dedicated to *Mission Action* available from *eng.chinamil.com.cn/special-reports/node_45418.htm*, and a Chinese-language webpage available from *chn.chinamil.com.cn/zt/2010smxd2010/index.htm*.

34. "Lanzhou Military Region Units Participate in '*Mission Action-2010B*' Maneuvers," CPP20101023072010, Beijing, China, *Xinhua Domestic Service* in Chinese 1208 GMT, October 23, 2010, translated by OSC.

35. Video, "Beijing MR Group Army in '*Mission Actions-2010*' Holds Maneuvering Exercise," CPP20101122017003, Beijing, China, *CCTV-7* in Mandarin 1130 GMT, October 14, 2010, translated by OSC.

36. Video, "Beijing MR Group Army in '*Mission Action-2010*' Conducts Combat Exercise," CPP20101122017006, Beijing, China, *CCTV-7* in Mandarin 1130 GMT, October 17, 2010, translated by OSC.

37. Video, "Beijing MR Troops in '*Mission Action-2010*' Complete Combat Preparation Work," CPP20101122017009, Beijing,

China, *CCTV-7* in Mandarin 1130 GMT, October 20, 2010, translated by OSC.

38. "Beijing Military Region Starts '*Mission Action-2010A*' Drills in Northeast China," CPP20101020005005, Beijing, China, *Xinhua Domestic Service* in Chinese 0912 GMT, October 20, 2010, translated by OSC.

39. "Participating troops of '*Mission Action-2010B*' exercise conduct anti-terror drill," *PLA Daily*, October 25, 2010, available from *eng.chinamil.com.cn/special-reports/2010-10/25/content_4320299.htm*.

40. PRC, "Lanzhou MR Successfully Holds Live Force Drills in '*Mission Action-2010*'," CPP20101028172006, Beijing, China, *Xinhua Domestic Service* in Chinese 0733 GMT, October 28, 2010, translated by OSC.

41. "General communication station vows to ensure smooth communication for '*Mission Action-2010*' exercise," *PLA Daily*, October 14, 2010, available from *eng.chinamil.com.cn/special-reports/2010-10/14/content_4314586.htm*.

42. "Participating Troops of '*Mission Action-2010*' exercise make forced crossing of Yellow River," *PLA Daily*, October 21, 2010, available from *eng.chinamil.com.cn/special-reports/2010-10/21/content_4318483.htm*.

43. PRC, "Chengdu MR Tests Counterattack Tactics in '*Mission Action-2010*' Exercise," CPP20101023704003, Beijing, China, *Jiefangjun Bao Online* in Chinese, October 23, 2010, p. 5, translated by OSC.

44. Video, "Chengdu MR Troops in '*Mission Action-2010*' Examine Systems Combat Methods," CPP20101122017014, Beijing, China, *CCTV-7* in Mandarin 1130 GMT, October 22, 2010, translated by OSC.

45. PRC, "Jinan MR Infantry Division Relies on Local Support in Long-Range Maneuver," CPP20101024702001, Beijing, China, *Jiefangjun Bao Online* in Chinese, October 24, 2010, p. 5, translated by OSC.

46. Xiang Yang and Luo Cheng (向阳、罗诚),"空军首次组织跨区跨海远程整建制兵力投送" ("The PLAAF for the First Time Organizes a Trans-regional, Cross-Sea, Long-Distance Full Organization Force Projection"), *PLA Daily*, April 4, 2011, available from *news.mod.gov.cn/headlines/2011-04/04/content_4235851.htm*.

47. "PLA Engineer Command College holds 1st cross-regional combined joint-training exercise," *PLA Daily*, June 2, 2011, available from *eng.chinamil.com.cn/news-channels/china-military-news/2011-06/02/content_4446730.htm*.

48. Clip: "Troops Move to '*Vanguard-2011*' Exercise Range in China's Henan," CPP20110604163005, Beijing, China, *CCTV-Xinwen* in Mandarin 0134 GMT, June 4, 2011; and Clip: "'Vanguard-2011' Exercise Shows Military Bridge Construction," CPP20110606163002, Beijing, China, *CCTV-Xinwen* in Mandarin 0642 GMT, June 5, 2011, translated by OSC.

49. "PLA conducts force projection drill with civilian aircraft," *PLA Daily*, July 22, 2011, available from *eng.chinamil.com.cn/news-channels/china-military-news/2011-07/22/content_4578003.htm*. Other air movement or multi-mode transportation exercises are conducted within MR boundaries. In 2011, Shenyang MR has held several such exercises, see Yang Zaixin, Liu Lingyue, Hou Huaming, and Li Nan, (杨再新 刘凌月 候华明 李楠), "某集团军运用民航远程输送实兵实弹" ("A Group Army Uses Civil Aviation for Long-distance Transport of Live Troops with Live Ammunition"), *PLA Daily*, August 26, 2011, available from *chn.chinamil.com.cn/wq/2011-08/26/content_4675716.htm*; and Clip: "Shenyang MR Conducts Long-distance Transportation Drill," CPP20110827003003, Beijing, China, *CCTV-Xinwen* in Mandarin 0100 GMT, August 26, 2011, translated by OSC.

50. PRC: "Shenyang MR Stages '*Tengfei-2011*' Emergency Air Transport Drill," CPP20110722787014, Beijing, China, *Zhongguo Qingnian Bao* Online in Chinese, July 22, 2011, translated by OSC.

51. *Ibid.*

52. Clip, "PRC People's Armed Police Force Conducts Air Loading, Transportation Drill," CPP20110705114001, Beijing, China, *CCTV-Xinwen* in Mandarin, July 4, 2011, translated by OSC.

53. "PLA transports troops in high-speed train," *PLA Daily,* July 19, 2011, available from *eng.chinamil.com.cn/news-channels/ china-military-news/2011-07/19/content_4538481.htm.*

CHAPTER 6

LOOKING GOOD ON PAPER: PLA PARTICIPATION IN THE *PEACE MISSION 2010* MULTILATERAL MILITARY EXERCISE

Daniel M. Hartnett

The remarks contained in this chapter are solely those of the author's, and do not represent the views of any organization with which he is or was affiliated. Special thanks for Ken Allen and the two anonymous reviewers who provided very helpful comments on earlier drafts of this chapter.

EXECUTIVE SUMMARY

This chapter presents an in-depth look at the Chinese military's participation in *Peace Mission 2010*, a multilateral military exercise of the Shanghai Cooperation Organization (SCO). It does this in order to determine what, if any, lessons the People's Liberation Army (PLA) may have learned to benefit its modernization efforts.

MAIN ARGUMENT

Although *Peace Mission 2010* appeared on paper to have been a complex and advanced military exercise, a closer look reveals it was actually a superficial exercise. Exercise weaknesses included a highly scripted nature and lack of realism, as well as rudimentary coordination among the participating forces. These weaknesses reflect the inherent nature of the SCO as a primarily political and not military institution. As such, the PLA likely gained little from other SCO militaries about how to further its military capabilities. Instead, the only benefits the PLA took away were the experiences it gained from deploying a large ground force complete with equipment to a neighboring country and projecting air power into China's periphery.

POLICY IMPLICATIONS

- The United States should not view SCO military exercises as providing the PLA with opportunities to learn from its fellow militaries. The nature of the SCO hinders the emergence of robust military exercises from which the PLA could learn. Instead, any progress the PLA makes will be due to its own efforts.
- The United States should consider the growing possibility that PLA ground forces may someday deploy outside of China's territory in the event of a regional crisis. When planning for regional crisis scenarios, such as a collapse of the North Korean regime, U.S. strategic planners should incorporate potential PLA ground force involvement rather than risk being caught unprepared.
- The United States should recognize that the PLA Air Force (PLAAF) is transforming into an incipient expeditionary air force. While still in its nascent phase, the PLAAF is slowly moving toward the ability and mindset necessary to project air power outside of China's territory. As such, regional security planners should increasingly incorporate the possibility of PLAAF operations in future crisis scenarios.

INTRODUCTION

In September 2010, roughly 1,000 personnel of the PLA deployed to Kazakhstan to participate in a multilateral exercise alongside the militaries of Kazakhstan, Kyrgyzstan, Russia, and Tajikistan. These five militaries participated in this nearly 2-week-long exercise, officially named *Peace Mission 2010 Joint Antiterrorism Military Exercise* (和平使命-2010联合反恐军事演习)[1] (hereafter, *Peace Mission 2010*), under the auspices of the regional security forum, the SCO. During the exercise, the militaries of the SCO states conducted a veritable cornucopia of modern combat operations: air raids, armor assaults, artillery strikes, helicopter raids, joint operations, and counterterrorism operations. At first glance, one gets the impression that this exercise provided the PLA with a wealth of observations, insights, and lessons that subsequently could be turned into lessons learned, thus strengthening the PLA's overall military modernization efforts.[2]

Upon closer look, however, the evidence presents a mixed bag in support of the claim that *Peace Mission 2010* significantly contributed to the PLA's long-term efforts to improve its military capabilities. Several weaknesses inherent in the exercise likely hindered any major opportunity for learning from the other participating militaries. These weaknesses primarily include the exercise's highly scripted nature and lack of realism, as well as the rudimentary nature of coordination among the participating forces. Yet, weaknesses aside, there were two areas in which the PLA could gain from its participation in *Peace Mission 2010*. The first is the experience and observations acquired from deploying a large number of ground forces complete with full equipment and vehicles into China's near periphery. Second, the PLA likely acquired valuable experience from conducting an offensive air strike outside its territory, since this was the first exercise to practice this capability since the founding of the People's Republic of China (PRC) in 1949. Taken together, it is likely that while tactically the PLA probably only made slight gains, strategically it may have acquired some useful experiences, should the PLA properly interpret and distill them into lessons learned.

Yet, given that the PLA doesn't exercise frequently with foreign militaries, especially when compared with other modern militaries, it is somewhat counterintuitive that *Peace Mission 2010* did not yield more lessons for the PLA to exploit. The primary reason for this lack of opportunities for tactical military advances likely lies with the nature of the SCO. First, because the SCO is a mechanism for cooperation and information sharing, not a military alliance, it places less emphasis on close military coordination. Second, and relatedly, the SCO's primary focus on coordinating efforts to counter transregional threats such as ethnic separatism and terrorism, rather than combating major military threats, limits the organization's push toward in-depth military interactions among its member states. Third, geopolitical factors—such as a low-level rivalry between Moscow, Russia, and Beijing, China, for influence in Central Asia, and regional distrust of China—also limit the likelihood that the other SCO states would be willing to develop closer military ties with China. So long as these structural factors remain, it is likely that SCO multilateral military exercises will be more about demonstrating political coordination than about military coordination.

This chapter seeks to answer the question of what, if any, insights the PLA could have gained from participating in *Peace Mission 2010*. It does that by conducting a deep dive into open-source reporting on the exercise, using English, Chinese, and Russian language sources. However, although all relevant sources were searched, the vast majority of sources are Chinese. Not only were Russian sources fewer in number; they also generally provided less information about the overall exercise and only superficial details about the PLA's participation. As with any study on China or the Chinese military using open sources, a critical eye must be used. Chinese media sources are likely to paint both the exercise and especially the PLA's participation in a positive light, regardless of the real situation. Furthermore, the information provided in the articles may not be complete, or even completely accurate. Therefore, it is necessary to cross-reference the information contained in the articles with other sources whenever possible. As a result, this chapter does not claim to provide the bottom line of exactly what occurred during the exercise. Instead, it provides one probable interpretation based upon the sources available.

EXERCISE OVERVIEW

From September 10-25, 2010, Kazakhstan hosted the militaries of its fellow SCO member states, China, Russia, Kyrgyzstan, and Tajikistan, for the multilateral military exercise, *Peace Mission 2010*. Uzbekistan, the sixth member of the SCO, declined to send troops to participate, although it was invited.[3] Kazakhstan held *Peace Mission 2010* at its Matibulak training area, located about 20 kilometers (km) north of the city of

Otar, approximately 140 km northwest of Kazakhstan's capital, Almaty, and 1,000 km west of Urumqi, China. According to media reports, a total of between 3,000 and 5,000 troops participated in this 2-week exercise, as well as a variety of ground and air force platforms. The exercise was conducted in a phased manner, gradually increasing in complexity, and culminated in a 1-day live-fire capstone event. This was the second time the PLA had deployed a relatively large number of troops and equipment on an expeditionary exercise, the first being the SCO's *Peace Mission 2007* multilateral exercise in Russia (discussed below). Another, possibly larger, milestone is that during this exercise, the PLAAF left from within China's borders to carry out offensive air strikes against ground targets in a neighboring country. Although the Chinese press claimed this as the first time China had conducted such an event, it is more accurate to state that this was the first time the PLA Air Force carried out such a *practice* event. In 1951, PLAAF bombers (Tu-2s) conducted two bombing missions against Taehwa-do Island during the Korean War, leaving and returning from an air base within China.[4] This was the last known time the PLAAF conducted such an operation.

Peace Mission 2010 was not the first or last multilateral military exercise the SCO held. Instead, it was the seventh SCO exercise and the fourth one named *Peace Mission*. The first SCO military exercise was a small, unnamed counterterrorism exercise in October 2002, held between the militaries of China and Kyrgyzstan. Every year since except 2004, 2008, and 2011, the SCO has held an annual multilateral military exercise. While it is unclear why there was no exercise in these years, it is possible that China's (and the PLA's) focus on internal security for the 2008 Summer Olympics in Beijing may have been a factor for that year. Previous bilateral or multilateral SCO military exercises[5] include the following:

- *Exercise-01*, a bilateral counterterrorism exercise between China and Kyrgyzstan, held in October 2002 along their shared border. This small, 2-day exercise with about 300 total troops was not only the first SCO multilateral exercise, but also the PLA's first participation in an international military exercise.
- *Joint-2003 (or Coalition-2003)*, the SCO's first multilateral counterterrorism exercise, was held on Chinese and Kazakhstani soil in August 2003. About 1,300 troops from China, Kazakhstan, Kyrgyzstan, Russia, and Tajikistan participated.
- *Peace Mission 2005*, the first named *Peace Mission* exercise, was a bilateral Sino-Russian counterterrorism exercise held in August 2005 in both Russia and China. This exercise was the SCO's largest multilateral exercise to date, with approximately 10,000 troops participating, of which reportedly 8,000 were Chinese.
- *Cooperation-2006* was a small bilateral Sino-Tajikistani counterterrorism exercise held in Tajikistan in September 2006.
- *Peace Mission 2007* was an August 2007 multilateral counterterrorism exercise held in Russia with about 5,000 Chinese, Kazakhstani, Kyrgyzstani, Russian, and Tajikistani troops participating. This was reportedly China's first time deploying a large number of troops and equipment for an exercise on foreign soil, with the PLA contingent reaching about 1,600 personnel.

219

- *Peace Mission 2009* was a relatively small (2,600-person) bilateral counterterrorism exercise between China and Russia. This exercise was held concurrently in both China and Russia.[6]

Although the SCO did not conduct a multilateral military exercise in 2011, it has scheduled one for later this year. According to media reports, Tajikistan will host *Peace Mission 2012* sometime in June 2012.[7]

As can be seen, although the exercises vary in name, size, and participants, three characters are common throughout. First, although the actual number of participants has shifted between two and five, China has been a participant in all of them. Second, the SCO military exercises have all focused on some type of counterterrorism scenario, which, as discussed further below, is the SCO's *raison d'être*. Third, although a full member of the SCO, Uzbekistan has never participated in a SCO multilateral military exercise. Uzbekistan did however, host, in March 2006, an SCO counterterrorism exercise with paramilitary and law enforcement forces, named *Vostok-Antiterror-2006*.[8]

The official goal of *Peace Mission 2010* was "to test the interoperability of the SCO armed forces in rendering assistance to a member state involved in an internal armed conflict or subjected to a mass terrorist attack."[9] The scenario for this exercise had the SCO responding to a mass terrorist attack in one of the states. In the scenario, a "terrorist force" of 1,500 people invades an SCO member state and takes control of some of that state's territory. In response to a request for aid from the invaded state, the militaries of the SCO member states, with authorization from the United Nations (UN), dispatch a coalition force to assist the invaded country "to destroy the terrorist armed forces and restore territorial integrity."[10]

Media reports vary on the number of troops who participated in *Peace Mission 2010*. Some articles note that approximately 5,000 troops were in attendance, while a few others note that there were only slightly more than 3,000. Most reports seem to agree that China, Kazakhstan, and Russia each sent roughly 1,000 personnel. These reports also note that Kyrgyzstan and Tajikistan, likely due to the smaller size and weaker capabilities of their militaries, contributed significantly fewer troops, although exact numbers are unclear.[11] If *Peace Mission 2007* is any clue, however, the Kyrgyzstani and Tajikistani contingent could be as small as a few dozen; both countries sent fewer than 100 troops to that earlier exercise.[12] Therefore, one possibility is that the 5,000 figure is inaccurate, and that the total size of the exercise was actually closer to 3,000 troops. Another possibility is that the numbers represent different categories, with the smaller amount signifying the number of troops actively participating in the exercise, and the larger number the total with supporting forces. Unfortunately, the author was unable to determine this definitively.

The order of battle for the participating forces varied by country, though media reports were not clear on the exact breakdown of troops and equipment that each participating nation sent. Kazakhstan appears to have dispatched the most equipment, which is logical given that it was the host nation. According to one source, Kazakhstani forces comprised at least two tank battalions, a motorized rifle company, an air assault battalion, a reconnaissance company, a tactical missile battery, a multiple-launch rocket battery, and a battalion of internal security forces. In addition, Kazakhstan contributed the most aviation forces, with a total of 20 fixed-wing and rotary aircraft.[13] Russia sent

230 pieces of equipment, which included 130 tanks, self-propelled artillery pieces, and infantry fighting vehicles and an additional 100 trucks and support vehicles. Russia also dispatched 10 fixed-wing and rotary aircraft, reportedly from its air base in Kant, Kyrgyzstan.[14] There is little available information on the composition of the Kyrgyzstani and Tajikistani forces that participated.

Reporting on the Chinese forces provided more, but unfortunately not exact, details. The roughly 1,000 participating PLA forces were organizationally divided into three different groups: an "army battle group" ("陆军战斗群"), an "air force battle group" ("空军战斗群"), and a "comprehensive logistics group" ("综合后勤群"). The PLA army battle group was primarily comprised of forces from the Beijing Military Region (MR), reportedly the first time the leadership of the Beijing MR and its forces participated in such an exercise. According to Major General Ma Xiaotian (马晓天), a deputy chief of the PLA general staff:

> For the army battle group, this is the first time the command organs (指挥机关) and forces of the Beijing MR have participated in this type of an exercise. Long-distance cross-border deployment, massing and spreading out in an unknown land, and entering into a live-troop exercise in a foreign land according to the exercise plan; are all brand new tasks (崭新的课题) for them.[15]

Although the various relevant media reports took pains to not provide a breakdown of the army battle group's order of battle, from various Internet photos and articles it appears that, at a minimum, it consisted of the following:[16]

2 companies of T-99 tanks
3 companies of light mechanized infantry
1 company of Type 87 assault guns
1 battalion of 122mm truck-mounted howitzers
100+ support vehicles
1 battery of PGZ95 air defense systems
2 Z-9 attack helicopters
2 Mi-17 helicopters
2 to 3 squads of special operations forces.

According to several articles, the subordinate units of the army battle group were organic units (成建制) that traveled complete with equipment and vehicles.[17]

The PLAAF dispatched an air force battle group to conduct offensive air operations along with Kazakhstani and Russian air forces. The air force battle group consisted of four H-6H bombers, two J-10 fighters, a KJ-2000 early warning and control aircraft, and an H-6U aerial refueling tanker.[18] Of import, and discussed more later on, the PLA's air force battle group actually never deployed to Kazakhstan, but rather took off from and returned to a PLA air base near Urumqi, Xinjiang (likely Changji Air Base), without landing in Kazakhstan—a roundtrip flight of about 2,000 km if flown along a straight path. It is unclear from where exactly the various aircraft originated; however, there are some clues based upon open-source literature. The tanker most likely came from the 22nd Air Regiment, 8th Bomber Division, at Leiyang Air Base, Hunan (Guangzhou MR), since this is the only location where the PLAAF has H-6U refueling tankers. In addition, pictures associated with the article show bombers with bort numbers[19] (4xx7x) that correspond to the 108th Air Regiment, 36th Air Division (Wugong Air Base, Shaanxi, Lanzhou MR).[20] Unfortunately, no further information is available on the other aircraft, including the J-10s, which participated in the exercise.

The third and final component of the PLA's contingent was the comprehensive logistics group, of which very little was said. The Xinjiang Military District (MD) also provided some logistics for this exercise. In order to prepare the support properly, the MD drafted a logistics support plan, set up a leading small group to coordinate the operation, and established a logistics support base at Alashankou, the crossing point on the Chinese side of the Sino-Kazakhstani border for the Chinese troops and equipment traveling via rail to Kazakhstan. In addition, the Xinjiang MD provided the participating troops with the following items: a train transfer flowchart, three cooking vehicles, 250 cots, dining tables for 480 personnel, 10 water tanks, and three field shower vehicles.[21] The PLA forces also relied upon the market to purchase supplies from vendors, although it is unclear whether these purchases were made in China while the troops were traveling or in Kazakhstan during the exercise.[22]

According to press reports, there was no overall commander for this exercise. Rather, command was carried out in a consultative fashion through two hierarchically distinct entities. The first, higher-level command organization was the joint exercise directorate (联合导演部), which consisted of representatives from all five militaries. This organization appears to be primarily responsible for the overall setup and coordination of the exercise, to include preliminary negotiations and consultations about the exercise scenario. Over the course of the year leading up to the exercise, the exercise directorate met four times for consultations.[23] Major General Ma represented the Chinese side in the joint exercise directorate.[24] The second organization, the joint campaign headquarters (联合战役指挥部), was more intimately involved in the day-to-day operations of the exercise. This organization, too, consisted of representatives from each military, and was the primary point of coordination among the five militaries. The Chinese side was led by Major General Li Shaojun (李少军), deputy commander of the Beijing MR.[25] Major General Meng Guoping (孟国平), deputy director of the PLA General Staff Department's First Department (Operations), assisted Major General Li as the deputy director of the joint campaign headquarters for the Chinese side.[26] According to the Chinese press, the joint campaign headquarters held conferences to reach agreements on all "operational intentions, decisions, and planning." Decisions at this level were made based upon negotiations and common agreements.[27] From this it appears likely that the joint campaign headquarters was the organization directly commanding the various forces during the exercise.

TIMELINE OF THE EXERCISE

As mentioned, the exercise officially took place from September 10 to 25, 2010. Over this 2-week period, the exercise was divided into several stages, with the addition of the deployment timeline prior to the actual exercise. Each of these stages is detailed below.

Stage 1: Deployment.

The participating military forces began deploying to Matibulak from the end of August through the first week in September, depending upon their original location. The Chinese forces, located the farthest away, officially began deploying on August 31, when the first of six batches of PLA troops departed via train from the combined arms training base in Zhurihe, Inner Mongolia. All Chinese forces, with the exception of the air force battle group, deployed via rail, with the last batch arriving in Otar on the afternoon of September 9.[28] Due to the difference in Chinese and Kazakhstani rail gauge sizes, the PLA had to unload at Alashankou all of its troops and equipment from the Chinese trains and switch to Kazakhstani trains.[29] In preparation for the deployment, the PLA constructed a mock platform at the Zhurihe combined arms training base (Inner Mongolia) to practice loading and unloading of the trains. Two new platforms were also constructed at the border crossing point to transfer the heavy equipment from the Chinese to Kazakhstani trains.[30] It remains to be seen whether these platforms are temporary in nature. Once all the troops arrived at Matibulak base, the official exercise commenced in three stages: strategic consultation, joint counterterrorism campaign preparation, and joint counterterrorism campaign implementation. Each of these is discussed below.

Stage 2: Strategic Consultation.

The strategic consultation stage occurred on the morning of September 10 in Almaty. This consultation appears to have been mostly a short, pro forma discussion among the heads of each nation's military. In attendance were the first deputy defense ministers from Kazakhstan, Kyrgyzstan, Russia, and Tajikistan, as well as Chief of the PLA General Staff Chen Bingde. During this meeting, the various representatives addressed the global and regional situation, laid out the exercise scenario, and expressed their views on the intent of the exercise. After this short, 1-1/2-hour meeting, the delegates broke up, and the focus of the exercise shifted to Matibulak.[31]

Stage 3: Joint Counterterrorism Campaign Preparation.

After 2 days — during which it is unclear exactly what transpired — on September 13 the exercise began its second official stage, the joint counterterrorism campaign preparation. This part of the exercise took up the bulk of the exercise, lasting 10 days. During this stage, the five militaries practiced the operations and maneuvers that they were to conduct in the final part of the exercise. The aim of this stage was to familiarize the troops with the terrain, the sequence of operations, and the means of coordination.[32] Throughout this stage, the forces held six joint practice drills, the latter four of which were live-fire exercises.[33] Each drill increased in complexity and difficulty in order to improve gradually the troops' capabilities. After each drill, the commanders of each participating military force evaluated the outcomes and worked together with their foreign colleagues in the joint campaign headquarters to make any necessary changes.[34] In between the joint drills, the individual militaries conducted separate training drills and held camaraderie-building events, such as singing and dancing events.[35]

Stage 4: Joint Counterterrorism Campaign Implementation.

The main event of *Peace Mission 2010* was the 1-day, live-fire joint exercise held on September 24. This event was the capstone of the previous 2 weeks of training, incorporating all the topics that the troops had so far been practicing. The exercise was divided into four phases: "firepower preparation and break-through" ("火力准备与突破"); "surround and suppress the enemy in a residential area" ("围剿居民地之敌"); "enter reserve forces into the fight" ("预备队投入交战"); and "nighttime suppression of the enemy's base" ("夜间清剿基地之敌"). Each phase will be discussed in turn.

Phase 1: Firepower Preparation and Breakthrough (火力准备与突破).

The exercise began at 11 a.m. local time, with the firepower preparation and breakthrough phase. The first component of this exercise was an air strike conducted in successive waves by (in order of wave) Kazakhstani, Russian, and Chinese fighters and bombers. For this exercise, the PLA's air force battle group, comprising four H-6H bombers, two J-10 fighters, an early warning and control aircraft, and at least one tanker, took off from an airbase outside of Urumqi (likely, Changji Air Base) in the morning.[36] The battle group was divided into two flights, with two H-6Hs, two J-10s, the KJ-2000 early warning and control aircraft, and the tanker in the first flight, and two unescorted H-6Hs in the second flight.[37] En route and prior to departing Chinese airspace, the J-10s refueled in the air.[38] At the border with Kazakhstan, two Kazakhstani Mig-29s met and escorted the second flight of Chinese

H-6H bombers to the training base.[39] During this exercise, media reports noted that neither the KJ-2000 nor the tanker left Chinese airspace.[40] Upon reaching the targets, each echelon conducted one attack run, dropping 12 bombs per bomber, while the escort fighters conducted simulated attacks and electronic suppression against the terrorist forces. It is worth noting that reports made no mention of the J-10s conducting live-fire operations during this exercise, although it is unclear why not. Upon completing their runs, the two flights immediately returned to their starting air base outside Urumqi, China.[41]

Media reports noted that command for the air operation was carried out by three separate entities during the air force battle group's portion of the exercise. Within China, command was exercised through a ground command post and an airport control tower (presumably both in Urumqi). Within Kazakhstan, there was also a command post, possibly the joint campaign headquarters at the Matibulak training base. For the entire route, the KJ-2000 early warning and control aircraft acted as a command and communications relay station, providing "early warning, command guidance, and communications relay support in real time" for the air force battle group.[42] Although this is not fully clear, it would appear then that the KJ-2000 simply passed commands from the various ground command posts to the aircraft, rather than providing instructions directly to the aircraft.

After the air raid, the joint forces conducted artillery strikes against the "terrorist forces."[43] A joint group of ground artillery was composed of a Kazakhstani and a Russian battalion of rocket artillery and a Kazakhstani and a Russian battalion of 122mm tracked self-propelled howitzers. For this component of the exercise, the Chinese forces consisted of a battalion of 122 mm truck-mounted howitzers.[44]

Once the artillery assault concluded, the forces began an armor assault along three approaches. The Russian-speaking forces attacked along the right and center approaches; a combined force of Russian and Kyrgyzstani troops attacked along the right flank, while a combined force of Kazakhstani and Tajikistani tanks moved up the center. The Chinese forces, divided into two assault teams—each composed of Type 99 tanks, Type 92B wheeled infantry fighting vehicles, Type 87 assault guns, and Type 92A wheeled armored personnel carriers—were responsible for the left flank.[45] Throughout the ground portion of this exercise, there was no mention of opposition forces.

Phase 2: Surround and Suppress the Enemy in a Residential Area (围剿居民地之敌).

Around noon, the second phase of the live-fire exercise began. Here, the SCO forces moved to liberate an urban environment occupied by the terrorists. Each nation sent in a small group of special operations forces to free the hostages and eliminate the terrorists. The troops were supported by "feigned helicopter attacks and sniper cover."[46] This is the only event of the day that appears to actually have used opposition forces, with a platoon of Kazakhstani internal security forces playing the role of the terrorists.[47]

Phase 3: Enter Reserve Forces into the Fight (预备队投入交战).

In the scenario's third phase, the terrorists, having been soundly beaten in the first two phases, "fell back" to their base area to regroup. In response, a combined ground force of Chinese and Russian armor and mechanized infantry forces sought to drive the terrorists into a circle. After the initial assault by the Chinese and Russian forces, two Kazakhstani tank battalions entered the fray and surrounded the enemy forces. Kazakhstani, Russian, and Chinese attack helicopters then conducted air strikes to assist the ground forces. At the same time, a joint artillery force cut off the terrorists' escape routes to the rear, thus isolating the remaining enemies. The goal was to set up for the final phase of the operation.[48]

Phase 4: Nighttime Suppression of the Enemy's Base (夜间清剿基地之敌).

The final phase of the September 24 live-fire exercise was a combined helicopter and armor attack at night to destroy the remnants of the terrorist forces trapped in their home base.[49] For the helicopter portion of the exercise, Kazakhstani, Russian, and Chinese attack helicopters formed three separate groups, each with two helicopters, to conduct a wave of attacks on the targets. The PLA formation, the last of the three waves, was comprised of two Army Aviation Z-9 attack helicopters.[50] Soon after the helicopters completed their mission, a joint armored assault force attacked the base area. This force was comprised of three groups, again divided along national and linguistic lines. On the left flank was a combined force of Kazakhstani and Tajikistani troops, while a combined Russian and Kyrgyzstani force attacked on the right flank. This time, however, the Chinese troops, consisting of a tank company, two mechanized infantry platoons, and a psychological operations vehicle, operated in the center between the Russian-speaking groups.[51]

Finally, at 8:30 p.m., the exercise ended.[52] Over the next week, the Chinese forces boarded six waves of trains to return home, again having to change trains at the Sino-Kazakhstani border due to the differences in rail gauges between the two countries.[53]

Exercise Assessment—A Mixed Bag for Lessons Learned.

In many ways, if the media reports about this *Peace Mission 2010* are even half accurate, the exercise was less than an ideal training event. In particular, this chapter identifies three characteristics of the exercise that detract from the overall benefits it could have provided to the PLA: its heavily scripted nature, its noticeable lack of realism, and the lack of in-depth co-ordination among the multinational forces. That being said, however, the exercise likely does provide experiences from which the PLA could learn, should it seek to do so. In particular, the PLA gained valuable observations and lessons for its ability to project power into its near periphery, be it land forces via rail or offensive air operations. Each aspect will be discussed in turn.

Overall, this exercise suffered from several limitations. The first, and in this author's opinion, most serious, limitation of this exercise for the PLA was its heavily scripted nature. As noted above, upon arriving at the base, the troops drilled for nearly 2 weeks on the exact set of plans they were to conduct for the September 24 capstone event. According to one source, on the first day of the drills (September 14), the troops actually "walked on foot" ("徒步") the area in formation so they could familiarize themselves with the terrain, sequence of the exercise, and positions of both themselves and the other forces during the actual exercise.[54] As Major General Li described:

> Each side's participating force, according to the joint live-troop activities plan, undertook the method of 'first bare-handed, then real equipment, finally live-ammo' ('先徒手, 后实装, 再带实弹'); proceeding step by step and gradually going deeper, and comprehensively breaking in the command procedures, operational methods, and communications means for the joint activities.[55]

Compounding this problem is the apparent long lead time the Chinese troops had to practice specifically for the exercise. For example, the air force battle group had several months of training to prepare, whereby they first practiced as individual components, and then slowly integrated the various platforms into one organic group.[56] The participating air defense detachment immediately began training for the exercise upon being alerted in March 2010.[57] Similarly, the Army Aviation regiment that was tasked to send the four helicopters to the exercise also worked hard to improve its ability to fulfill the requirements of the exercise, namely, nighttime raids. In order to successfully complete this task, which according to one account, is not covered in PLA training regulations, over several months the crew studied these types of operations, interviewed factory experts about the nighttime capabilities of the helicopters and the rockets, and participated in several nighttime live-fire exercises at the Zhurihe combined arms training base in Inner Mongolia.[58] Taken together, it is probably more accurate to refer to the six practice drills and capstone exercise as dress rehearsals leading up to the main event, in which the troops learned their actions by rote memorization, not unlike the way an actor learns his lines in a play.

The second and related limitation was the overall lack of realism in *Peace Mission 2010*. For example, the only evidence of opposition forces in this exercise was a platoon of Kazakhstani internal security forces acting as terrorists in the second phase of the September 24 capstone exercise.[59] In addition, there were no reports about the use of intelligence and reconnaissance assets in *Peace Mission 2010*, which is surprising, given the PLA's near-fanatical emphasis on the value of information operations. Furthermore, the short nature of each phase of the capstone exercise also detracted from its realism. China's participation in the bombing portion of the exercise, for example, lasted about 10 minutes for both waves (excluding the flight time there and back). Even more shocking, when the first three phases of the capstone exercise are combined, it only extends the length to just over an hour.[60]

Another sign that this exercise lacked realism was its phased nature. In *Peace Mission 2010*, each event was clearly delineated from the others, and began only after the preceding event ended. While such an approach to training may be good for exercising the individual component phases, it bears little resemblance to modern combat operations, where events often blur together. Finally, throughout the various reporting, there was no mention of casualties or wounded for either side. While it is not necessarily a leap of faith to maintain that no prisoners were taken by the SCO forces, it is a bit too much to imagine that the terrorist forces were unable to wound or kill any of the SCO forces. It leaves one to wonder, in the event of a real mass terrorist attack, could the SCO forces, including the PLA, respond to their own casualties? If so, how would they react?

A third issue that limits any benefits the PLA could acquire from this exercise was the level of coordination among the SCO forces. As far as can be ascertained, all coordination among the five militaries was limited to that which occurred through the joint campaign headquarters. Decisions made in a consultative fashion were then relayed down to the forces, with little or no direct coordination between the actual troops. When problems arose during the drills, rather than solve them on the spot, they appear to have been passed up to the joint campaign headquarters for discussion, evaluation, and decisionmaking—after the drill concluded. Once a collection decision was agreed upon, the joint campaign headquarters then passed the decision back down to the units for inclusion in the next round of practice, which was sometimes the next day. There also appeared to be a language barrier between the Russian- and Chinese-speaking forces. For example, according to one news report, Kazakhstani Mig-29 pilots were unable to communicate with the pilots of the Chinese H-6H bombers that they escorted due to the language barrier. Instead, the fighters had to use their wings to communicate, tilting them left or right in order to signal to the bombers.[61] Coordination difficulties in earlier practice drills also existed between the Chinese pilots and Kazakhstani and Russian pilots.[62] While language barriers can be a problem in almost any multinational exercise, it seems overly dangerous for air units to be unable to communicate with each other, especially when operating together. It is also interesting that the PLAAF did not ensure that Chinese Russian-speaking pilots, or at least one translator, participated in this exercise. While not directly stated, this language barrier may have been the reason Chinese ground forces operated somewhat distinctly from the rest of the (Russian-speaking) forces in the capstone exercise.

However, to dismiss this exercise totally is to throw the baby out with the bathwater. There are definitely lessons in *Peace Mission 2010* that the PLA could draw upon to improve its overall ability to conduct combat operations. First, the clearest benefit is the likely experience the PLA gained from deploying a thousand troops complete with equipment to a neighboring country. Although the deployment relied primarily on rail, with no apparent use of air transport, the observations and lessons that the PLA made have the potential to provide it with a foundation for improving its ability to mobilize troops over long distances and abroad. As PLA Senior Colonel Li Zhujun (李祝俊), deputy director of the external affairs coordination team for *Peace Mission 2010*, noted:

> The Chinese side's rail transport of its participating units in the '*Peace Mission 2010*' multilateral military exercise was another rather large, cross-border, long-distance projection of organic units organized by our military during peacetime, and one which accumulated useful experiences for the long-distance projection of our military.[63]

The beneficial experiences included transporting a large force across China's borders; moving the units complete with their equipment, including heavy equipment such as the T-99 tanks; dealing with the issue of different rail gauges; and providing logistical support for the troops en route—all of which could provide lessons for future PLA deployments. Indeed, it would appear that any deployment lessons from *Peace Mission 2010* would be a natural extension of lessons observed from the PLA's growing fascination with long-range transregional exercises over the past few years, as Dennis Blasko discusses more fully in his chapter in this volume.[64]

A second takeaway for the PLA is the experience the air force gained from conducting a long-range air strike against a target outside of China's borders. Although tactically this action was of relatively small value given its simplistic and scripted nature—essentially a there-and-back bombing mission without opposition—there are still potential lessons for the PLAAF to learn, should it make the effort to do so. The coordinated use of escort fighters, aerial refueling tankers, and an early warning and control aircraft likely provided the PLAAF with some valuable lessons on how to improve such operations in the future. The experience and observations gained from passing command between several command stations also could benefit the PLAAF's ability to conduct long-range operations. Finally, the successful completion of this mission conferred on the PLAAF a sense of confidence that it could conduct similar operations in a future combat scenario. In part, the PLAAF's participation in this exercise represents fulfillment of a new set of strategic guidance issued to the air force in 2004. This new guidance, referred to as "simultaneous offensive and defensive operations," calls upon the PLAAF to be able to conduct offensive air operations outside of Chinese territory—the first such official requirement since the founding of the PRC in 1949.[65] The air force battle groups' successful bombing raid against mock targets in Kazakhstan clearly demonstrates the ability to conduct "simultaneous offensive and defensive operations."

WHY NOT A MORE EFFECTIVE MILITARY EXERCISE?

So why wasn't *Peace Mission 2010* a more effective military exercise? Why was the exercise not carried out in a more rigorous manner, which in turn could have translated into increased qualitative and quantitative lessons for the PLA to absorb? A likely answer to these questions lies with the nature of the SCO as a multilateral organization. First, the organization is more political than military, and 10 years after its creation remains more of a forum for consultation and cooperation than a military alliance. Second, and related to the first, the stated goal of the SCO is to focus on combating regional transnational threats such as terrorism, extremism, and separatism; rather than on military threats that would require a more concerted and focused military response. Third, discordant interests *within* the organization likely hinder any moves toward a stronger military focus, even if such desires among the six member states existed. Each will be discussed in turn.

At its very core, the SCO is a forum for consultation and cooperation on regional security concerns. Several Western scholars refer to the organization with more ambiguous terms, such as an "intergovernmental network," "multilateral security dialogue," "discussion forum," and "regional political-security arrangement."[66] One thing most observers agree on, however, is that the SCO is not a military alliance. This point has been consistently and repeatedly reaffirmed by the SCO member states since the SCO's establishment in 2001, and was most recently made during the April 2012 SCO meeting of defense ministers, the news release of which reiterated "that the SCO is not a military or political alliance. . . ."[67] Instead, according to the Secretariat of the SCO:

> The main goals of the SCO are strengthening mutual confidence and good-neighborly relations among the member countries; promoting effective cooperation in politics, trade and economy, science and technology, culture as well as education, energy, transportation, tourism, environmental protection and other fields; making joint efforts to maintain and ensure peace, security and stability in the region, moving towards the establishment of a new, democratic, just and rational political and economic international order.[68]

While this may be construed by many as simply empty words, the key point here is that the SCO is not the equivalent of a military alliance. In many ways, the consultative and egalitarian method with which command was carried out throughout *Peace Mission 2010* demonstrates the organization's stronger focus on political coordination than on military coordination. Had the SCO been a true military alliance, it is likely that command would be carried out in a more hierarchical manner.

On a related note, the SCO's core focus is on countering transnational security concerns, rather than more traditional, hard military threats such as invasion. In part, this stems from its legacy of being built upon an earlier confidence-building organization, the Shanghai Five. In 1996, China, Kazakhstan, Kyrgyzstan, Russia, and Tajikistan established the Shanghai Five as a regional confidence-building mechanism to resolve then-existing border disputes among the five states. By the late-1990s, having solved these issues, the Shanghai Five began to shift its focus to addressing mutually held concerns about religious extrem-

239

ism, ethnic separatism, and terrorism.[69] This focus carried through to the 2001 creation of the SCO, which is essentially the Shanghai Five expanded to include a sixth member, Uzbekistan. As the SCO's founding convention, the Shanghai Convention on Combating Terrorism, Separatism, and Extremism, states, the SCO primarily seeks to have member states "cooperate in the area of prevention, identification and suppression of" terrorism, separatism, and extremism—what the Chinese press commonly refer to as the "Three Evils" or "Three Forces" ("三股势力").[70] In order to promote joint efforts to combat these "Three Evils," Article 6 of the SCO's convention calls upon its member states to cooperate along several paths:

- Exchange information concerning the "Three Evils" with other member states;
- Prevent, identify, and suppress terrorist, separatist, and extremist acts; to include such activities that might be launched from one's own territory against another SCO member state;
- Prevent financial, training, and other types of support for such activities;
- Exchange legal and regulatory information;
- Exchange experiences combating these acts;
- Train experts to counter these threats; and,
- Implement other forms of cooperation and support, such as providing practical assistance to combat terrorism, separatism, and extremism.[71]

As such, while the SCO convention does promote countering the "Three Evils," it does not specifically mention the need to develop each other's military capabilities. In fact, official SCO documents mention neither military capacity building nor military modernization.[72] Were it more focused on military threats, the SCO likely would conduct more frequent and more complex military exercises, as well as promote other types of military cooperation efforts. Since the SCO's founding in 2001, however, it has conducted at most one military exercise per year, for a total of seven military exercises, with an eighth scheduled for later in 2012. By way of comparison, the North Atlantic Treaty Organization (NATO), which is indeed a military alliance, conducted at least four named exercises in 2010 alone. Furthermore, a key function of a military alliance's exercises is for members to learn from each other's defense reforms. However, the official documents of the SCO fail to mention the notion of sharing military "best practices," other than exchanging information and knowhow on countering terrorism.[73]

The consultative and coordinative nature of the SCO, as well as the SCO's primary fixation on transnational security threats, can be clearly seen in China's stated goals of *Peace Mission 2010*. As Major General Ma described:

> China's objectives in taking part in this exercise are . . . to implement the consensus reached by the heads of states of the various SCO member states; further strengthen practical cooperation in all areas, including cooperation in defense affairs, among the various SCO member states; safeguard the security, peace and stability of the region; as well as further demonstrate in full their determination, willpower and ability to jointly oppose terrorism, separatism, and extremism. At the same time, taking part in the joint military exercise can also further enhance mutual political trust among the member states as well as strengthen understanding and friendship among the troops of the different countries.[74]

A final structural factor that prevented *Peace Mission 2010*, and likely other SCO multinational military exercises, from emerging as a more rigorous military exercise, arises from a divergence of interests and a lack of trust within the organization. Key among these disparate views are those of the two largest players in the organization, China and Russia. While the two countries are not antagonistic, several scholars note that an important interest for both Beijing and Moscow is to balance the other in Central Asia.[75] Furthermore, China and Russia have divergent end goals for the SCO. China seeks to expand the SCO's focus to also include economic and energy-related issues, while Russia resists this direction. As the Stockholm International Peace Research Institute notes:

> Given the inevitability of Chinese economic penetration into Central Asia, the growing Chinese need for energy, and the region's objective need for Chinese investment if it is to grow without over-dependence on the West, it makes eminent sense for Russia to capture the process in an explicit institutional framework in which it can hope to retard any premature breakthrough, such as a free-trade area.[76]

Russia instead takes a more ambivalent view of the SCO, and puts more focus and effort on another regional security organization, the Collective Security Treaty Organization (CSTO).[77] The CSTO, which includes Russia, Belarus, Armenia, Kazakhstan, Kyrgyzstan, Tajikistan, and Uzbekistan, is a regional mutual defense alliance established in 1992, shortly after the breakup of the Soviet Union.[78] Unlike the SCO, the CSTO has a much stronger military focus, and specifically seeks "to ensure the collective defense of the independence, territorial integrity and sovereignty of the member states. . . ."[79] Furthermore, the CSTO calls for the establishment of coalition groupings of forces and military infrastructure, joint training of military staff, and support for military procurement—all things not covered under the SCO.[80] The Russian aviation forces that participated in *Peace Mission 2010*, for example, came from an air base in Kant, Kyrgyzstan, which is a CSTO air base.[81] Finally, from a geopolitical aspect, Russia prefers the CSTO over the SCO primarily because Russia dominates the alliance, and China is not a member.[82]

Other structural aspects of the SCO also inhibit the level of military coordination and support among the SCO states. Among the smaller Central Asian member states, for example, there are disagreements over the SCO and its value. All tend to use the SCO to play the two much larger and much-more-powerful China and Russia against each other. At the same time, however, the Central Asian states have their individual interests and do not want to be fully tied to either China or Russia.[83] Furthermore, all the former Soviet states have a historical distrust of China, which, according to Martha Olcott, a senior associate at the Carnegie Endowment for International Peace, implies that "for the foreseeable future it is impossible to imagine China becoming an equal security partner of any of the Central Asian states or of Russia."[84] Therefore, while Russia and the Central Asian states are likely to conduct military exercises with China, the former Soviet states are likely to keep the exercises at a lower level of complexity than they are capable of doing. It is worth noting that the 2011 CSTO military exercise, *Center-2011* (Ценмр-2011), was a significantly larger and more complex exercise than the typical SCO multinational military exercise. In this CSTO multilateral military exercise, more than 12,000 troops from Armenia, Belarus, Kyrgyzstan, Kazakhstan, and Russia conducted military operations simultaneously in four different nations (Russia, Kazakhstan, Tajikistan, and Kyrgyzstan).[85]

CONCLUSIONS

On paper and at first glance, China's participation in *Peace Mission 2010* appears to have provided the PLA with a wealth of experience. Coordinated air strikes, joint operations, rapid assaults, and nonlinear operations held during the exercise bear the hallmark of advanced, modern combat operations. If the PLA were to turn these lessons into learned — in effect, enforcing a change in the way it conducts military operations — the PLA's efforts to improve its military capacities would likely receive a significant boost. However, aside from the difficulty that any military, let alone a highly bureaucratic military such as the PLA, would have in turning lessons into lessons learned, there are other flaws in this picture. Several characteristics of the exercise hindered the PLA from benefiting from this multinational exercise. These characteristics included the exercise's highly scripted nature, its distinct lack of realism, and its highly centralized means of coordination among the participating forces. Taken together, these characteristics likely made this exercise little more than a chance to practice the PLA's driving, flying, and shooting skills.

These limitations and weaknesses in *Peace Mission 2010* are primarily driven by the structural nature of the SCO. First, the SCO does not prioritize promoting stronger military coordination among its members.

Instead, at its heart, the SCO remains an international consultation and coordinating mechanism at best. It is primarily a political organization that seeks to promote a certain level of cooperation on threats to regional stability, such as terrorism, extremism, and separatism. While military means are indeed one tool for dealing with these threats, the SCO appears to realize that it is neither the only nor the main tool in the tool box. Finally, internal disagreements and an overall lack of trust among its members limits the chance that SCO multilateral military exercises will be anything more than basic confidence-building and demonstration exercises. In other words, the level of complexity achieved in *Peace Mission 2010* may be exactly what the participating nations were looking for all along. It is quite likely that tactical military efficiency was a secondary goal behind the primary goal of demonstrating a basic level of political coordination among the SCO states.

However, one should not totally dismiss *Peace Mission 2010* as a complete waste of the PLA's efforts. There are definitely lessons in the exercise that the PLA could draw upon to improve its overall ability to conduct military operations. First, the PLA likely acquired significant experience from deploying 1,000 troops complete with equipment to a neighboring country. Although singularly relying on rail for this deployment, the observations and lessons that the PLA made have the potential to further its ability to mobilize troops over long distances and potentially send them into China's near abroad. Loading and unloading large numbers of men and heavy equipment, dealing with the issue of different rail gauges, providing logistical support for the troops en route all could provide lessons for future PLA long-range, transnational deployments. Indeed, it would appear that any deployment lessons from *Peace Mission 2010* would be a natural extension of lessons observed from the PLA's growing fascination with long-range transregional exercises over the past few years. Although *Peace Mission 2010* took place in Central Asia, it is not difficult to imagine a different scenario whereby PLA forces — possibly also from the Beijing MR — are dispatched via rail to another part of China's periphery in response to a regional crisis. A collapse of the North Korean regime, for example, comes quickly to mind.

A second positive takeaway for the PLA is the experience the air force gained from successfully conducting a long-range bombing outside of China's borders. Tactically, this action was relatively minor, given its simplistic and scripted nature. However, the bombing is much more significant at the strategic level, and signifies the fact that the PLAAF is moving, albeit slowly, toward being able to fulfill the strategic requirement for an offensive air capability outside of China's territory. The PLAAF's portion of *Peace Mission 2010* may also solidify the notion within the Chinese Communist Party elite that the PLA Air Force is gradually morphing into an *incipient expeditionary air force*. The significance of changing the mindset of Chinese and PLA leadership should not be understated, since this is a crucial step into transforming a lesson into a lesson learned. Of course, whether the PLA grasps this fact and brings about an actual change in its operating procedures remains to be seen. However, if recent events are any clue, in some ways it is already accomplishing this task. In late-February 2011, as the fighting between pro-Gaddafi and anti-Gaddafi forces in Libya escalated, some 35,000 Chinese citizens working in Libya increasingly came under threat. In order to rescue its citizens and arguably stave off any domestic criticism of perceived Party or PLA impotence to act, the Chinese government conducted its "largest and most complicated overseas evacuation ever," and the first to involve the PLA.[86] Of importance for this chapter, the PLAAF dispatched four IL-76 transport aircraft to assist in the evacuation process.[87] These aircraft, dispatched on February 28 from China, began evacuating people from Sabha, Libya, to Khartoum, Sudan, the next day.[88] Although the PLAAF evacuated only a small percentage of the total number of Chinese in Libya, its successful participation in this event was a crucial demonstration of an expeditionary air mindset within China, and a possible harbinger of similar events in the future.

POLICY IMPLICATIONS FOR THE UNITED STATES

So what does this all mean for the United States? There are three key takeaways for U.S. policymakers. First, the United States should not view the SCO multilateral exercises as automatically providing the PLA with significant operational experiences to improve its combat capabilities. While there are definitely lessons the PLA could learn from its fellow participant militaries, these lessons are likely to be limited at best, and to appear better in media reports than in reality. Structural aspects of the SCO will inhibit the PLA from acquiring major benefits from these exercises, at least for the near to medium term. In addition, the core focus of the SCO on improving capacities to combat terrorism in the region does not fully translate into abilities to counter a highly advanced military force, such as the U.S. military.

Second, U.S. policymakers and strategic thinkers should consider the growing possibility that PLA ground forces may someday deploy outside of China's territory in the event of a crisis. *Peace Mission 2010* shows that the PLA is slowly expanding its capacity to project power into China's periphery. When planning for regional crisis events, such as a collapse of the North Korean regime, U.S. strategic planners should not dismiss outright the notion that Beijing may call upon the PLA to dispatch forces to the region. A more detailed study looking at exactly what China and the PLA are doing to improve their long-range deployment capabilities may shed further light on this possibility.

Third, the United States and other regional actors should recognize that the PLAAF is transforming into an incipient expeditionary air force. Gone are the days when the PLAAF was a territorial defense air force. While still in its nascent phase, the PLAAF demonstrated during *Peace Mission 2010* and other recent events that it is slowly acquiring the ability and mindset to conduct air operations, offensive and other, beyond China's borders. Therefore, for better or worse, regional planners should incorporate in future crisis scenarios outside of China's territory the possibility of PLAAF participation.

ENDNOTES - CHAPTER 6

1. Although Chinese English-language articles on this exercise used the term "antiterrorism" ("反恐") to describe this exercise, given that it comprised 3,000-5,000 personnel, long-range bombing and airstrikes, battalions of armor, etc., it is probably more accurate to refer to it as a "counterterrorism" exercise. However, in order to be consistent with Chinese English-language reporting, the term "antiterrorism" is retained.

2. For the purpose of this chapter, lessons learned are distinct from lessons. A lesson refers to the knowledge or understanding gained by experience or observation, and can be either negative or positive. A lesson learned, on the other hand, signifies that an individual or organization has internalized the lesson, resulting in a noticeable change in behavior.

3. Some observers maintain that Uzbekistan may have refused, due to its "love-hate relationship" with the SCO, and that it generally shies away from supporting any multilateral military exercise. Julie Boland, *Learning from the Shanghai Cooperation Organization's 'Peace Mission 2010' Exercise*, Washington, DC: The Brookings Institution, October 29, 2010, available from *www.brookings.edu/opinions/2010/1029_asia_war_games_boland.aspx*.

4. I am indebted to Ken Allen for his insight into this point. For more on PLAAF operations in the Korean War, see Zhang Xiaoming, *Red Wings over the Yalu: China, the Soviet Union, and the Air War in Korea*, College Station, TX: Texas A&M University, 2002, especially pp. 156-62.

5. This list includes only military exercises and excludes paramilitary or law enforcement exercises.

6. Dennis J. Blasko, "People's Liberation Army and People's Armed Police Ground Exercises with Foreign Forces, 2002-2009," in Roy Kamphausen, David Lai, and Andrew Scobell, eds., *The PLA at Home and Abroad: Assessing the Operational Capabilities of China's Military*, Carlisle, PA: Strategic Studies Institute, U.S. Army War College, June 2010, pp. 381-405; *China Daily*, "China and Kyrgyzstan Launch Anti-terrorism Exercises," September 11, 2002, available from *yaleglobal.yale.edu/content/china-and-kyrgyzstan-launch-anti-terrorism-exercises*; Zheng Shouhua and Hua Ji (郑守华，花吉), "系列军演成为'品牌'" ("A Series of Military Exercises Becomes a 'Trademark'"), 环球军事 (*Global Military*), No. 231, October, 2010, pp. 10-13; *People's Daily*, "Peace Mission 2007," July 27, 2007, available from *english.people.com.cn/90002/91620/91644/6225832.html*; "Chinese, Russian troops showcase Anti-terror Power in Joint Military Exercise," *Xinhua*, July 26, 2009, available from *eng.mod.gov.cn/SpecialReports/2009-07/27/content_4016983.htm*.

7. Luo Zheng, "SCO Defense Ministers Meet with Chinese and Foreign Reporters," *People's Daily*, April 26, 2012, available from *english.peopledaily.com.cn/90786/7800245.html*; "SCO to Hold Joint Military Drill in Tajikistan," Xinhua, April 26, 2012, available from *europe.chinadaily.com.cn/china/2012-04-26/content_ 15153461.htm*.

8. Radio Free Europe—Radio Liberty, "Newsline," March 10, 2006, available from *www.rferl.org/content/article/1143591.html*.

9. "*Peace Mission 2010* to be held in Kazakhstan from September 9th to 25th," *RIA Novosti*, July 21, 2010, available from *en.rian. ru/mlitary_news/20100721/159892157.html*.

10. Guo Jianyue, Lü Desheng, Tan Zhaoping, and Zhang Jifeng (郭建跃, 吕德胜, 覃照平, 张吉峰),"打响联合反控新战役: 目击 '和平使命-2010'联合反恐军演实兵演练" ("Starting a New Antiterror Joint Campaign: Seeing with our Own Eyes the Live Troop Drill of the '*Peace Mission 2010*' Joint Antiterror Military Exercise"), 解放军报 (*PLA Daily*), September 25, 2010, p. 4.

11. "Russian Defense Minister Hails Results of SCO Counterterror Exercises," Interfax-AVN, September 27, 2010, available from *www.militarynews.ru*; "SCO Counter-terror Exercises Show High Level of Armed Forces' Training—Kazakh Defense Minister," Interfax-AVN, September 27, 2010, available from *business. highbeam.com/407705/article-1G1-238187915/sco-counterterror-exercises-show-high-level-armed-forces*; Zhang Chunyou (张春友), "上合组织反恐亮剑" ("The Shanghai Cooperation Organization's Shining Sword of Antiterrorism"), 光明日报 (*Guangming Daily*), September 26, 2010, p. 8.

12. Zheng and Hua, p. 12.

13. Kong Lingqiang and Li Daguang (孔令强, 李大光) "参演五国尽遣精锐" ("The Five Participating Nations All Send Crack Troops"), 环球军事 (*Global Military*), No. 231, October, 2010, pp. 8-9.

14. *Ibid.*, p. 9.

15. Li Xuanliang and Yue Lian'guo (李宣良，岳连国), "中方战役指挥部副总指挥: 中方陆军参演部队实现三大突破" ("Chinese Campaign Headquarters Deputy Commander: The Chinese Ground Forces Participating in the Exercise Achieved Three Big Breakthroughs"), 新华社 (*Xinhua*), September 23, 2010, available from *news.xinhuanet.com/mil/2010-09/23/c_12598979.htm*.

16. Wang Jianmin (王建民), "鸟瞰'和平使命-2010'野战兵营" ("Getting a Bird's Eye View of the Field Camp at '*Peace Mission 2010*'"), 新华社 (*Xinhua*), September 18, 2010, available from *news. xinhuanet.com/photo/2010-09/17/c_12579883.htm*; Sun Yanxin (孙彦新), "现场：和平使命-2010军演装备大亮相" ("The Scene: The Equipment of the *Peace Mission 2010* Military Exercise Strikes a Pose"), 新华社 (*Xinhua*), September 15, 2010, available from *news. xinhuanet.com/mil/2010-09/10/content_14156631.htm*.

17. Li and Yue, "Chinese Campaign Headquarters Deputy Commander," in Kong and Li, p. 8.

18. 中国民航飞行学院学报 (*Journal of Civil Aviation*), "镜头里的'和平使命-2010'" ("'*Peace Mission 2010*' in the Camera Lens"), No. 1, 2011.

19. Bort numbers refer to the unique identification numbers on the fuselage or tail of an aircraft.

20. *Sinodefence.com*, "H-6 Inventory," April 21, 2008, available from *www.sinodefence.com/airforce/groundattack/h6-inventory.asp*; Orbat, "Order of Battle: Air Force," available from *www.scramble. nl/mil/7/china/plaaf-orbat.htm#ZB94*.

21. Liu Guohui, Yang Xiaoyong, and Zhou You (刘国辉, 杨小永, 赵友), "新疆军区首次完成跨国兵力投送后勤支援保障" ("The Xinjiang Military District for the First Time has Completed a Logistics Support Guarantee for a Transnational Military Deployment"), 新疆日报 (*Xinjiang Ribao*), October 13, 2010, p. 11.

22. 团结报 (*The United Daily*), "'和平使命-2010'联合反恐军事演习" ("'*Peace Mission 2010*' Joint Antiterror MilitaryExercise"), 党政干部参考 (*Party and Government Cadre Reference*), No. 11, 2010, p. 45.

23. Li and Yue, "The Chinese Side's 'Main Characters,' " p. 66.

24. Li Xuanliang and Yue Lian'guo (李宣良， 岳连国), "中方'关键人物'揭秘'和平使命-2010'" ("The Chinese Side's 'Main Characters' Uncover 'Peace Mission 2010'"), 瞭望东方周刊 (Oriental Outlook), No. 39, September 30-October 6, 2010, p. 66; The United Daily, p. 45; 中国新闻周刊 (China News Weekly), "上合组织军演步入机制化轨道" ("The Shanghai Cooperation Organization Military Exercise Walks Onto the Path of Mechanization"), October 4, 2010, p. 59.

25. Guo Jianyue and Lü Desheng (郭建跃、吕德胜), "'和平使命-2010'军演进行首次全程全要素实弹演练" ("'Peace Mission 2010' Military Exercise Carries out its First All-Course, All-Factor Live-Fire Practice"), 解放军报 (PLA Daily), September 19, 2010, available from news.mod.gov.cn/action/2010-09/19/content_4194713.htm.

26. The United Daily, p. 45.

27. Ibid.

28. It is unclear how or when the PLA's helicopters arrived at the exercise area. China News Weekly, pp. 58-59.

29. China railroads use standard gauge, with a width of 1,435 mm, while all the former Soviet Union states use a wider gauge of 1,520 mm.

30. Li Xuanliang and Yue Lian'guo (李宣良, 岳连国), "和平使命-2010铁路输送为我军远程投送积累经验" ("Railroad Transport during Peace Mission 2010 Accumulates Experiences for our Military's Long-distance Projection"), 新华 (Xinhua), September 22, 2010, available from news.xinhuanet.com/world/2010-09/22/c_12597172.htm.

31. Guo Jianyue and Lü Desheng (郭建跃，吕德胜), "上合组织成员国总参谋长举行战略磋商" ("Chiefs of the General Staff of the SCO Member States Conduct a Strategic Consultation"), 解放军报 (PLA Daily), September 10, 2010, available from news.163.com/10/0910/22/6G8M992T00014JB5.html.

32. "*Peace Mission 2010* Concludes, Opens New Page for SCO Cooperation," *Xinhua*, September 26, 2010, available from *english. cpc.people.com.cn/66102/7150416.html*.

33. Li and Yue, "Chinese Campaign Headquarters Deputy Commander."

34. Guo Jianyue, Lü Desheng, and Zhang Jifeng (郭建跃, 吕德胜, 张吉峰) "联手反恐突出实战性：目击＇和平使命-2010'联合军演首次实兵合练" ("Joining Hands To Oppose Terrorism by Stressing Actual Combat: Seeing with Our Own Eyes Real Troops Training Together for the First Time in the '*Peace Mission 2010*' Joint Military Exercise"), 解放军报 (*PLA Daily*), September 15, 2010, p. 4; Guo Jianyue, Lü Desheng, Cao Zhuanbiao, and Zhang Jifeng (郭建跃, 吕德胜, 曹传彪, 张吉峰), "出征哈萨克斯坦的中国军人" ("The Chinese Military Personnel Going on an Expedition to Kazakhstan"), 中国国防报 (*China Defense News*), September 21, 2010, p. 17; Li Jing, "Chinese J-10 Fighters in First Joint Drill of '*Peace Mission 2010*' Exercise," *PLA Daily*, September 16, 2010, *english.pladaily.com.cn*; CCTV, "中方参加上合军演轰炸机演练低空轰炸" ("Chinese Bomber Participating in the SCO Military Exercise Drills Low-altitude Bombing"), September 14, 2010, available from *www.360doc.com/content/10/0914/22/16546_53697195.shtml*; Guo and Lü, "'*Peace Mission 2010*' Military Exercise Carries out its First All-Course, All-Factor Live-Fire Practice;" Sun Zifa (孙自法), "'和平使命-2010'进行全要素全过程实兵合练" ("'*Peace Mission 2010*' Conducts an Allelement, All-process, Real-troop Combined Exercise"), 中新社 (China News), September 19, 2010, available from *www.chinanews.com/gn/2010/09-19/2541525.shtml*; Sun Zifa, "'和平使命-2010' 联合反恐军演举行最后一次合练" ("'*Peace Mission 2010*' Joint Antiterrorism Military Exercise Carries out the Final Combined Exercise"), *Xinhua*, September 23, 2010, available from *www.chinanews.com/gn/2010/09-23/2550565.shtml*.

35. "Art performance Staged during Anti-terror Drills in Kazakhstan," *Xinhua*, September 19, 2010, available from *eng.mod. gov.cn/SpecialReports/2010-09/16/content_4194068.htm*; Oleg Gorupay (Олег Горупай), "Плечом к Плечу" ("Shoulder to Shoulder"), *Krasnay Zvezda* (Red Star), September 17, 2010, available from *old.redstar.ru/2010/09/17_09/1_01.html*.

36. Guo *et al.*, "打响联合反控新战役" ("Starting a New Anti-terror Joint Campaign"), p. 4.

37. *China News Weekly*, pp. 58-59.

38. Li Jianwen, Shen Jike, and Cao Zhuanbiao (李建文, 申进科, 曹传彪) "雷霆出击—空军战斗群参加'和平使命-2010'联合反恐演习侧记" ("A Thunderbolt Attacks—Sidelights of The Air Force Battle Group Participating in *'Peace Mission 2010'* Joint Antiterror Exercise"), 国防部网站 (Website of the Ministry of National Defense), September 25, 2010, available from *news.mod.gov.cn/action/2010-09/25/content_4196308.htm*.

39. Li, Shen, and Cao, "A Thunderbolt Attacks;" Zhang Yuqing, Li Kaiqiang, and Cao Chuanbiao (张玉清, 李开强, 曹传彪), "中方机群境外一次性轰炸成功: 精准轰炸引外军猜测" ("The Chinese Air Group First Overseas Bombing Success: Accurate Bombing Attracts Foreign Military Guesses"), 新华 (*Xinhua*), September 26, 2010, available from *news.ifeng.com/mil/special/hepingshiming2010/content-1/detail_2010_09/26/2633543_0.shtml*.

40. Li and Yue, "The Chinese Side's 'Main Characters,'" p. 67.

41. Zhang, Li, and Cao, "The Chinese Air Group First Overseas Bombing Success."

42. Zhang, Li, and Cao, "The Chinese Air Group First Overseas Bombing Success."

43. Guo *et al.*, "打响联合反控新战役" ("Starting a New Anti-terror Joint Campaign"), p. 4.

44. *Ibid.*

45. *Ibid.*; *China News Weekly*, p. 59.

46. Guo *et al.*, "Starting a New Antiterror Joint Campaign," p. 4.

47. Kong and Li, p. 9.

48. Guo *et al.*, "Starting a New Antiterror Joint Campaign", p. 4.

49. Guo, Lü, Cao, and Zhang, p. 17.

50. *China News Weekly*, p. 59.

51. *Ibid.*; Guo *et al.*, "Starting a New Antiterror Joint Campaign," p. 4.

52. Guo *et al.*, "打响联合反控新战役" ("Starting a New Anti-terror Joint Campaign"), p. 4.

53. Zhang Jifeng (张吉峰), "'和平使命—2010'联演第一梯队官兵回国" ("The First Echelon of Troops Returns Home from 'Peace Mission 2010' Joint Exercise"), 解放军报 (*PLA Daily*), September 28, 2010, p. 4.

54. Guo, Lü, and Zhang, p. 4; Guo, Lü, Cao, and Zhang, p. 17; Li, "Chinese J-10 Fighters;" CCTV, "Chinese Bombers."

55. Li and Yue, "The Chinese Side's 'Main Characters,'" pp. 66-67.

56. Guo, Lü, Cao, and Zhang, p. 17; Zhang, Li, and Cao, "The Chinese Air Group First Overseas Bombing Success."

57. Li Xiao, Luo Zizhuang, and Huang Bo (李啸, 罗子壮, 黄波) "防空利剑扬威异国演兵场" ("A Sharp Sword of Air Defense Flaunts its Strength on a Foreign Drill Ground"), 解放军报 (*PLA Daily*), November 22, 2010, available from *chn.chinamil.com.cn/xw-pdxw/2010-11/22/content_4339461.htm*.

58. *China News Weekly*, p. 59; Guo, Lü, Cao, and Zhang, p. 17.

59. Kong and Li, pp. 8-9.

60. Zhang Chunyou (张春友), p. 8.

61. CCTV-7, "军事纪实" ("Military Report"), September 29, 2010, *cctv.cntv.cn/cctv7/.*

62. Gorupay, "Shoulder to Shoulder."

63. Li and Yue, "Railroad Transport during *Peace Mission 2010.*"

64. See also David Chen, "2011 PLA Military Training: Toward Greater Interoperability," *China Brief,* Vol. 11, No. 2, January 28, 2011.

65. Roger Cliff, John Fei, Jeff Hagen, Elizabeth Hague, Eric Heginbotham, and John Stillion, *Shaking the Heavens and Splitting the Earth,* Arlington, VA: RAND Corporation, 2011, pp. 45-46.

66. Jing-Dong Yuan, "China's Role in Establishing and Building the Shanghai Cooperation Organization," *Journal of Contemporary China,* Vol. 19, No. 67, November 2010, pp. 855-869; Alyson J. K. Bailes, Pal Dunay, Pan Guang, and Mikhail Troitskiy, "The Shanghai Cooperation Organization," *SIPRI Policy Paper,* No. 17, May 2007; U.S. Congress, "The Shanghai Cooperation Organization: Is It Undermining U.S. Interests in Central Asia?" Hearing before the Commission on Security and Cooperation in Europe, 109th Congress, 2nd sess., September 26, 2006, Washington, DC: U.S. Government Printing Office, 2008, p. 37.

67. "SCO Defense Ministers' Meeting Held in Beijing," *Xinhua,* April 25, 2012, available from *english.cntv.cn/20120425/110451. shtml.*

68. "Brief Introduction to the Shanghai Cooperation Organization," website of the Secretariat of the Shanghai Cooperation Organization, available from *www.sectsco.org/EN/brief.asp.*

69. Yuan, "China's Role in Establishing and Building the Shanghai Cooperation Organization," pp. 855-869.

70. Summarized from "The Shanghai Convention on Combating Terrorism, Separatism and Extremism," website of the Secretariat of the Shanghai Cooperation Organization, June 15, 2001, available from *www.sectsco.org/EN/show.asp?id=68.*

71. *Ibid.*

72. Bailes, Dunay, Pan, and Troitskiy, p. 21.

73. "The Shanghai Convention on Combating Terrorism, Separatism and Extremism."

74. Li Xuanliang and Yue Lian'guo (李宣良, 岳连国), "中方总导演马晓天空军上将详解 '和平使命—2010'" ("General Director of the Chinese Side, PLAAF Major General Ma Xiaotian, Explains in Detail 'Peace Mission 2010'"), 新华 (Xinhua), September 17, 2010, available from *news.xinhuanet.com/society/2010-09/17/c_12578059. htm.*

75. Bailes, Dunay, Pan, and Troitskiy, p. 10; Yuan, "China's Role in Establishing and Building the Shanghai Cooperation Organization," p. 863; Commission on Security and Cooperation in Europe, pp. 35, 37.

76. Bailes, Dunay, Pan, and Troitskiy, pp. 10-11.

77. Yuan, "China's Role in Establishing and Building the Shanghai Cooperation Organization," p. 863; Commission on Security and Cooperation in Europe, p. 29.

78. John A. Mowchan, "The Militarization of the Collective Security Treaty Organization," *Issue Paper* v. 6-09, Carlisle, PA: Center for Strategic Leadership, U.S. Army War College, July 2009.

79. "Charter of the Collective Security Treaty Organization," May 15, 1992, available from *www.ieee.es/Galerias/fichero/ Varios/2002_Carta_de_la_OTSC.pdf.*

80. *Ibid.*

81. "Russian Air Base in Kyrgyzstan Prepares for Formal Opening Ceremony," *EurasiaNet.org,* October 21, 2003, available from *www.eurasianet.org/departments/insight/articles/eav102203. shtml.*

82. Yuan, "China's Role in Establishing and Building the Shanghai Cooperation Organization."

83. Commission on Security and Cooperation in Europe, p. 35.

84. *Ibid.*, p. 37.

85. "Крупнейшие учения «Центр-2011» начинаются на территории четырех стран" ("First in a String of *Center-2011* Exercises starts on the Territories of Four Countries"), *RIA News* (РИА Новости), September 19, 2011, available from *ria.ru/ defense_safety/20110919/439662892.html.*

86. Adam Rawnsley, "Chinese Missile Ship Races to Libya," *Wired.com*, February 25, 2011, available from *www.wired.com/ dangerroom/2011/02/chinese-missile-ship-races-to-libya-for-rescue- duty/*; Josh Chin, "China vows to Protect Chinese in Libya," *The Wall Street Journal*, February 25, 2011, available from *online.wsj. com/article/SB10001424052748703905404576164321645905718. html*; "35,860 Chinese Evacuated from Unrest-torn Libya," *Xin- hua*, March 3, 2011, available from *news.xinhuanet.com/english2010/ china/2011-03/03/c_13759456.htm.*

87. Although not discussed here, the PLAN also dispatched a frigate to escort civilian ships charted to evacuate Chinese citizens by sea.

88. According to Chinese reports, the aircraft flew over Paki- stan, Oman, Saudi Arabia, and Sudan before landing in Sabha. During the flight to Libya, the aircraft refueled on the ground twice, in Karachi, Pakistan, and Khartoum. Tan Jie, "PLA Air Force Transporters Evacuate Compatriots from Libya," *PLA Daily*, March 2, 2011, available from *eng.mod.gov.cn/Defense- News/2011-03/02/content_4228001.htm.*

CHAPTER 7

PLA ENGAGEMENT WITH INTERNATIONAL PARTNERS: PLA INVOLVEMENT IN INTERNATIONAL PEACEKEEPING AND HUMANITARIAN ASSISTANCE AND DISASTER RELIEF

Chin-Hao Huang

The author is deeply grateful to Anton Wishik II of The National Bureau of Asian Research for his excellent research assistance in the completion of this chapter.

EXECUTIVE SUMMARY

This chapter looks at the Chinese security forces' increasing participation in two major engagements with international counterparts—peacekeeping operations and humanitarian assistance and disaster relief—over the past 10 years. The chapter also explains some of the main motivating factors undergirding China's security approach, and identifies some of the major and recent developments in terms of military capabilities and security challenges.

MAIN ARGUMENT

In recent years, the People's Liberation Army (PLA) has taken on a broader perspective on security challenges to include both traditional warfare as well as nontraditional security threats. This chapter focuses on the evolving Chinese perspectives and responses to some of these nontraditional security challenges, particularly in the areas of humanitarian crises and natural disasters. As a result of this evolution, the Chinese armed forces have expanded their involvement in international peacekeeping operations and humanitarian assistance and disaster relief (HADR) exercises, all the while increasing their ability to carry out military operations other than war (MOOTW) abroad. Continued deployments in such exercises are transforming the PLA's skills and capabilities and merit closer observation and analysis of their significance and implications for regional and global security, as well as for U.S. national security interests in the Asia-Pacific and beyond.

POLICY IMPLICATIONS

The analysis calls for greater U.S.-China cooperation on international peacekeeping and HADR. While some may question whether improving the Chinese armed forces' MOOTW capabilities could in turn become a challenge to the U.S. military and the security interests of its allies in the region, peacekeeping and HADR training and other capacity-building exercises serve as useful platforms to build confidence, mutual trust, and understanding between the two militaries — aspects of bilateral military relations that, when lacking, contribute to misunderstanding and miscalculation. Moreover, engaging with China in peacekeeping and HADR exercises provides an invaluable opportunity to gain greater insights into and assessments of the PLA's structural strengths and weaknesses, especially regarding the state of its joint command system, training, and integrated support capabilities.

INTRODUCTION

In recent years, the PLA has taken on a broader perspective on security challenges to include both traditional warfare as well as nontraditional security threats. This chapter focuses on the evolving Chinese perspectives and responses to some of these nontraditional security challenges, particularly in the areas of humanitarian crises and natural disasters. As a result of this evolution, the Chinese armed forces have expanded their involvement in international peacekeeping operations and HADR exercises, all the while increasing their ability to carry out MOOTW abroad. Continued deployments in such exercises are transforming the PLA's skills and capabilities and merit closer observation and analysis of their significance and implications for regional and global security, as well as for U.S. national security interests in the Asia-Pacific and beyond. This chapter takes a broad-brush approach in discussing some of the key motivating strategic and political factors behind China's increasing involvement abroad in peacekeeping and HADR exercises. It will also take stock of some of the recent developments—both within China and external events—in which these motivating factors have materialized. The chapter will conclude with an analysis that includes policy implications and recommendations.

KEY STRATEGIC AND POLITICAL FACTORS

China's expanding participation and evolving role in international peacekeeping operations and HADR exercises helps project a more positive and reassuring side to its rising prominence and power on the global stage. The Chinese leadership is acutely aware that there are still regional uncertainties about the PLA's capabilities and intentions, particularly with regard to whether a rising China will pursue a more assertive, aggressive, and potentially disruptive foreign and security policy. Concerned with its status, image, and global reputation, Beijing understands that China needs to be more responsive to international expectations, minimize tensions and conflict, and make tangible contributions to international peace and security. Peacekeeping and HADR have thus become important priorities, helping to put into action the call by senior Chinese officials for the country to demonstrate its "peaceful development" and commitment to a "harmonious world."[1] China's increased activities in these two areas provide an opportunity to display a more constructive side of the PLA's capabilities, reassuring neighbors about its peaceful intentions and at the same time signaling that China is further integrating into the international community and acting as a responsible power.[2]

As China becomes increasingly engaged in global security affairs, a widening array of voices within the Chinese academy and policymaking realms also call for Chinese foreign and security policy to be defined beyond material power interests. An editorial in the widely Chinese Communist Party domestic and foreign affairs journal, *Liaowang*, pointed out:

> Compared with past practices, China's diplomacy has indeed displayed a new face. If China's diplomacy before the 1980s stressed safeguarding of national security and its emphasis from the 1980s to early this century is on the creation of excellent environment for economic development, then the focus at present is to take a more active part in international affairs and play a role that a responsible power should on the basis of satisfying the security and development interests.[3]

There is also an understanding that China's growing integration with the rest of the world means increasing linkages between international conflicts and national security. Zhang Yesui, formerly China's vice-foreign minister, remarked at the 2007 Munich Conference on Security Policy that China's increasing involvement in United Nations (UN) peacekeeping missions, for example, "reflected China's commitment to global security given the country's important role within the international system and the fact that its security and development are closely linked to that of the rest of the world."[4] There is also growing recognition that as China's international role evolves and expands, its interests will likewise become more global in nature. China's security is thus becoming intrinsically linked to a stable and peaceful international environment, and this in turn is an important factor in China's taking a more cooperative stance and supportive role in international peacekeeping and HADR exercises.

More importantly, peacekeeping, anti-piracy missions, rescue-and-relief operations, counterterrorism exercises, post-conflict reconstruction, energy security, and climate-change dialogues have all become major components of China's increasingly complex and dynamic international strategy.[5] These activities are broadly defined as nontraditional security issues, and their growing importance parallels the PLA's interest in mobilizing its resources and preparing for MOOTW both at home and abroad. This reflects President Hu Jintao's call for the security forces to perform and engage more adequately in MOOTW as part of the PLA's *New Historic Mission*.[6] Doing so would help safeguard national interests, as well as contribute to regional and global peace, security, and development. Overseas, nontraditional security threats, given their unpredictability and potential negative impact on China's national security and economic development, are increasingly perceived as equally, if not more, challenging and dangerous in comparison with traditional security threats.[7]

To be sure, there are also rational and utility-maximizing considerations behind China's participation in peacekeeping and other humanitarian exercises and operations abroad. As such, China's Armed Forces have professionalized, testing their power projection capabilities through MOOTW as the nation seeks to become a major regional and global power. The PLA and the PLAN, in particular, have become more innovative and are learning through three notable areas.[8] They are briefly summarized below and will be subsequently drawn out and integrated into a more detailed discussion of China's engagements in peacekeeping and various HADR exercises abroad. China's evolving approach toward peacekeeping and humanitarian operations is thus supported by a combination of strategic and national security considerations.

- Improving the PLA's training methodology. As outlined in the 2010 *Defense White Paper*, the PLA is intensifying the joint training of its armed forces, placing increasing emphasis on training in complex and unfamiliar terrains and varied weather conditions. By taking part in humanitarian operations and exercises, the PLA is becoming more adept at getting better acquainted with the formations and procedures of preparing for both combat and noncombat exercises. In June 2009, for example, the Central Military Commission (CMC), the PLA, and five of the seven military region commands met in Beijing to strengthen and improve the PLA's peacekeeping role and HADR participation, discussing ways to streamline the selection, organization, training and rotation of Chinese forces abroad.[9]

- Improving operational command systems. The PLA General Staff Department recently announced that it would strengthen the PLA's emergency response system and rapid deployment capacity to respond to the various MOOTW.[10] As part of its modernization program, the PLA has been seeking to become more agile and efficient in its operational capability. Taking part in peacekeeping operations and HADR activities has provided a valuable opportunity for China's security and naval forces to interact closely and more systematically with international counterparts. The lessons learned from these external missions have allowed the PLA to speed up the building of a more integrated joint operational command system to address emergency contingencies. The recent naval deployments by the PLA Navy (PLAN) in carrying out humanitarian missions abroad demonstrate some of the important lessons learned in this area (discussed in greater detail below).

- Expanding integrated support capabilities. Recent defense White Papers have described how the Chinese military has been seeking to enhance the support capabilities that will allow the armed forces to carry out their missions more effectively during wartime as well as non-combat operations at home and abroad.

The 2010 *Defense White Paper*, in particular, highlights this important emphasis.

Following the principle of providing systematic, precise and intensive support, the PLA strengthens the construction of composite combat and support bases, optimizes battlefield-support layout, and improves position facilities for the following services: command and control, reconnaissance and intelligence, communication, surveying and mapping, navigation, meteorological and hydrological support as well as rear storage facilities, military communication and equipment maintenance facilities—thus forming an initial battlefield-support capability that matches the development of weaponry and equipment and satisfies the needs of combat units in offensive and defensive operations.[11]

PEACEKEEPING

The deployment of Chinese troops abroad to take part in international peacekeeping missions carries inherent practical benefits for the Chinese security forces. Training and operating alongside other troop-contributing countries' forces provides invaluable experience that will allow Chinese troops to improve their responsiveness, riot control capabilities, coordination of emergency command systems, and ability to carry out MOOTW more effectively. Over time, participation in peacekeeping missions abroad will also help to modernize and professionalize the security forces. For example, a sustained effort to deploy troops in Africa has meant that PLA forces are gaining greater operational knowledge of different operating environments, an advantage that few counterparts in other countries have. To date, nearly three-quarters of China's peacekeeping contributions are currently based in the African continent, providing critical support for peace enforcement and post-conflict reconstruction in Liberia, the Democratic Republic of the Congo (DRC), Southern Sudan, and Côte d'Ivoire. The sustained rotations and deployments also provide the PLA with "more knowledge about logistics, ports of debarkation, lines of communication, lines of operation, operational intelligence, local 'atmospherics' and *modus operandi* and means of sustaining forces in Africa over prolonged periods."[12] All these measures allow the Chinese security forces to display their professionalism and operational competence on the one hand, while also demonstrating their growing deterrent capability on the other.[13]

China currently deploys troops that carry out important backbone engineering, medical, and logistical support in UN peacekeeping operations, giving the troops special access and increased know-how on expanding integrated support capabilities for the PLA. More than half of China's current peacekeeping contributions are dedicated to providing engineering, logistical, and transportation support. Several peacekeeping operations (e.g., the UN Mission in Liberia), depend solely on the Chinese troops for transport, fuel, equipment, and infrastructure support. Over the years, the Chinese troops have, in essence, carved out a niche area of expertise in their peacekeeping contributions. PLA engineering units, as such, have developed into a critical multifunctional support force that is becoming more rapid in response, has been tried and tested, and can be used both in peacetime and in war. Along these lines, these peacekeeping operations have also strengthened the PLA's special capabilities in emergency rescue and disaster relief. As such, PLA capabilities in integral combat support and MOOTW exercises have been deeply enhanced. China's interest in contributing to the management of international peacekeeping was marked in 2002 by an important agreement to join the UN Standby Arrangement System — whereby the Ministry of Defense has a 525-strong engineering battalion, a 25-strong medical unit, and two 160-strong transport companies on standby and ready for deployment with other UN forces within 90 days.

Equally important, in recent years, China has also shown an interest in providing military experts to peacekeeping operations. These military experts, normally at the rank of lieutenant colonel or colonel, are tasked with the duty of collecting local intelligence for the UN operational headquarters. Repeated and long-term deployments in this regard help sharpen the PLA's intelligence-gathering capabilities at the operational and tactical levels.

With nearly 2 decades of continuous and active participation in international peacekeeping operations, the PLA has been steadily trying to professionalize and improve the overall image, reputation, and caliber of its peacekeeping troops — thus getting them better prepared in line with the international standard operating procedures maintained by the UN Department of Peacekeeping Operations (DPKO).[14] Though Chinese troops' English- and French-language proficiency generally remains weak, limiting their levels of interaction with other contingents and local populations, Chinese officials appear to have recognized these shortcomings and are placing increased emphasis on preparation for peacekeeping. As part of the PLA budget, Chinese policymakers have sought to improve and expand Chinese peacekeeping training facilities. In June 2009, China unveiled a new peacekeeping training center in Huairou in suburban Beijing.[15] The new facility is used for pre-deployment training and also serves as the main venue for international exchanges on peacekeeping. The facilities include simulation rooms, shooting and driving ranges, and simulated UN peacekeeping camps and demining training grounds. In Langfang, a city in suburban Beijing, the Ministry of Public Security has also established the Civilian Peacekeeping Police Training Centre to train police officers and formed police units (FPU).

In recent years, China has also become more open to increasing interfaces with foreign counterparts to help expand its peacekeeping capacity. Chinese security personnel have participated in joint peacekeeping training and exchanges with other countries, including Australia, Bangladesh, Canada, France, Germany, India, Indonesia, Mongolia, New Zealand, South Africa, Sweden, Switzerland, Thailand, and the United Kingdom (UK).[16] Through these joint training exercises, the PLA has requested foreign military counterparts to provide more in-depth pre-deployment training assistance programs and joint training and simulation drills.[17]

Beijing has also hosted a number of international seminars on peacekeeping, bringing in foreign experts, scholars, and practitioners to exchange views and share lessons learned from previous peacekeeping experiences. The international seminars with the UK, as well as with Norway and Sweden, for example, have opened avenues for joint collaboration in peacekeeping. The International Committee of the Red Cross has also been tasked by the security forces to provide pre-deployment briefings for peacekeepers to help train and better prepare personnel on issues related to international humanitarian law.[18]

Within the region, China is stepping up coordination for multilateral peacekeeping activities, sponsoring and taking part in such events as the China–Association of Southeast Asian Nations (ASEAN) peacekeeping seminar in 2007.[19] China has also engaged in a series of drills and simulation exercises with Russia and Central Asian countries. *Peace Mission 2005* was one of the largest joint military exercises China has ever carried out on a bilateral basis.[20] The exercise involved nearly 10,000 Army, Air Force, and naval personnel and included headquarters and command-post exercises in Vladivostok, coordination of warship movements around the Shandong Peninsula, and amphibious landings. While bilateral training with Russia may not be directly related to UN peacekeeping per se, it helps the PLA to improve its mobilization capabilities and to conduct a range of operation types that could be applicable to multilateral peacekeeping missions — encouraging China to provide more contributions to peace operations, particularly troops, as the PLA's capabilities and the caliber of its troops improve. Some observers also indicate that such military exercises are contingency plans for managing a possible humanitarian crisis (e.g., preventing a flood of would-be refugees into China's borders) in neighboring North Korea.[21]

China's evolving approach toward UN peacekeeping is thus supported by a combination of factors. Through increasing interaction with the international community, China has become more willing to accept global norms and to contribute to peace and stability. At the same time, participation in peacekeeping allows China to professionalize its armed forces, to test its power projection capabilities through MOOTW, and to help attain its aspirations to become a major global power. In light of these important principles, where is this evolving Chinese approach toward peacekeeping activities seen in action, and where is more needed? Equally important, it should be noted that the degree to which China has internalized these peacekeeping norms remains an unresolved debate. There are serious limitations to Chinese contributions to peacekeeping and, at times, instances of resistance and obstructive behavior. In particular, the episodic reversals in Chinese normative behavior tend to occur when China displays a more confident and assertive self-image, complemented with strained relations abroad, that tracks closely with realpolitik ideology.

On the whole, China needs to engage more substantively in UN peacekeeping operations. In terms of its financial contribution, China provides about 3 percent of the peacekeeping budget, significantly less than most other Security Council members. According to the UN Multi-Donor Trust Fund Office, China has also contributed a total of $4 million to the UN Peacebuilding Fund from 2006 to 2012,[22] but has yet to provide financial support for other aid programs or trust funds that are critically needed. Consequently, China will need to increase its financial contributions if it wishes to play a role commensurate with its Security Council and global status.

Moreover, China's increasing involvement in the UN peacekeeping regime means that there will be expectations of China to expand its troop commitments in areas where there are critical needs. China initially offered to deploy troops to the Lebanon in 2006, and officials are on record as saying that China remains open to the idea of deploying troops if the DPKO requested them, though it remains to be seen whether China would respond favorably. Likewise, some UN officials have called for China to contribute such force enablers as light tactical and transport helicopters and more ground transport units to help sustain and facilitate operations. In short, as China seeks to play a more active role in shaping and influencing UN peacekeeping affairs, it could consider increasing personnel, financial, and logistical contributions.

When confronted with important questions related to foreign policy and international security, Chinese policymakers tend to take a case-by-case approach. As such, although rhetoric and government policies seem to have supported UN peacekeeping, traditional ideas about state sovereignty persist. There are instances in which China has supported intervention on humanitarian grounds, including in East Timor in 1999, through a non-UN force led by Australia. China also contributed a civilian police contingent to support the subsequent UN mission. In 2003, in response to growing instability in the Democratic Republic of the Congo and Liberia, the Ambassador to the UN, Zhang Yishan, argued that the UN should intervene in such conflict areas earlier, faster, and more forcefully. China's more active participation in peacekeeping thus came at a time of growing debates on how the international community should reconcile the imperatives of global stability and justice and strike the right balance between state sovereignty and human rights. From these debates, a loose consensus emerged by the 2000s, especially in the West, that there is political and moral currency for the "international community" to take exceptional measures at times of need in addressing human rights concerns, especially when the state does not fulfill its responsibility to protect its citizens.[23]

Although China was a relative newcomer to these debates, the issue gained a degree of traction within China as well, with a number of international-law scholars and foreign-policy experts pointing to the changing nature of peacekeeping and the circumstances that warrant a more flexible interpretation and understanding of the principles related to sovereignty.[24] For example, a widening circle of policy elites began to debate issues such as state sovereignty and conditions for interventionism. Of particular interest are the increasing number of influential Chinese academic, scholarly, and policy-oriented journals that printed and circulated these discussions. Such journals include: 中国法学 (*Chinese Legal Studies*); 西部法学评论 (*Western Law Review*); and 法制与社会 (*Legal System and Society*). These journals printed an increasing number of articles discussing a state's obligations to its citizens and arguing that a failure to uphold these responsibilities warrants the international community to intervene to protect individuals, while other articles have also argued that human rights are moral issues increasingly shaped by the international community and that all states have a right to monitor these concerns. Allen Carlson's research has led him to conclude that an increasing number of Chinese researchers, scholars, experts, and policymakers have adopted more flexible views of sovereignty and the conditions under which UN peacekeeping operations should be sanctioned to help enforce the peace in conflict regions and protect civilians. Moreover, Carlson finds that some of these policy elites have also gained important access to key policymakers and top leaders within the Chinese foreign and security policy apparatus and that they are shaping the foreign policy discourse on peacekeeping.

It is too early to gauge whether China has internalized and accepted these global norms, but Chinese official policy and rhetoric with regard to sovereignty, intervention, and peacekeeping have become more flexible. Traditionally, China has objected to authorizing or extending the mandates of UN peacekeeping missions in countries that recognized Taiwan. In January 1997, China vetoed a proposed mission to Guatemala until the Guatemalan government gave assurances that it would no longer support a General Assembly vote on admitting Taiwan to the UN. The Verification Mission in Guatemala (MINUGUA) could then proceed. In 1999, China vetoed the continuation of the UN Preventive Deployment in Macedonia (UN-PREDEP) 2 weeks after suspending diplomatic ties with the country over its recognition of Taiwan, bringing an end to that experiment in conflict prevention. Some Chinese peacekeeping specialists later acknowledged that "this was a difficult lesson for China" and that the government should have "considered Macedonia's interests more than its own national interests."

In 1999, at the height of the crisis in the Balkans, China was adamantly opposed to authorizing a peacekeeping force for Kosovo. Chinese opposition was in a large part accentuated when the U.S.-led North Atlantic Treaty Organization (NATO) air raids mistakenly hit the Chinese Embassy in Belgrade. Chinese objections turned to indignant outrage as the Chinese general public as well as the regime insisted that the NATO bombing was deliberate and intended to contain China.

In the case of Haiti, notwithstanding the lack of full diplomatic relations with Beijing, China supported the UN from 2004 to 2010 with deployments of FPU. However, China apparently used the threat of curtailing the mission to warn Haiti against any high-profile diplomatic exchanges in support of Taiwan. Some observers contend that Haiti's continued recognition of Taiwan was a reason for the withdrawal in 2010, while others have indicated that China was uncomfortable with the overwhelming U.S. civilian and military presence following the earthquake. The Haiti case indicates that there are still gaps in and limitations to China's overall commitment to peacekeeping. As in Kosovo, the resurgence of realpolitik ideology seemed to have trumped the broader underlying trend of more active engagement and participation in peacekeeping operations.

Beijing's position on the Darfur question, however, provides a prominent example of constructive engagement, in which China has yielded to widespread regional and international pressure. Responding in large part to mounting criticism of its relations with the Sudanese government, in 2006 China began exerting pressure on Sudan to allow UN and African Union (AU) peacekeepers into Darfur. In November 2006, with the humanitarian situation worsening, former Chinese Ambassador to the UN Wang Guangya was widely credited in gaining Sudanese acceptance of the UN/AU hybrid peacekeeping force of 20,000 troops in Darfur. Subsequently, China also became the first permanent member of the UN Security Council to commit and deploy more than 300 troops there and was widely applauded by African leaders. In February 2007, President Hu Jintao visited Sudan and met President Omar al-Bashir. The visit drew widespread criticism internationally, particularly from the United States, since China was seen as abetting alleged genocidal acts committed in Darfur. However, Hu reportedly intervened to press al-Bashir to abide by international commitments. While this could be interpreted as mere rhetoric, it is about as close as a Chinese leader has come to publicly warning and chiding a foreign leader. What the senior-level leadership says about these sensitive issues is important, because it reflects in a large part China's changing behavior and understanding of peacekeeping and noninterventionism. Its quest to play a leadership position in the developing world, particularly in Africa, means that China needs to be more attuned and attentive to African public opinion and concerns. As seen here with its peacekeeping contributions to Darfur, ideational factors thus altered China's foreign policy calculus and its own identity and interests so that they are more consistent, or at least not at odds with, regional and global norms.

More recently, in the wake of the political demonstrations and uprisings in North Africa and the Middle East, China's approach has been cautious, and its policy demonstrated a degree of flexibility as well as limitations on compromising the principle of sovereignty and interventionism. To be sure, there were economic interests at stake, with more than 30,000 Chinese citizens and 75 Chinese firms in Libya. China also relies on Libyan oil for roughly 3 percent of its domestic energy consumption. But more importantly, the Ministry of Foreign Affairs was carefully assessing and monitoring the Libyan situation at every turn. As expected, it initially voiced support for the Gaddafi regime, as China's overall concern was the political stability and unity of Libya as a whole. As developments unfolded and it became apparent that the rebel forces were gaining increasing legitimacy and support throughout Libya and the international community, China and the National Transitional Council began to open up communication channels. With divergent views between the AU and the Arab League on how best to manage the conflict in Libya, China preferred a multilateral, diplomatic approach that would bring the major stakeholders to the negotiation table. According to interviews with senior Chinese officials monitoring the Libyan situation, Beijing's primary concern throughout the Libyan case was what it saw as the excessive involvement and the especially prominent role NATO was playing from the inception of the Libyan crisis. Given the historic sensitivity in NATO-China relations during the Kosovo crisis of 1998-1999 and the subsequent U.S. bombing under NATO's purview of the Chinese Embassy, in Belgrade, China had misgivings and serious concerns about NATO's expanding role in interventions into Northern Africa. The historical analogy dictated Chinese officials to take a critical stance on the Libyan situation, because they associated NATO's involvement with malign intent and belligerent hegemony.

The Libyan case provides a mixed picture at best of where China stands on humanitarian intervention and sovereignty. It supported the UN Security Council Resolution 1970, placing an arms embargo on Libya, a freezing of Libyan funds and assets, and referral to the International Criminal Court (ICC) to investigate crimes against humanity. At the same time, China was also wary of what it perceived as excessive NATO involvement in Libya. These developments point to the fact that China is in a steep learning curve in managing and responding to calls for humanitarian interventions. China's traditional defense of the notion of sovereignty will not always necessarily stand in the way of achieving its overall national security interests. In particular, at times of need to support intervention, especially where there is consensus among the relevant parties at stake to do so, China tends to be supportive.

HUMANITARIAN ASSISTANCE AND DISASTER RELIEF

Gulf of Aden Escort Operations.

The Gulf of Aden escort operations to counter piracy activities have become an important part of the PLAN's MOOTW mission. China first dispatched naval ships to conduct escort operations in the Gulf of Aden in December 2008. In each rotational deployment, the Chinese escort fleet includes up to three ships and is equipped with two ship-based helicopters, dozens of Special Operation Force soldiers, and more than 800 crew members who were tasked with overseeing and maintaining the security of Chinese merchant and commercial ships and personnel passing through the Gulf of Aden and Somali waters, as well as the safety of international ships delivering food, water and other humanitarian supplies through the World Food Program (WFP) and other international humanitarian organizations. To date, the PLAN has provided escort for more than 3,600 merchant vessels from 48 countries through joint-area patrol and onboard escort. More interestingly, the escort of foreign ships now constitutes more than two-thirds of the merchant convoys the PLAN escorts in the Gulf of Aden, compared to less than one-third when it first started its convoy-escort mission.

The PLAN's participation in the counter-piracy activities indicates that it is actively seeking an off-shore defense strategy as a strategic imperative. Over time, through these activities the PLAN will gain enhanced capabilities to carry out strategic deterrence and counterattacks, operate in distant waters, and manage nontraditional security threats. The Gulf of Aden operation marks an important milestone in its power projection capabilities. It is an important test and training ground for deploying the PLAN's forces and material assets for an extended period of time at such a great distance from its onshore naval bases.

The PLAN is improving its operational capabilities, and its expanding role and interactions with foreign counterparts in the Gulf of Aden point to increasing confidence. Chinese escort fleets have established mechanisms for regular intelligence exchange and sharing with such counterparts as Japan, NATO, the Netherlands, Russia, and South Korea. Since 2008, the PLAN has also conducted joint escort operations with Russian fleets and joint maritime exercises with South Korean escort ships. More recently, there have been more regularized exchanges and coordination with the European Union Naval Force Somalia (EU NAVFOR) in deterring, disrupting, and suppressing piracy in the Horn of Africa. There is also a perceived interest from the Chinese side in increasing its cooperation with the other task forces in the Gulf of Aden, including a rotational role in the coordination of counter-piracy operations and a possibility of increasing the number of its vessel deployments.[25] China has also expressed a willingness to co-chair a Shared Awareness and De-confliction (SHADE) meeting, an important forum in which international navies and organizations share information on disrupting and preventing counter-piracy activities off the coast of Somalia. The meeting is traditionally co-chaired by the U.S.-led Combined Maritime Forces (CMF), the EU, and/or EU NAVFOR.[26] While the PLAN has yet to step up in taking on a greater role in SHADE meetings, during Major General Chen Bingde's visit to the

United States in May 2011, he left the door open for the prospects of closer engagement and participation of Chinese naval forces with the United States and other international naval forces involved in counter-piracy operations in the Horn of Africa.[27] On other fronts, there are also increasing interfaces between the U.S. and Chinese naval forces in the region. As part of the Commander Engagement Program of Combined Task Force 151 (CTF 151), the U.S. Commander of CTF 151, Rear Admiral Harris Chan, visited the Chinese escort ships in May 2011 to help broaden and extend the network for information sharing and operational cooperation between independent deployments and coalition forces.[28]

In short, the PLAN naval forces remain interested and involved in the multilateral efforts in the counter-piracy operations but have yet to formally enlist in permanent coalition forces with Western or other Asian navies operating in the Horn of Africa. Through continued coordination with international partners, the PLAN is gradually improving its capability to enhance multinational interoperability and in turn to help strengthen its operational capacity to deploy naval assets abroad over a lengthened period of time. It currently relies on foreign sources and bases in the region for refueling and logistics support, primarily at three locations: the Port of Salalah in Oman, Port of Djibouti in Djibouti, and Port of Aden in Yemen. PLAN ships have also conducted at least 19 friendly port calls during their naval deployments, and during five of these port visits, the PLAN conducted joint maritime drills with the Italian, Pakistani (twice), Singaporean, and Tanzanian navies. Chinese officials have raised the idea of establishing a permanent port in the Seychelles for refueling and providing logistical support for its naval deployments. In private, however, Chinese officials recognize the technical and operational difficulties, as well as the potentially negative reactions, the Seychelles naval base plan might raise. They have also opined that such a plan would only move forward if endorsed and supported by the Seychellois government and the AU.[29]

Even without the establishment of a naval base, it remains to be seen how quickly the experiences gained from such deployments abroad will translate into the PLAN's development into a "blue-water navy." The PLAN has been going through internal reviews of the lessons learned from the naval deployments and the immediate priorities that need to be taken to strengthen its future deployments, including cultivating the ability to implement increasingly diversified naval tasks, instructional courses on complex HADR naval exercises on the high seas in its naval academies and other military-related institutions, strengthening the PLAN's joint command capabilities, and investing in new equipment and technology as well as in the human capital of its naval officers (e.g., foreign languages and international humanitarian law).[30]

Medical Ships, Disaster Relief, and Search and Rescue Exercises.

Chinese security forces have been seeking to improve their military capabilities through regularized and systematic training in complex environments and terrains. In addition to the counter-piracy operations, the PLAN has been organizing naval vessels for humanitarian drills in distant waters, further developing training missions for MOOTW operations. New types of naval assets have been deployed to test the

PLAN's capabilities. For example, in 2008 the PLAN successfully launched its first 10,000 deadweight tonnage hospital ship, also known as the "Peace Ark," and medical transport helicopters, and is working to further improve its logistical support capabilities for carrying out and sustaining such maritime missions as disaster relief and other emergency search and rescue exercises beyond the vicinity of China's territorial waters. The Chinese medical ship's operations seek to parallel what the USNS *Mercy* and *Comfort* have been engaged with for several years, providing flexible and rapid emergency and other humanitarian services.

In 2009, China sent its medical ship to Africa to hold a joint humanitarian mission with Gabon in the Gulf of Guinea. This was the first joint medical operation conducted by the Chinese military and the first bilateral joint operation carried out by the Chinese in Africa. The Chinese medical detachment engaged in medical training and search and rescue exercises with its Gabonese counterpart. In 2010, the "Peace Ark" carried out an 87-day medical mission to the Gulf of Aden and Indian Ocean, making port calls and providing free clinical and medical services to the local communities in Bangladesh, Djibouti, Kenya, the Seychelles, and Tanzania. The medical ship then embarked on "Harmonious Mission 2011," making its first visit to Latin America with port calls in Cuba, Costa Rica, Jamaica, and Trinidad and Tobago.

China's international disaster relief efforts have also broadened to include other elements of its China's security forces, including the People's Armed Police Force (PAPF), regional military commands, the Chinese International Search and Rescue (CISAR) team, and the China Earthquake Administration. According to the 2010 *Defense White Paper*, China has carried out more than 28 humanitarian aid missions abroad and provided assistance to 22 disaster-stricken countries with emergency relief materials since 2002.[31] Most recently, in the wake of the earthquake in Haiti, a CISAR and PLA medical and epidemic prevention team was jointly dispatched to Haiti to carry out search and rescue tasks, medical work, and epidemic-prevention operations. In September 2010, in addition to a CISAR and PLA medical team, a helicopter rescue formation was dispatched to Pakistan to conduct humanitarian rescue operations.

The Chinese armed forces have also been playing an active role in international exchanges and disaster relief training exercises . They hold regular seminars and joint operations on humanitarian rescue with regional armed forces, many of which fall under the ASEAN Regional Forum and the ASEAN Plus Three workshops on personnel training and on establishing the legal rules for regional armed forces' participation in international disaster relief operations. The PLAN has also taken part in regional maritime exercises held within the framework of the Western Pacific Naval Symposium.

Engaging in such humanitarian missions abroad has become an important priority for the PLA, particularly as it seeks to be more flexible and have a greater rapid deployment and emergency response capability. Regular participation in these missions abroad provide important lessons to help improve the PLA's training and effectiveness, especially in establishing a cohesive joint command system and greater interoperability across the Chinese armed forces. Perhaps even more important, the training and joint exercises abroad provide the PLA and the armed forces with the necessary skill sets and firsthand experiences to strengthen their capabilities to manage humanitarian disasters on the home front, including earthquakes, floods, droughts, and hurricanes. A series of domestic laws and regulations have been enacted to reflect this increasing emphasis and priority for the PLA to respond better to nontraditional security threats. In January 2009, China formed eight state-level emergency response professional units, including a total of 50,000 personnel specializing in flood control and emergency rescue; earthquake rescue; nuclear, biological and chemical emergency rescue; urgent air transportation, rapid road and infrastructural repair; maritime emergency search and rescue; emergency mobile communication support; and medical aid and epidemic prevention. Likewise, in March 2009, a document entitled "Opinions on Strengthening Political Work in MOOTW" was promulgated, stipulating that the PLA should have a stronger understanding of the characteristics and laws related to MOOTW and explore new areas and functions of the supporting role of such work. Subsequently, in November 2010, the CMC passed the "Regulations on Emergency Command in Handling Emergencies by the Armed Forces." The new regulation calls for the armed forces to streamline their organization's, command, force deployment, integrated support, and civil-military coordination while responding to and managing humanitarian disasters and other emergencies. In effect, these recent legislations reflect the calls by President Hu for the PLA to demonstrate its performance legitimacy, to carry out its *New Historic Missions* effectively, and to be able to address both traditional and nontraditional security challenges at home and abroad.[33]

POLICY IMPLICATIONS AND RECOMMENDATIONS

This brief analysis on China's increasing involvement in international peacekeeping operations and HADR points to a number of important policy implications for the United States. To ensure that the Chinese armed forces continue down this path of constructive development, the United States should consider policy options aimed at deepening these encouraging trends, shaping and influencing Chinese policies and military modernization in a positive direction. In so doing, it is also worth raising an equally important and relevant point: Why should the United States work with China on peacekeeping and HADR issues? Some may question whether improving the Chinese armed forces' MOOTW capabilities could in turn become a challenge to the U.S. military and the security interests of its allies in the region, all the while extending unnecessary leverage to the PLA.[34] At the same time, however, peacekeeping and HADR training and other capacity-building exercises serve as useful platforms to instill confidence, mutual trust, and understanding between the two sides—aspects of bilateral military relations that, when lacking, contribute to misunderstanding and miscalculation.[35] Moreover, engaging with China on peacekeeping and HADR exercises provides an invaluable opportunity to gain greater insights into and assessments of the PLA's structural strengths and weaknesses, especially regarding the state of its joint command system, training, and integrated support capabilities. Given these developments, the United States should implement policies aimed at deepening the encouraging trends related to Beijing's involvement with peacekeeping operations and HADR—areas that are considered soft security issues but nonetheless important for testing the Chinese security forces' capabilities and intentions—as well as to help build greater communication and practical engagement for both sides. There has been some thinking in this direction for some time now. On peacekeeping operations, former U.S. Secretary of Defense William Cohen indicated in a speech in Beijing in 2000: "U.S. and Chinese service members may one day find themselves working side by side in peacekeeping missions."[36] Likewise, at a recent track-1.5 dialogue on U.S.-China security issues, former U.S. Secretary of Defense William Perry also suggested that the two armed forces should cooperate more closely on humanitarian operations and peacekeeping missions.[37]

More important, the high-profile military visits between the United States and China in 2011 resulted in several key bilateral agreements that would pave the way for closer engagement and cooperation between the two militaries in such practical areas as peacekeeping and HADR. During Major General Chen Bingde's visit to the United States in May 2011, for example, both sides agreed to conduct joint naval exercises in the Gulf of Aden as part of the international anti-piracy effort. Two other important agreements reached included the decision to conduct a humanitarian disaster rescue and relief joint training exercise in 2012, and an agreement to conduct joint medical rescue training exercises.

The Barack Obama administration's emphasis on multilateral diplomacy, as well as on encouraging China to step up and contribute to global commons and security issues, opens the door for greater cooperation between the United States and China in regions where both countries have increasing security interests. Underpinning this thinking and rationale is the recognition that both the United States and China gain more security when both countries cooperate to address international security challenges — traditional and nontraditional security threats — that are of mutual and global concern. In recent years, China's support in the areas of international peacekeeping and HADR has played a constructive role in areas of conflict and other regional hot spots, such as Haiti, sub-Saharan Africa as well as the Horn of Africa, and the Gulf of Aden. There will be continued expectations for China to deploy its military assets in these parts of the world to help provide regional and global security and stability. The Chinese leadership's continued concerns with its status, image, and global reputation (especially in light of China's perceived maritime assertiveness and aggressiveness in the South China Sea of late)[38] serve as important reminders that China needs to be more sensitive, responsive, and attuned to international expectations; minimize tensions and conflict; and make tangible contributions to international peace and security. As such, peacekeeping and HADR have been and will continue to be important priorities as part of the PLA modernization program, as the military seeks to put into action the call by senior Chinese officials for the country to demonstrate its "peaceful development." In short, U.S. policy should thus recognize that China's leadership appears to understand the value of multilateral security and confidence-building measures, conforming to regional and global norms, and measured steps to demonstrate constructive intentions.

At the same time, there is a need to understand that Chinese decisionmakers' choices to take more positive measures on peacekeeping and HADR will derive from their own realization that it is in China's interests to do so. The occasional reversals in Chinese normative behavior tend to occur when China displays a more confident and assertive self-image, complemented with strained relations abroad. Hence, an effective strategy of embedding China more closely into a role in which it takes a more constructive approach toward such global commons issues as conflict resolution, peacekeeping, counter-piracy, and humanitarian relief must make a convincing case that China's commitment to becoming a more responsible stakeholder and a legitimate great power is not only in the interests of the international community, but equally, or even more so, in China's own interest.

Looking ahead, external observers and U.S. policymakers alike should be cognizant of the fact that engaging with the Chinese on managing U.S.-China military and security relations will be met with frequent frustrations, even regarding MOOTW and non-combat exercises. However, the stakes are too high for such frustrations and temporary setbacks to become excuses for inaction. The following policy considerations seek to engage China more strategically so as to deepen Beijing's commitment to global security and stability and help shape its policies in a more constructive direction:

- Institutionalize regularized and substantive contacts between the two militaries. The resumption and continued institutionalization of contacts between the U.S. and Chinese armed forces, such as the Defense Consultative Talks and the Defense Policy Coordination Talks, serve as important channels of communication between the two sides to have more focused discussions on the practicalities of cooperation and to build military-to-military communication and trust. Senior military officials from both sides agreed in January 2011 to cooperate on HADR. The operationalization of these agreements could follow up with a clearer and more-in-depth focus on sharing information about each side's emergency response capabilities and decisionmaking structure and processes and providing access and visits to training sites for humanitarian operations.

- Engage in military-to-military training and other capacity-building exercises. The Defense Authorization Act of 2000 and the Foreign Assistance Act do not explicitly restrict military-to-military interaction for peacekeeping and HADR training exercises, but they do restrict the scope and scale of bilateral military engagement. This adds a degree of caution within Washington to avoid any risks to national security.[39] However, there have been past precedents when Chinese civilian and military delegations have been invited to partake either as observers or full participants in U.S. capacity-building exercises related to peacekeeping and HADR issues. These developments should be further encouraged, with the justification that continued Chinese participation in these training and capacity-building exercises provides greater access to current Chinese capabilities, including the PLA's strengths and weaknesses in its emergency response and humanitarian operations and disaster assistance.

- Coordinate with international partners to work with China on peacekeeping and HADR activities. With regard to the counter-piracy efforts in the Gulf of Aden, the United States should work with the EU, the AU, and other key states in the region to encourage greater Chinese involvement in the maritime operations. A collective approach with broad consensus among the key stakeholders can help persuade the PLAN to consider sending more naval vessels and to take up a rotating co-coordinating role in the counter-piracy operation. The same consensus-based approach can be replicated in soliciting greater Chinese support for UN-sanctioned peacekeeping operations, including logistical and financial contributions — providing such force enablers as light-transport helicopters and trucks, and combat troops on the ground. Likewise, Washington, together with ASEAN member countries can jointly encourage China to forge closer humanitarian relief-coordination efforts and plan for joint contingency response mechanisms to regional natural disasters and other related humanitarian crises.

ENDNOTES - CHAPTER 7

1. "Hu Jintao Says China Pursues Peaceful Development," *People's Daily*, September 3, 2005.

2. See Wang Yizhou (王逸舟), 磨合中的建构：中国与国际组织关系的多视角透视 (*Construction in Contradiction: A Multiple Insight into Relationships Between China and International Organizations*), Beijing, China: China Development Press, 2003; Jing-Dong Yuan, "Multilateral Intervention and State Sovereignty: Chinese Views on UN Peacekeeping Operations," *Political Science*, Vol. 49, No. 2, 1998, pp. 275–295; Alastair Iain Johnston and Robert Ross, eds., *New Directions in the Study of China's Foreign Policy*, Stanford, CA: Stanford University Press, 2006; Evan Medeiros and M. Taylor Fravel, "China's New Diplomacy," *Foreign Affairs*, Vol. 82, No. 6,

2003, pp. 22–35; Bates Gill, *Rising Star: China's New Security Diplomacy*, Washington, DC: Brookings Institution Press, 2007; Robert Sutter, *Chinese Foreign Relations: Power and Policy Since the Cold War*, Lanham, MD: Rowman & Littlefield, 2008.

3. "PRC's 'New Diplomacy' Stress on More Active International Role," *Liaowang*, July 11, 2005.

4. "China Bolsters Peacekeeping Commitment," *Jane's Defense Weekly*, February 14, 2007.

5. See Chin-Hao Huang, "Principles and Praxis in Chinese Peacekeeping," *International Peacekeeping*, Vol. 18, No. 3, pp. 259–272; Zhongying Pang, "China's Changing Attitude to UN Peacekeeping," *International Peacekeeping*, Vol. 12, No. 1, 2005, pp. 87–104; "Wang Jisi Discusses Issues in PRC Foreign Policy Strategy," Open Source Center, trans., *Guoji Zhengzhi Yanjiu*, November 25, 2007; "Chinese Expert Views Army Counteracting Non-traditional Security Threats," BBC Monitoring Service, International Reports, trans., *Zhongguo Xinwen She*, June 20, 2007.

6. James Mulvenon, "Chairman Hu and the PLA's 'New Historic Missions,'" *China Leadership Monitor*, No. 27, 2009, pp. 1–11; Cynthia Watson, "The Chinese Armed Forces and Non-traditional Missions: A Growing Tool of Statecraft," *China Brief*, Vol. 9, No. 4, 2009, pp. 9–12.

7. Susan L. Craig, *Chinese Perceptions of Traditional and Nontraditional Security Threats*, Carlisle, PA: Strategic Studies Institute, U.S. Army War College, March 2007.

8. See Dennis J. Blasko, *The Chinese Army Today*, New York: Routledge, 2006; and David Shambaugh, *Modernizing China's Military: Progress, Problems, and Prospects*, Berkeley, CA: University of California Press, 2002; Bernard Cole, *The Great Wall at Sea: China's Navy in the Twenty-first Century*, Annapolis, MD: Naval Institute Press, 2010.

9. "PLA Peacekeeping Work Conference Held in Beijing," *People's Liberation Army Daily*, June 26, 2009.

10. "PLA Constructs MOOTW Arms Force System," *People's Liberation Army Daily*, May 14, 2009.

11. *China's National Defense in 2010*, Beijing, China: State Council Information Office, March 2011.

12. Philip Rogers, "China and UN Peacekeeping Operations in Africa," *Naval War College Review*, Vol. 60, No. 2, 2007, p. 89.

13. "The Deterrence Function of Launching Military Training Exercises," *Jiefangjun Bao*, April 29, 2008.

14. "Chinese Deputy Military Chief on Raising Army's Peacekeeping Role," *Zhongguo Xinwen She*, June 22, 2007.

15. "China Opens First Peacekeeping Training Center," *China Daily*, June 25, 2009.

16. Ping Zhang, "Remarks on the People's Liberation Army's Participation in UN Peacekeeping Operations," speech at conference on "Multi-Dimensional and Integrated Peace Operations: Trends and Challenges," Beijing, China, March 26–27, 2007.

17. *Ibid.*

18. International Committee of the Red Cross, *Annual Report 2009*, Geneva, Switzerland, May 2010, pp. 3–4.

19. "Defense Ministry Touts Deepened China-ASEAN Security Cooperation," *Xinhua News*, March 30, 2009.

20. Alyson J. K. Bailes, *The Shanghai Cooperation Organization*, Stockholm, Sweden: Stockholm International Peace Research Institute, 2007; Marc Lanteigne, "Security, Strategy and the Former USSR: China and the Shanghai Cooperation Organization," in Shaun Breslin, ed., *A Handbook of Chinese International Relations*, London, UK: Routledge, 2010, pp. 166–176.

21. Stephen Blank, "Peace Mission 2009: A Military Scenario beyond Central Asia," *China Brief*, August 20, 2009, pp. 7–9.

22. United Nations Development Group, "Contributor/Partner Fact Sheet," available from *www.unpbf.org/donors/contributions/*.

23. Gareth Evans, "Responding to Atrocities: The New Geopolitics of Intervention," Chap. 1, *SIPRI Yearbook 2012*, Oxford, UK: Oxford University Press, 2012; and Taylor Seybolt, *Humanitarian Military Intervention: The Conditions for Success and Failure*, Oxford, UK: Oxford University Press, 2007.

24. Allen Carlson, "China's Approach to Sovereignty and Intervention," in Alastair Iain Johnston and Robert Ross, eds., *New Directions in the Study of China's Foreign Policy*, Stanford, CA: Stanford University Press, 2006, pp. 217–241.

25. See, for example, Shi Yinhong (时殷弘), "论二十世纪国际规范体系" ("A Discussion of the System of International Norms in the Twentieth Century"), 国际论坛 (*International Forum*), No. 6, 2000, pp. 8–10; Liu Jie (刘杰), 人权与国家主权 (*Human Rights and State Sovereignty*), Shanghai: Shanghai Renmin Chubanshe, 2004; Allen Carlson, *Unifying China, Integrating with the World: Securing Chinese Sovereignty in the Reform Era*, Stanford, CA: Stanford University Press, 2005; Li Buyun (李步云), "人权的两个理论问题" ("Two Theoretical Human Rights Issues"), 中国法学 (*Chinese Legal Studies*), No. 3, 1999, pp. 38–42; Cheng Shuaihua (成帅华), "国家主权与国际人权的若干问题" ("Issues Involving International Human Rights and State Sovereignty"), 欧洲 (*Europe*), No. 1, 2000, pp. 32–35; Cheng Hao (程浩), "联合国维和行动中的主权让渡问题分析" ("An Analysis on UN Peacekeeping Operations and Sovereignty"), 法制与社会 (*Legal System and Society*), No. 5, 2009, pp. 1-7.

26. EU NAVFOR, "EU Meets China in Gulf of Aden," available from *www.eunavfor.eu/2009/11/eu-meets-china-in-gulf-of-aden*.

27. Combined Maritime Forces, "CMF hosts 21st SHADE Meeting," available from *www.combinedmaritimeforces.com/2011/09/27/cmf-hosts-21st-shade-meeting*.

28. "Hit Pirates on Land, Says Top China General,' " *South China Morning Post*, May 20, 2011.

29. Combined Maritime Forces, "Commander CTF 151 Visits Chinese Independent Warship," available from *www.combined-maritimeforces.com/2011/05/15/commander-ctf-151-visits-chinese-in-dependent-warship*.

30. Remarks at a conference on "China's Role in the Horn of Africa," Nairobi, Kenya, January 11-12, 2012.

31. "One Year of GoA Convoys: What the PLAN has Learned," *Xinhua*, December 14, 2009.

32. *China's National Defense in 2010*, Beijing, China: State Council Information Office, March 2011.

33. For related and a more comprehensive analysis on civil-military relations and the "nationalization" of the PLA, see Andrew Scobell, "China's Evolving Civil-Military Relations: Creeping Guojiahua," *Armed Forces and Society*, Vol. 31, pp. 227-244; and Michael Kiselycznyk and Philip Saunders, *Civil-Military Relations in China: Assessing the PLA's Role in Elite Politics*, Washington, DC: National Defense University Institute for National Strategic Studies, 2010.

34. Shirley Kan, "U.S.-China Military Contacts: Issues for Congress," Washington, DC: Congressional Research Service, available from *www.fas.org/sgp/crs/natsec/RL32496.pdf*.

35. *Quadrennial Defense Review Report*, Washington, DC: U.S. Department of Defense, available from *www.defense.gov/qdr/images/QDR_as_of_12Feb10_1000.pdf*.

36. "Chinese Military Students, Family Member Query Cohen," Washington, DC: U.S. Department of Defense, available from *www.defenselink.mil/news/newsarticle.aspx?id=45322*.

37. "China, U.S. Armed Forces Vow to Enhance Cooperation," *Xinhua News*, June 30, 2008.

38. Eric McVadon, "The Reckless and the Resolute: Confrontation in the South China Sea," *China Security*, Vol. 5, No. 2, Spring 2009.

39. On the Defense Authorization Act of 2000, see Kenneth Allen, "U.S.-China Military Relations: Not a One-way Street," Washington, DC: Henry L. Stimson Center News Advisory, December 13, 1999. Insights into the challenges of the Foreign Assistance Act to U.S.-China mil-to-mil relations are based on the author's research interviews with U.S. officials at the State Department and the Department of Defense.

CHAPTER 8

PLA LOGISTICS 2004-11:
LESSONS LEARNED IN THE FIELD

Abraham M. Denmark

The author is greatly indebted to the research team led by Anton Wishik II at The National Bureau of Asian Research for its excellent research and translation assistance.

EXECUTIVE SUMMARY

This chapter describes advances in the People's Liberation Army (PLA) logistics capabilities from 2004 to 2011 as demonstrated by exercises and responses to domestic and foreign security challenges.

MAIN ARGUMENT

As the PLA has been required to respond to a diverse set of military tasks across an increasingly broad geography, PLA logistics has been rapidly adjusting. From responding to domestic natural disasters to rescuing civilians in Libya, PLA logisticians have been gradually improving their ability to support operations in the field. Concurrently, PLA strategists are attempting to modernize their logistical systems by introducing complex information systems; incorporating market forces; improving civil-military and interservice logistical integration; enhancing readiness for diverse military roles; and ensuring logistical support for operations on land, sea, air, space, and in the electronic domain. Still, PLA logistics continue to confront significant challenges across the board, and its ability to support operations far from the Chinese mainland remains significantly reliant on a peaceful and accommodating international environment.

POLICY IMPLICATIONS

- China has significantly improved its domestic and external logistical capabilities.
  - Logistical systems have been somewhat modernized, logistical processes have been somewhat rationalized, and decisionmaking has been streamlined.
  - PLA logisticians have demonstrated an improved ability to improvise.
  - Chinese logistics benefits tremendously from the utilization of civilian resources.
- Although the PLA's logistics system has come a long way, it still has a long way to go.
  - Insufficiently resilient infrastructure and a lack of prepositioned resources have in the past hampered logistics supporting responses to domestic security challenges.
  - Inefficiencies and a lack of power projection capabilities hamper external logistics.
- Until China establishes a network of foreign bases, China's ability to project and sustain power beyond its immediate periphery will remain significantly dependent on a peaceful and accommodating external environment.
  - During a time of conflict or crisis — when the external environment may be hostile to Chinese power projection efforts — the PLA's effective power projection capability will likely shrink to Chinese territory and its immediate periphery.

Modern wars are all about support. Without a strong comprehensive support capability, it is very hard to win combat victory. When logistics support is in place, victory is a sure thing.

> President Hu Jintao,
> People's Republic of China,
> Addressing a PLA logistics work meeting.[1]

INTRODUCTION

As it is for any military, logistics has been an important aspect of the operational thinking of China's PLA. The authoritative 1995 study, *Science of Military Strategy* (战略学), identifies "Strategic Logistical Support" as a key element of military power, and emphasizes that the intense materiel demands of modern warfare, likely due to the adversary's targeting of PLA logistics nodes and supply routes, would test China's economic productivity capacity as well as the PLA's organizational capabilities.[2] *The Science of Military Strategy* sets basic requirements for logistics, which include the integration of central and local government organs responsible for economic activity, prioritizing logistical efforts to those most in line with China's strategic objectives, and the importance of planning and coordination.

Recent years have been extremely busy for the PLA. Once a force preoccupied with Taiwan, territorial integrity, sovereignty, and the maintenance of internal stability, the PLA has been repeatedly called upon to address a wider range of challenges, across a broader geography, than it ever has before. From conducting disaster response operations in Southern China to evacuating Chinese civilians from a fast-

299

crumbling Libya, the PLA has attempted to transform itself in a few short years to a military with a greater role both inside China and in the outside world.

These new demands have necessarily tested the PLA's logistical support system. New tasks, new missions, and new geographies present radically different challenges. For the first time, PLA logisticians have been forced to consider how to deliver fuel, food, and transport rapidly to forces and civilians thousands of miles away. They are also being expected to provide for soldiers and civilians alike when the PLA responds to an increasingly diverse set of tasks, often referred to as "military operations other than war" (MOOTW; "非战争军事行动"), which can include preserving internal stability, search and rescue, disaster relief, international peacekeeping, emergency response, and epidemic prevention and response.

The need to adapt to these expanding demands is certainly not unique to the PLA's logisticians, yet they do have the unique opportunity to learn and experiment in the real world, and not through exercises alone. The PLA's experiences in recent years have taught Chinese military analysts a great deal about the logistical challenges involved in power projection and MOOTW; these analysts have attempted to promulgate these lessons learned and translate them into new doctrine and operational concepts.

This chapter will discuss how the PLA has used its experiences since 2004 to improve its logistical capabilities. It will detail the major logistical challenges the PLA has faced since 2004 and the lessons PLA analysts learned from these experiences. The chapter will then discuss doctrinal changes implemented by the PLA over this period, and will conclude by analyzing trends, improvements, and continuing logistical challenges facing the PLA.

LOGISTICS AND MILITARY OPERATIONS OTHER THAN WAR, 2004-11

Writing on this subject in 2000 for a previous iteration of this conference, Mr. Lonnie Henley detailed contemporary PLA reforms intended to improve its logistics support structure and its operational doctrine in order to cope better with a fast-moving, modern opponent.[3] Henley first described a group of decisions aimed at standardizing military operations and training. Chief among these was the issuance in January 1999 of new "combat regulations" or "operational ordinance" designed to standardize PLA doctrine, tactics, techniques, and procedures for combat operations. Henley also detailed a 10-year PLA effort to restructure the logistical system of the entire PLA announced by General Logistics Department (GLD) director General Wang Ke in November 1998.

In January 2000, the PLA officially created an Integrated Logistics System "with the military region as the foundation, with zone support and force structure support combined, and general support and special support combined."[4] Writing later that year, Henley concluded that "even if successful, these reforms may not significantly increase China's power projection capability, but they will improve its ability to move and sustain forces within China and around its periphery."[5]

Over the next decade, these conclusions were tested by a series of operations that forced PLA strategists and logisticians to learn in the field. An examination of the PLA's major activities in the intervening decade demonstrates that, while China's power projection capabilities were significantly limited as the decade began, the PLA was able to learn from experience and gradually improve logistical capabilities to support a series of missions of increasing complexity and ambition.

Indian Ocean Tsunami (2004).

In December 2004, a 9.3 earthquake struck the Indian Ocean, killing more than 230,000 people in 14 countries. As several nations rushed to aid the millions of survivors, the power projection capabilities of the responding nation's militaries were inadvertently put on full display. While the U.S. military demonstrated its robust ability to deploy rapidly over vast distances and sustain those forces over time, the PLA's performance demonstrated that significant gaps in its power projection capabilities remained—just as Henley had predicted.

The PLA's response to the tsunami indicated a capability that was not nearly up to the task of projecting power beyond China's immediate periphery.[6] The PLA procured items domestically and provided logistical support inside China, but military supplies were flown from civilian airports in China by civilian aircraft to the affected areas.[7] The PLA's foreign commitments to the affected areas were limited to a People's Armed Police (PAP) medical unit and an engineering unit from a Beijing Military Area Command, both of which deployed to Indonesia. A Western analysis attributed the PLA's lack of experience beyond its own waters to continued logistical deficiencies in power projection.[8]

Sichuan Earthquake (2008).

The next major test for the PLA's logistics system came in the form of an 8.0 earthquake that struck Mianyang, north of Chengdu in Sichuan Province, in May 2008. The earthquake reportedly killed roughly 88,000, injured over 368,000, and forced the evacuation of more than 15 million people, mostly in Sichuan Province.[9] The earthquake also severely damaged transportation and communication networks, significantly complicating response operations. The PLA was tasked with conducting rescue and recovery operations, providing emergency relief to affected populations, repairing damage, and clearing away debris.

Despite these efforts, the PLA's response was widely regarded as significantly deficient. Damage to roads and airports hampered the PLA's ability to quickly send massive numbers of troops and equipment. It reportedly took 44 hours for troops to arrive in large numbers, and even then they did not possess the heavy machinery necessary to rescue people in the first critical hours after the disaster.[10] In the immediate hours after the earthquake, only 15 out of 6,500 paratroopers that were deployed to Sichuan were reportedly able to actually drop into the disaster zone, due to poor weather conditions. Additionally, the lack of heavy-lift helicopters prevented the PLA from removing large pieces of debris from collapsed buildings.

In July 2008, the Chengdu Military Region (MR) — which was on the frontline of coordinating the PLA's response to the earthquake — published a summary of the logistical work it had accomplished and the lessons it had learned as a result of the earthquake in *Zhanqi Bao* (战旗报), the official newspaper of the Communist Party Committee [CPC] of the Chengdu Military Region).[11] In an article likely designed to answer criticism about the MR's disappointing disaster response, the article highlighted claims that the Chengdu MR had:

> rapidly reacted, scientifically commanded, participated in the entire process, and efficiently guaranteed troop mobile transport, the transfer of materials and equipment, and the diverting of the masses from the quake-hit areas. [The Military Transportation Department of the Chengdu Military Region Joint Logistics Department] fought a campaign of joint support in military transportation, and completely fulfilled all the tasks assigned by the joint command made up of the Central Party Committee, the General Headquarters, and the Chengdu Military Region.[12]

During the earthquake disaster response, the Chengdu MR Logistics Department dispatched more than 300 transportation vehicles, carrying 50 sets of Beidou satellite command stations, 40 sets of unilateral radio transmitters, and 130 sets of walkie-talkies, to transport the first batch of nearly 8,000 disaster relief troops from railroad stations to affected areas.[13] It also requisitioned more than 4,000 civilian cars, more than 8,000 trucks, and tens of large-sized platform trailers. More than 20,000 civilian vehicles were used for emergency road transport support, transporting more than one million people.[14]

According to the Chengdu MR, the quake relief effort was managed by a three-tiered command structure involving joint command, zone-of-responsibility command posts. However, the Logistics Department in the Chengdu MR lamented that the various zones of responsibility did not have corresponding logistical command mechanisms or elements, and they had no way of leading the logistical support missions in their zones of responsibility.[15] Despite these problems in command and control, the Logistics Department focused on determining damage to ground transportation infrastructure—contacting military and civilian air transport organizations, establishing supply depots, and concentrating needed vehicles away from unimportant areas (i.e., Tibet) and focusing them on disaster-affected regions.[16]

The article also identified continuing deficiencies in disaster response logistics:

> in formulating pertinent disaster prevention and relief action plans, in rationalizing and unblocking command relations, and in building the emergency reaction capacity of the large-sized military transportation equipment . . . in strengthening targeted training, rationalizing work relations between organs and relevant local departments, and in quickening the pace of transforming traditional military transportation to modern military transportation.[17]

The Chengdu MR identified key capabilities necessary for effective internal disaster responses: civil-military integration, sub-commander initiative (referred to as "unconventional measures" ["超常措施"]), streamlined procurement, and centralized command and control enabled by a distributed communications network. Elsewhere, the Chengdu MR stated that satellite communications—necessary for coordination when traditional land-based communications are damaged—were apparently unavailable in the required quantities, implying the need for more satellite communications equipment.[18]

In an after-action review published in the same publication 1 month later, the Chengdu MR emphasized the lesson that MOOTW "have already become an important and frequent mode of employing military forces. Strengthening logistical preparations for military operations other than war is a extremely important and pressing matter of practical significance."[19]

The review emphasized logistical challenges as especially pressing in addressing MOOTW. Reexamining the earthquake-related disaster response operations of the previous months, the Chengdu MR bemoaned the "lack of focused logistical preparations with regard to things such as the formulation of emergency support plans, constructing a command system, and building up equipment and supplies."[20] It argued that constant MOOTW responsibilities had prevented its units from bringing to bear its combat capabilities, largely due to a lack of logistical preparations during peacetime. Highlighting a report from the 17th National Party Congress that called for military units to "deal with diverse security threats and accomplish diversified military tasks" ("应对多种安全威胁，完成多样化军事任务"), Chengdu highlighted the need for increased logistical support for MOOTW.[21] Specifically, it called to focus improvement in four areas:

1. Fast response and rapid support capabilities. Chengdu emphasized the need for speed in providing disaster relief in an urgent situation and called for improved logistical information, decisionmaking, planning, organization, resource prepositioning, coordination, and control. Chengdu proposed the creation of "field depot logistical equipment" ("野战兵站后勤装备") that is suited to the demands of military operations other than war, which are of a highly unexpected nature and have high timeliness [requirements].[22]

2. Military-civilian integration and joint support capabilities. When the Chengdu MR discussed "jointness" ("联合"), it was not referring to improved integration between the PLA's ground, air, and naval assets. Instead, Chengdu emphasized the importance of "joint" coordination of military and civilian logistical assets to conduct MOOTW effectively.[21] Civilian resources and logistics are necessarily more distributed and robust than the PLA's, making them useful for disaster relief operations. "This quake relief effort was a disaster relief and rescue operation under the unified leadership and deployment of the local party committees and governments, and was carried out jointly with military, police, and civilian integration as well as integration among the military services." Chendgu called for improved civil-military integration and joint support capabilities and identified civil-military interoperability and a joint logistics and logistical mobilization system such as economic mobilization and traffic control, an improved joint command mechanism for civil-military emergency response logistics, and "improving the political, military, social, and economic benefits of logistical support."[22]

3. Accompanying, follow-along, and mobile support capabilities. Given the requirements to concentrate and distribute forces and materiel across large disaster-affected areas, Chengdu identified the need for "full-spectrum mobile support" ("全方位机动保障"), involving "the adjustment of support forces as disaster relief units maneuvered and the adjustment of support focal points as disaster relief missions changed." Chengdu called for the PLA to strengthen development in areas such as "command information systems and logistical equipment and materials, satisfying the requirements for on-the-move command,

coordination, and support, and achieving transitions from fixed-point support to accompanying, follow-up support, and from regional support to comprehensive mobility."[23]

4. Focus on requirements and special procurement support capabilities. Finally, Chengdu emphasized the wide variety of resource and geographical challenges associated with conducting MOOTW and the correspondingly robust and diversified logistical system required. "In this quake relief effort, various missions were interwoven, including fighting the earthquake, preventing epidemics, preventing flooding, and rescue operations; there were varying environments including plains, plateaus, and mountains; and there were alternating weather conditions including extreme heat, extreme cold, and humidity." Chengdu therefore called for a special procurement system to allow for ample stockpiles and fast resource distribution.[24]

Ultimately, Chengdu called for focusing on efforts regarding "emergency response command mechanisms, logistical supplies stockpiles, building up logistical equipment and materials, and logistical training and exercises, striving to improve logistical support capabilities for military operations other than war."[25]

Also in 2008, the Chengdu MR co-hosted, with the Military-Wide Logistics Academic Research Center, a symposium "commemorating 30 years of reform and opening up," in which "they looked back over the glorious history of military logistics reform, and centered around the key points of promoting reform and transformation in the comprehensive building of modern logistics."[26] The symposium reached the following conclusions:

- The logistics system must be reformed and upgraded to adequately support a small, fast-paced military force.
- Interservice, civil-military, and "peace-and-war" ("平战结合") logistical integration must be improved.
- Market-style logistics practices should be adopted to improve efficiency.
- Preparations should be made for logistically supporting a greater diversity of military tasks (i.e., MOOTW).

Gulf of Aden Operations (2008-11).

In December 2008, Beijing announced its decision to send ships to the Gulf of Aden to conduct counter-piracy operations—the first modern deployment of Chinese naval assets outside the Pacific.[27] Chinese officials cited the problem piracy posed to Chinese shipping in these vital waterways as the primary motivation for this move, and emphasized the importance of a UN-sponsored multilateral mandate in providing political justification for such action.

For the PLA, counter-piracy operations presented a unique opportunity to learn lessons in power projection through experimentation, and to build experience in out-of-area operations for the PLA Navy (PLAN). The PLAN sent the most capable platforms in its surface fleet, rotating several warships from a variety of classes to ensure that experience was maximized throughout the force.

Logistically, the PLA learned a great deal from over 3 years of continuous operations in the Gulf of Aden. According to a major naval publication, questions of providing food and fresh water, fuel, and spare parts were "the focus of attention of people around the world."[30] The article emphasized several logistical innovations developed in these operations:

- For the first time, a foreign port was used to carry out commercialized replenishment. Several thousand tons of goods in all varieties purchased by the PLAN's advance team were successively replenished to ships in 2 days at Port Salalah, Oman. This was the first time the ship *Weishanhu* berthed at Oman's commercial port to carry out comprehensive replenishment, and it was the third time the escort task force relied on a foreign port for replenishment.

- For the first time, large-scale material replenishment at sea was carried out with the help of a cargo ship, and it proved to be a flexible replenishment method. Soon after the deployment began, Zhongyuan Group's *Wanhe* line brought the Chinese task force more than 2,000 kilograms of vegetables.

An American study of several PLA reactions and lessons learned from the Gulf of Aden mission identified five categories of challenges confronting the PLAN: distance, duration, capacity, complexity of coordination, and hostility of environment.[31] After analyzing the PLAN's deployment to the Gulf of Aden, the study concluded:

> Among expected factors making out of area deployments especially challenging, we note that the Gulf of Aden deployment illustrated how duration, capacity, and distance continue to bedevil PLAN long-distance operations. Duration is important because the Chinese have yet to resolve the problem of preserving foodstuffs and other consumables over long periods.

Distance figures prominently because China lacks nearby facilities and bases to which it can send vessels for maintenance and repair. And operations tempo/capacity is relevant because China currently lacks enough ships to simultaneously deploy out of area and in waters proximate to the Chinese mainland in the event of a domestic contingency.[32]

According to the same American study, PLA analysts proposed various solutions to these challenges, including:

- Gaining access to port facilities;
- Significantly increasing the number of surface combatants and providing a stable capacity of ships to normalize the deployments to out-of-area regions;
- Providing SATCOM for all out-of-area deployments; and,
- Producing additional and new underway replenishment ships.[33]

Libya Evacuation (2011).

The outbreak of unrest in Libya in February 2011 created another opportunity for the PLA to test and demonstrate its logistical capabilities, this time to evacuate more than 35,000 Chinese diplomats, tourists, entrepreneurs, and students. On February 22, the day a speech by Muammar Gaddafi signified (to Beijing) the inevitability of civil war in Libya, Chinese President Hu Jintao directed relevant departments to "go all out to ensure the safety of Chinese nationals in Libya."[34] Hu and Premier Wen Jiabao requested the creation of an emergency command headquarters in Beijing, directed by Vice Premier Zhang Dejiang, to manage a "three-dimensional coordinated evacuation plan combining sea, land, and air operations."[35]

311

The evacuation thus utilized several methods of transportation. The first chartered flight sent by China took off on February 23 and arrived the next morning, demonstrating China's ability to deploy resources quickly. Thereafter, Chinese airlines (Air China, China Eastern Airlines, China Southern Airlines, and Hainan Airlines) sent aircraft from several airports throughout China to airports in Libya and Egypt.[36] Concurrently, the Chinese Embassy in Libya directed Chinese citizens to travel to Tripoli and Benghazi, where ocean liners rented by the Chinese government on February 24 began transporting them, 2,000 at a time, to Greece and Malta. Protecting these ships was the missile frigate *Xuzhou*, which was dispatched from patrol duty in the Gulf of Aden on February 25. Approximately 20,000 Chinese nationals in Libya had been evacuated by February 27, and all 35,000 Chinese nationals in Libya had been safely evacuated from Libya by March 10.[37] The PLA was also directly involved in the evacuation, deploying four Il-76 heavy transport aircraft.

Chinese writers were exuberant in highlighting the evacuation's large scale. For example, a publication affiliated with the Ministry of Foreign Affairs noted:

> China dispatched a total of 91 Chinese civilian chartered flights, 35 foreign chartered flights and 12 flights using military airplanes, and chartered 11 foreign ships, five cargo ships of the China Ocean Shipping (Group) Company [COSCO] and the China Shipping Container Lines Company [CSCL], one military vessel, and over 100 bus trips; evacuated the Chinese nationals indirectly through third countries; and made use of A4-sized papers to serve as the emergency travel documents of the Chinese nationals.[38]

This civilian evacuation was notable for several reasons. As noted by several Chinese scholars, it was the largest and fastest evacuation of Chinese citizens in the history of the People's Republic of China (PRC), and was conducted at the greatest ever distances with the greatest ever diversity of resources.[39] It was also a highly complex operation for China, involving assets in Libya, Tunisia, Egypt, Sudan, the United Arab Emirates, Greece, and Malta, as well as eight or nine airports.

The PLA's role was emphasized as historic as well; this was (according to Chinese media) the first time that the PLAN sent a warship to participate in an operation to evacuate Chinese nationals, the first time that the Chinese Navy dispatched a warship to the Mediterranean Sea, and the first time that the Chinese Air Force sent large transport aircraft abroad to participate in the collection and transportation of Chinese nationals.[40]

Finally, Chinese scholars celebrated the speed and effectiveness of China's decisionmaking. According to the scholars, on February 23 — when China's evacuation was already underway — the governments of the United States, France, Britain, and Turkey were still considering their options.[41] They argued that the success of China's evacuation operations demonstrated the steady improvement of China's overall national strength (including surpassing Japan's gross domestic product [GDP] in 2010), an elevation of China's international prestige, an expanded ability to mobilize China's diplomatic resources, an expansion in the quantity of China's large heavy equipment, and the improvement of the quality of life of Chinese nationals abroad.[42]

Identifying exactly how many Chinese were evacuated on which conveyances is complicated by the fact that Chinese sources provide widely inconsistent information.[43] Yet, while authoritative, exact numbers may be unavailable, certain broad trends are easily identifiable. First, the significant role of civilian assets, operating at government direction, cannot be overemphasized. The vast majority of Chinese citizens were evacuated by civilian aircraft and ocean liners, operating at Beijing's request. Even the PLA was reliant upon civilian airports for refueling on the long flight to Libya. Indeed, it is clear that the role of the PLA was far smaller than the coverage it attracted in Chinese (and especially PLA-affiliated) media reports. Deploying the frigate *Xuzhou* and four Il-76 transport aircraft was a rather slow and small-scale reaction, especially compared with the massive civilian response that was quickly mobilized.

Yet, the Libya evacuations demonstrated that both the PLAN and PLA Air Force (PLAAF) have expanded capabilities and ambitions. The *Xuzhou* reached the Mediterranean Sea after sailing over 2,600 nautical miles, a relatively significant accomplishment for a Navy without a tradition of extended-range power projection. An article in *Modern Navy* emphasized that the voyage of the *Xuzhou* signaled the PLAN's transformation into a blue-water navy capable of performing diversified tasks at war and at peace.[44] As for the PLAAF, its four IL-76 transporters flew nearly continuous civilian evacuation flights from Urumqi, Xinjiang—flying over Pakistan, Oman, Saudi Arabia, Sudan and Libya, the Arabian Sea and the Red Sea; crossing six time zones in one-way flights of over 12 hours; and making stopovers for refueling at Khartoum, Sudan, and Karachi, Pakistan.[45] This was the first time the PLAAF participated in the evacuation of civilians at this range.

Exercises.

In addition to real-life experiences in the field, PLA logistics were tested by regular exercises. While examining specific exercises is necessarily iterative, a broad examination of exercises involving logistics reveals certain broad trends of emphasis.

For example, joint operations, force projection, and diversified military tasks were all major themes for exercises in 2010. That year, the director for training in the PLA's General Staff Department (GSD) recognized two joint training activities as the focus of joint training in 2010: *Joint-2010* and *Mission Action-2010* ("使命行动-2010"), both of which emphasized large joint combat formations.[46] Similarly, several military regions also held combined arms battalion exercises; for example, a November article in *PLA Daily* described a Lanzhou Military Region firepower strike exercise that involved a "joint tactical formation" comprising PLA ground forces, PLAAF elements, and even forces from the Second Artillery Corps.[47]

In April 2011, the Lanzhou MR hosted a live military exercise, code-named *Joint Logistics Mission 2011*.[48] The purpose of the exercise was to "comprehensively examine the emergency support capabilities of the logistics units in the context of informatization," specifically focusing on command and planning, maneuver and deployment, and support.[49] The exercise involved the establishment of a joint logistics sub-department under the MR, which centralized command and control for logistical elements. According to a published review of the exercise, the Lanzhou MR had benefited from previous exercises by building an "integrated command information system for logistics, a safety protection system, and a comprehensive logistics database and achieved interconnectivity among different information resources." This year, units have been tasked with applying "informatized means of support," including a "dynamic troop monitoring and command system, [a] field goods yard [sic] information management system, [and a] remote medical consultation system."[50] Also in 2011, the Chinese CPC and the staff of North Sea Fleet Aviation sought to modernize naval logistics "against the general background of the overall transformation in the construction of the Navy" by enhancing "information system-based 'system of systems'" capabilities and identifying three goals: standardization, informatization, and detail [quality].[51]

Implications for Warfighting.

The development and improvement of PLA logistical capabilities has several important implications for its ability to fight a war. First and most importantly, these improvements — though significant in themselves — demonstrate the PLA's continued challenges in projecting power and rationalizing logistical processes. The challenges faced by PLA logisticians in Sichuan Province in 2008 highlight these continued deficiencies, especially when real world obstacles force improvisation and deny the PLA easy access.

Difficulties would likely be intensified beyond China's borders, especially if China's external environment were hostile to the use of Chinese military power. Chinese MOOTW logistical support to the Libya evacuation — for example — absolutely depended upon the utilization of civilian airports, ships, and neighbor airspace. At this time, the PLA does not have the ability to force open denied air and sea space far from Chinese territory — thus shrinking the effective operational range of PLA logistics in a hostile external environment to China's territory and its immediate periphery.

That being said, PLA logistics have seen a marked improvement in capabilities since 2004. Their processes have been somewhat rationalized, their systems have been somewhat modernized, and logisticians have demonstrated a limited ability to adjust their processes to accord with the realities and demands of the operation — as they did in Sichuan Province in 2008. These improvements will somewhat enhance the ability of the PLA to support military operations during a time of conflict.

LESSONS LEARNED: DOCTRINAL AND OPERATIONAL ADAPTATION

As the PLA was busily responding to crises inside and outside China, Chinese strategists were attempting to translate lessons learned in the field to PLA doctrine and operational practices. Interestingly, though the PLA's GLD and other PLA organizations regularly issued guidance on the future of logistics, this guidance did not significantly evolve over time. Instead, the GLD seemed to be repeating its own guidance to the PLA's logisticians in various formulations. What follows are the major strategic and doctrinal adjustments related to logistics that issued by the PLA in recent years.

The Four Great Transformations (2006).

Six years after inaugurating the Integrated Logistics System and 2 years after the PLA's limited response to the Indian Ocean tsunami, the PLA's GLD issued what it referred to as "the Four Great Transformations" ("四大变革"), which were described as ushering in a "new era of logistics transformation strategic conceptualization."[52] According to this concept, PLA logistics must possess "the ability to ensure operational capabilities in multidimensional space including on land, at sea, in the air, in space and electronically, and other military operational capabilities including reacting to crises, maintaining peace, containing wars and winning wars."[53] Specifically, the Four Great Transformations are described as:

1. From autonomous to three armed services joint logistics (从自成体系到三军联勤);

2. From self-guarantee to socialized (i.e., integrated with the civil economy) guarantee (从自我保障到社会化保障);

3. Informatization constructs new logistics platforms (信息化构筑后勤新平台); and,

4. Scientification transforms traditional logistics management (科学化改造传统后勤管理).

MOOTW Logistics.

As China's national interests have expanded in recent years, so too have the mandates for the PLA. The State Council emphasized the importance of MOOTW for the PLA, issuing documents entitled "Opinions Regarding Comprehensively Strengthening Emergency Response Management Work" and "Methods for Responding to Incidents That Suddenly Occur."[54]

Similarly, in 2008, since the PLA was in a historically active state as it responded to internal and external challenges, the importance of nontraditional security threats and "non-war military actions" ("非战争军事行动") were emphasized by Chinese President Hu Jintao, who was quoted by a PLA journal as declaring:

> [We] must put MOOTW capability building into the overall situation of military modernization and military struggle preparation with scientific planning and implementation, and strive to markedly improve the PLA's MOOTW capabilities. Military logistics not only plays a vital role in support units' successful implementation of MOOTW, it also directly plays a leading role, and can even independently carry out tasks, in public health relief, international peacekeeping and humanitarian assistance, rescue and relief, and restoration and rebuilding. In essence, non-war military logistics operations are a kind of MOOTW style in a specific context, and the logistics support force is the main force of the operation.[55]

As MOOTW capabilities have become increasingly important to the PLA, so too have logistical capabilities designed to support and enable MOOTW. A PLA journal identified several logistical challenges posed by MOOTW:[56]

- A broad set of mandates (e.g., counterterrorism, maintaining internal stability, peacekeeping, and disaster relief) will create complex logistical demands.
- The ability to respond quickly in several areas at once requires preparation, prepositioning, and distribution.
- Internally, logistical supplies and capabilities should be distributed to account for the natural disasters they will be likely to face. For ex-

ample, Hainan and Guangdong areas should prepare for typhoons and emergency relief by prepositioning food, medical supplies, generators, etc. The Yangtze River Basin and other areas near major lakes and rivers should prepare to resettle large populations and provide food, medicine, and shelter. Hunan, Hubei, and northern Guangxi Districts should prepare to fight large blizzards by stockpiling electricity, space heaters, food, and clothing. Fuel depots should be established along the primary transit routes of a given area.

- Improve training, incorporate logistics equipment into a given organizational structure, and standardize logistics equipment management procedures.
- Improve civil-military and interservice integration by establishing a mechanism to share resources as well as command and control.
- Establish an early warning system that can communicate between regions and between organizations, be they civil or military.

Improving Procurement.

According to Zhou Linhe, Director of the Quartermaster, Materials, and POL Department of the GLD, the PLA in 2009 attempted to accelerate the pace of reform in military procurement, and set up a three-tier logistics procurement management system organized by major units, logistics departments, and troop units.[57] The PLA also attempted to establish a standardized set of rules and regulations for procurement in order to improve procurement centralization, apparently in order to improve efficiency.[58] A PLA journal highlighted the fact that from mid-2008 to mid-2009, the GDL organized a reform experiment in regional joint procurement for military goods and materiel in 13 cities, reportedly procuring goods valued at 1.4 billion yuan and saving 18 percent.[59] Procurement has been computerized in order to "evaluate bids," to improve transparency and improve efficiency. The same PLA article claimed computerizing procurement also contains and prevents "black-box operations," a likely reference to corruption. Separately, but in the same spirit, in 2010, the PLA experimented with allowing international bidding to provide medical and health equipment for 100-plus military hospitals, an endeavor the PLA claimed attracted 13 bids from Chinese and foreign business, saving roughly 10 million yuan.[60]

Building Modern Logistics in an All-Around Way.

In November 2010, at the conclusion of a logistics conference, CMC member and GLD Director Liao Xilong exhorted the PLA to "basically accomplish the task of building modern logistics in an all-round way."[61] Specifically, Liao pointed out that the PLA logistics system will:

> quicken the steps of reform on military support outsourcing, establish and improve the normal-state mechanism and effective channel to include military support outsourcing into the national and local economic and social development programs, establish a military-civilian joint storage model for disaster relief and stability maintenance general materials, a trinity of the military, state and local government.[62]

Liao also called on the PLA to improve "strategic projection capabilities" ("战略投送能力") by improving coordination of national traffic and transportation systems, establishing a military logistics information system based on the national logistics system, and improving civil support resources.[63]

Hu's Expositions.

In 2010, Hu Jintao issued "Important Expositions on Development of PLA Logistics," which the journal *China Military Science* exhorted its readers to study as "fundamental guidance for the development of PLA logistics."[64] Hu highlights instability and uncertainty in China's security environment, driven by "hostile Western forces [that] do not want to see China develop and grow stronger"; increasing complexity and volatility on China's periphery; and increasing domestic challenges driven by a higher number of mass incidents, environmental degradation, natural disasters, terrorism, energy security and information security.[65] He pairs these increasing challenges with expanded national interests that "are gradually going beyond the traditional sphere of territorial land, sea, and airspace, and keep expanding and extending to the ocean, the space, and the electromagnetic domain," and calls on the PLA to "develop a modern logistics with strong comprehensive support capabilities" that "not only can provide support for winning the local wars under informatized conditions, but also can provide support for various nonwar military actions; not only can support homeland defense operations, but also can support the units in safeguarding the security of maritime, space, and strategic routes, and in safeguarding national interests in other areas."[66]

According to the same PLA article, Hu's expositions highlighted areas in which the PLA must improve its logistical capabilities:

- Expanding capabilities beyond the traditional, army-oriented support structure, and adapting to demands for the PLA to operate in the sea, air, space, and electromagnetic domains;
- Enhancing logistical capabilities from mechanized and semi-mechanized support to informatized means, allowing for rapid, precision support;
- Developing capabilities to respond to multiple security threats and accomplish diversified military tasks requires the PLA to intensify reform of socializing logistics support and pushing forward military-civilian integrated development with Chinese characteristics—advancing reform of joint logistics and adhering to orientation of tri-service integrated support, strengthening the armed forces by applying science and technology, insisting on putting the people first and generating grassroots support, emphasizing scientific management and a cost-effective path of development for national defense and PLA modernization building, and regarding energy conservation as a basic national policy and military rule and building the armed forces through struggles, diligence, and thrift.[67]

Framework for Overall Advancement.

At the beginning of 2011, the GLD issued the "Framework for the Overall Advancement of Comprehensively Building Modern Logistics Experimental Goals and Tasks," which was intended as a baseline for future improvement in the PLA's logistical system.[68] Yet, the framework, which emphasizes the importance of integration, socialization, informatization, and scientization, is nearly identical to the Four Great Transformations from 5 years previously. The Framework did, however, add five aspects to logistics: supply, manage, build, train, and reform (供, 管, 建, 训, 改).[69]

CONCLUDING ANALYSIS

Examining PLA logistics in 2000, Lonnie Henley concluded that reforms enacted to that point "may not significantly increase China's power projection capability, but they will improve its ability to move and sustain forces within China and around its periphery."[70] More than a decade later, it is clear that Mr. Henley was prescient: Though still profoundly limited in several important ways, the PLA has significantly improved its logistical capabilities, enhancing its ability to move and sustain forces internally and throughout its periphery in a nascent power projection capability.

China's ability to deploy a small force over great distances quickly and sustain that force for a long period of time, was demonstrated by its operations in the Gulf of Aden and the Libya evacuation. Indeed, the activities and doctrinal changes discussed above are very informative about China's logistical capabilities and where PLA logistics are going.

China derives a significant logistical benefit from its ability to utilize civilian assets for national purposes. While the PLA's response to Beijing's order to evacuate more than 35,000 Chinese citizens in Libya was slow and small, civilian airlines responded quickly and massively. Interestingly, Chinese citizens in Libya who could not contact the PRC embassy were still able to be rescued by utilizing the Chinese micro-blogging service, QQ.[71] Using civilian resources has the added benefit of not generating the concern abroad that military units often engender in populations concerned about neo-imperialism or aggression.

China also demonstrated an improved ability to improvise and adapt to the particulars of a given situation. In contrast to its efforts in Sichuan in 2008 — in which thousands of troops were relegated to marching into the area on foot and digging with their hands — China demonstrated in Libya and in the Gulf of Aden the ability to use new sources of information and respond to events on the ground in real time, without necessarily relying on Beijing for tactical guidance.

It is difficult to predict improvements accurately in China's internal logistics system without real world demonstrations of capabilities. Still, if the PLA is able to preposition supplies successfully and distribute forces throughout the country in a way that accounts for damaged transportation and communications infrastructure, a more rapid and robust response to future disasters is likely. Improvements to domestic transportation and communications infrastructure will certainly help in this regard, as well.

Despite these accomplishments, the PLA's logistical capabilities remain remarkably limited. Foremost among them is the PLA's total reliance on a stable and accessible external environment. Civilian airliners, ships in the Gulf of Aden, and PLAAF transport ships all rely upon access to friendly ports and airports that would likely not be available in a less peaceful environment. Civilian aircraft have no ability to operate in a denied environment, and the PLA at this time has not demonstrated the capability to defend itself against anything more formidable than Somali pirates. A hostile environment would immediately limit China's reach to its immediate periphery, where it enjoys secure internal lines of communication and shore-based defenses.

Moreover, the PLA's logistical capabilities are simply limited in size and sophistication. The PLAN lacks significant numbers of oilers and resupply ships capable of operating at great distances, and the PLAAF lacks mid-air refueling capabilities necessary for extended-range air power projection. This deficiency can be solved with regular investment and continued modernization, but it will likely take a long time.

At the heart of these deficiencies is a continued lack of international basing. Friendly ports, even those built by China, cannot be relied upon as friendly during times of conflict or crisis. The PLA would simply be unable to operate at distance in a hostile environment without reliable access to safe areas. Even if the PLA significantly expands its fleet of supply ships and aerial refuelers, its reach will still be significantly limited—especially in the strategically vital areas of the Indian Ocean and Middle East.

Indeed, the logic of distributing supplies and forces throughout China in order to adequately respond to domestic crises also applies to China's international posture. If China seeks to sustain an international presence that is capable of exerting influence according to Beijing's interests, it requires supplies and forces to be readily and safely accessible. Relying on a peaceful and accommodating international environment, while likely a safe bet for the near future, is a significant gamble, given China's reliance on access to foreign markets and resources.

The PLA seems to know where it wants to go with its logistics system. Generally, strategic and doctrinal revisions in recent years all point to a rather straight-forward path ahead for PLA logistics. There is a clear interest in improving civil-military and interservice logistical integration, including logistical command and control as well as shared resources. The PLA is also committed to expanding the use of information "system-of-systems" in order to improve logistical efficiency and speed. There is also a great deal of emphasis on improving "multidimensional" capabilities in the land, sea, air, space, and electronic domains. Most importantly, though, is the general realization that a military being tasked with an increasingly diverse set of tasks and missions requires a logistical system that is flexible, distributed, and nimble — both domestically and internationally.

Ultimately, logistics is at the heart of any military's power. A modern military requires a modern logistical system — even one of the world's largest and most innovative economies cannot adequately support a military in a hostile international environment. A military looking at power projection and an expanded set of missions other than combat requires a logistics system geared toward power projection and diverse military tasks.

IMPLICATIONS FOR THE UNITED STATES

The deliberate and continuous improvement of the PLA's logistical capabilities has significant implications for American military planning and for U.S. efforts to integrate China into the international system as a power that substantially contributes to the health and success of the existing international order. Although China was once a country focused entirely internally, an improved ability of the PLA to operate far beyond China's borders means that the world will soon be forced to reckon directly with an increasingly capable Chinese military. Yet, capability does not necessarily equal intention, and the future mode of the outside world's interaction with the PLA remains very much unclear.

It is likely that PLA logistical improvements will primarily be focused on domestic MOOTW and security challenges along China's periphery — Taiwan, North Korea, and, most likely, the South China Sea. A further expansion of PLA logistical capabilities to project power further afield from its shores would require a significant investment in both resources to procure and develop modern logistical systems and an investment in time to build, utilize, and adjust these capabilities in the real world.

While some may view this development as inherently threatening, the ultimate implications of these emerging capabilities will largely be determined by the missions that the PLA will be sent on. If the PLA is ordered to secure sea lanes, counter piracy and proliferation, and otherwise uphold international stability and freedom of navigation on the high seas, an expansion of PLA logistics capabilities may be a boon for international stability and prosperity. On the other hand, missions to deny freedom of navigation or prevent international efforts to counter proliferation or other threats to international security will demonstrate to the world that PLA logistics do not benefit the international system.

Given the PLA's current reliance on a peaceful and accommodating external environment to project and sustain power, the last thing it needs is hostility or suspicion. It is therefore incumbent on the PLA to demonstrate that its expanding power is not a threat to the outside world and, indeed, is intended to contribute to international public good. Similarly, it is incumbent on the United States to hold the PLA accountable for its actions, and to ensure that PLA logistics are put to good and constructive use.

ENDNOTES - CHAPTER 8

1. "军队后勤建设发展的根本遵循-学习胡锦涛关于军队后勤建设的重要论述" ("Fundamental Guidance for Development of PLA Logistics - Study Hu Jintao's Important Discussion of Military Logistics Construction"), 中国军事科学 (*China Military Science*), No. 6, 2010, p. 25-31.

2. Peng Guangqian and Yao Youzhi, eds., *The Science of Military Strategy*, Beijing, China: Academy of Military Science, 1995, p. 354.

3. Lonnie Henley, "PLA Logistics and Doctrine Reform, 1999-2009," in Susan M. Puska, ed., *People's Liberation Army After Next*, Carlisle, PA: Strategic Studies Institute, U.S. Army War College, 2000, pp. 55-77.

4. "Promoting the Logistics Transformation with Deepened Reform," *Jiefangjun Bao*, November 4, 2008, p. 6, OSC CPP20081104710007.

5. Henley, pp. 55-77. For the sake of brevity, this chapter does not detail every mission or exercise undertaken by the PLA in this time period, but rather focuses on major activities in order to track progress and identify key lessons learned.

6. "Tsunami Relief Reflects China's Regional Aspirations," *China Brief*, January 17, 2005, available from *www.jamestown.org/programs/chinabrief/single/?tx_ttnews%5Btt_news%5D=3708&tx_ttnews%5BbackPid%5D=195&no_cache=1.*

7. *Ibid.*

8. *Ibid.*

9. "China earthquake death toll rises to 69,016," *Xinhua*, June 2, 2008, available from *news.xinhuanet.com/english/2008-06/02/content_8300457.htm*.

10. Jake Hooker, "Quake Reveals Grave Insufficiency of China's Military," *The New York Times*, July 2, 2008.

11. "牢牢掌握军交运输主动权" ("Firmly Grasp the Initiative in Military Transport"), 战旗报 (*Zhanqi Bao*), July 30, 2008, p. 6.

12. *Ibid.*

13. *Ibid.*

14. *Ibid.*

15. "着眼特殊保障需求加大后勤准备力度" ("Focus on Special Guarantee Requirements Increasing Logistics Preparation Level"), 战旗报 (*Zhanqi Bao*), August 15, 2008, p. 3.

16. "牢牢掌握军交运输主动权" ("Firmly Grasp the Initiative in Military Transport"), 战旗报 (*Zhanqi Bao*), July 30, 2008, p. 6.

17. *Ibid.*

18. *Ibid.*

19. "着眼特殊保障需求加大后勤准备力度" ("Focus on Special Guarantee Requirements Increasing Logistics Preparation Level"), 战旗报 (*Zhanqi Bao*), August 15, 2008, p. 3.

20. *Ibid.*

21. *Ibid.*

22. *Ibid.*

23. *Ibid.*

24. *Ibid.*

25. *Ibid.*

26. *Ibid.*

27. *Ibid.*

28. "Promoting the Logistics Transformation with Deepened Reform," *Jiefangjun Bao,* November 4, 2008, p. 6, OSC CPP20081104710007.

29. This subject is well-covered in Andrew S. Erickson, "Chinese Sea Power in Action: the Counter-Piracy Mission in the Gulf of Aden and Beyond," in Roy Kamphausen, David Lai, and Andrew Scobell, eds., *The PLA at Home and Abroad: Assessing the Operational Capabilities of China's Military,* Carlisle, PA: Strategic Studies Institute, U.S. Army War College, and National Bureau of Asian Research, July 2010, pp. 295-376.

30. 郭益科，曹海华和侯亚铭 (Guo Yike, Cao Haihua, and Hou Yaming), "远洋保障之路越走越宽广" ("The Further Down the Road to a Far Ocean Guarantee the Broader It Becomes"), 人民海军 (*Renmin Haijun*), July 22, 2009, p. 3.

31. Christopher D. Yung and Ross Rustici, *China's Out of Area Naval Operations: Case Studies, Trajectories, Obstacles, and Potential Solutions,* China Strategic Perspectives, Washington, DC: Institute for National Strategic Studies, No. 3, December 2010, p. 19.

32. *Ibid.*

33. *Ibid.*

34. Zhang Lili, "An Analysis of China's All-Out Efforts To Evacuate Chinese Nationals From Libya," *Dangdai Shijie,* April 5, 2011, p. 21-23, OSC CPP20110518671001.

35. *Ibid.*

36. *Ibid.*; Bo Xu, "A Record-Breaking Major Evacuation," *Shijie Zhishi,* April 1, 2011, OSC CPP20110609671003.

37. Zhang Lili, "An Analysis of China's All-Out Efforts To Evacuate Chinese Nationals From Libya," *Dangdai Shijie*, April 5, 2011, p. 21-23, OSC CPP20110518671001.

38. Bo Xu, "A Record-Breaking Major Evacuation."

39. Zhang Lili, "An Analysis of China's All-Out Efforts To Evacuate Chinese Nationals From Libya," *Dangdai Shijie*, April 5, 2011, p. 21-23, OSC CPP20110518671001.

40. *Ibid.*

41. *Ibid.*

42. *Ibid.*

43. For example, the same article published by an office affiliated with the Ministry of Foreign Affairs claimed that 26,240 people were evacuated on civilian airliners, while civilian ocean liners transported more than 18,000—already adding up to far more than the 35,000 evacuated overall, and not accounting for those evacuated over land or on PLA aircraft.

44. "中国海军维护我海外利益新航程" ("China's Navy's New Voyage Protecting China's Overseas Interests"), 当代海军 (*Modern Navy*), No. 4, 2011, pp. 10-11.

45. 谭结 (Tan Jie), "空军4架飞机抵利比亚接运我人员" ("4 Air Force Planes Reach Libya to Transport Personnel"), 解放军报 (*Jiefangjun Bao*), March 2, 2011.

46. "总参: 2010我军训练主抓一个试点三个演习" ("GS HQ: In 2010 PLA Training Concentrates on One Testing Point, Three Exercises"), 新华网 (*Xinhua Wang*), January 29, 2010; "军事报道" ("Military Report"), *CCTV-7*, October 22, 2010; "军事报道" ("Military Report"), *CCTV-7*, February 26, 2010; Video, "A Group Army of Jinan MR Group Army Explores New Mechanisms for Basic Campaign Corps," *CCTV-7*, October 29, 2010, OSC FEA20110124013666.

47. Video, "Lanzhou MR Holds First Combined Arms Battalion-Based Confrontation Exercise," *CCTV-7*, July 26, 2010,

OSC FEA20100916009357; Video: "A Mechanized Division of Shenyang MR Examines Combat Effectiveness of Combined Arms Battalions Through Day-Into-Night Training," *CCTV-7*, October 30, 2010, OSC FEA20110124013666; Video, "A Brigade of Jinan MR Explores New Models of Combined Arms Battalion Training," *CCTV-7*, August 28, 2010, OSC FEA20101101010898; Video, "A Division of Xinjiang MD Elevates Core Informatized Military Competences Through Live-Context Exercise," *CCTV-7*, November 8, 2010, OSC FEA20110225014874; Ma Sancheng, "Joint Operational Training Covering the Tactical Level—Lanzhou Military Region Organizes First Live Joint Tactical Army-Corps Firepower Strike Training Exercise," *Jiefangjun Bao*, November 2, 2010, p. 5, OSC CPP20101102787007.

48. Fan Yongqiang and Li Zhigang, "Lanzhou Military Region Holds *'Joint Logistics Mission 2011'* Live Exercise," *Xinhua*, April 28, 2011, OSC CPP20110428045009.

49. *Ibid.*

50. *Ibid.*

51. 齐为跃, 康志军和李斌富 (Qi Weiyue, Kang Zhijun, and Li Binfu), "找准撬动保障力跃升的支点" ("Identify and Leverage the Fulcrum for a Leap in Guarantee Capability"), 人民海军 (*Renmin Haijun*), February 14, 2011, p. 1.

52. "Four Great Transformations' Perspective on China's National Defense's 'Comprehensive Establishment of Modern Logistics'" ("四大变革透视中国国防' 全面建设现代后勤'"), 新华 (*Xinhua*), January 12, 2007, available from *news.xinhuanet.com/mil/2007-01/12/content_5596304.htm*.

53. *Ibid.*

54. *Ibid.*

55. 戴焕 (Dai Huan), "加强非战争军事后勤行动准备初探" ("Initial Exploration of Strengthening Non-War Military Logistics Operations Preparations"), 战士报 (*Zhanshi Bao*), April 24, 2008, p. 3.

333

56. *Ibid.*

57. 刘明学(Liu Mingxue), "我军现代军事物流体系建设发展迅速" ("PLA Modern Military Logistics System Construction Develops Rapidly"), 解放军报 (*Jiefangjun* Bao), September 18, 2009.

58. *Ibid.*

59. *Ibid.*

60. *Ibid.*

61. Fan Juwei and Zhang Jinyu, "Liao Xilong Sets a Requirement in His Speech at the All-Army Logistics-Related Work Conference: Promote Innovative Development in Comprehensive Construction of Modern Logistics from a New Starting Point," *Jiefangjun Bao*, November 19, 2010, OSC CPP20101119702008.

62. *Ibid.*

63. *Ibid.*

64. "军队后勤建设发展的根本遵循-学习胡锦涛关于军队后勤建设的重要论述" ("Fundamental Guidance for Development of PLA Logistics - Study Hu Jintao's Important Discussion of Military Logistics Construction"), 中国军事科学 (*China Military Science*), No. 6, 2010, pp. 25-31.

65. *Ibid.*

66. *Ibid.*

67. *Ibid.*

68. Peng Zhenhai and Fan Juwei, "The General Logistics Department Launched the 'Framework for the Overall Advancement of Comprehensively Building Modern Logistics Experimental Goals and Tasks'," *Jiefangjun Bao*, January 3, 2011, p. 1, OSC CPP20110103787006.

69. *Ibid.*

70. Henley, pp. 55-77.

71. Bo Xu, "A Record-Breaking Major Evacuation," *Shijie Zhishi*, April 1, 2011, OSC CPP20110609671003.

CHAPTER 9

THE AGONY OF LEARNING: THE PLA'S TRANSFORMATION IN MILITARY AFFAIRS

David Lai

EXECUTIVE SUMMARY

This chapter examines Chinese learning from other peoples' wars and military transformation and the impact of this learning on China's military thoughts, traditions, and the overall PLA institution.

MAIN ARGUMENT

For well over a century, the Chinese have been learning from the outside world to modernize China's military machine. However, due to their ideological and cultural barriers, the ability of the Chinese to learn from other peoples' wars and military transformation has been selective and tortuous. Chinese military modernization consequently is still on a winding and uncertain journey. In their latest efforts on this mission, the Chinese have adopted the U.S. military's integrated joint operations as a model for China's military transformation. This chapter finds that while the learning of this U.S. model and its implementation would help the Chinese military to improve its fighting capabilities, the impact of this learning on China's military thoughts and traditions is limited.

POLICY IMPLICATIONS

It is important for the United States to see the Chinese learning from other peoples' wars and military transformation and predicaments the Chinese have in their learning process. The United States should also prepare to meet the challenges from China and its military, who have gone through this agonizing learning process.

Due to its selective learning of the military "hardware" (the capabilities) but rejection of the "software" (the political, economic, and cultural underpinnings) from the U.S.-led West, China will improve its military's fighting capability but continue to set itself apart from the United States and other Western powers. A China with a more capable military that still does not share the fundamental values with the U.S.-led West is a great challenge in the future.

The ideological and cultural divide will continue to prevent China and the U.S.-led West from dealing with each other in good faith. Engagement with the Chinese military will continue to be difficult.

While the impact of Chinese learning from other peoples' wars and military transformation on China's military capability is significant, it is less so on China's military institution and the Chinese military traditions —namely, the Chinese way of war, about which U.S. leaders still have only limited understanding. It is imperative that the United States take measures to meet this challenge in the future.

INTRODUCTION

China test-sailed its first aircraft carrier on August 10, 2011. The maiden voyage was remarkably low key,[1] yet its significance is far reaching.

China's journey to this début started in the mid-1990s when it approached Ukraine for the possibility of acquiring the half-built but practically abandoned Soviet aircraft carrier *Varyag*. This warship had its keel laid in 1985 and was intended to be an addition to the Soviet Pacific Fleet. The collapse of the Soviet Union in 1991 brought the construction to an abrupt halt. Ukraine, home to the Soviet Union's warship industry, kept the unfinished carrier as a "divorce asset," though it had no intention or money to complete the project.

China eventually got the *Varyag* through a Hong Kong-based business tycoon, who purchased the hulk with a $20 million auction bid in 1998.[2] At the time, this sea monster was literally a rusty shell with all of the equipment forcefully removed, including the rudder.[3] China, however, was determined to bring it back to life.

In the 3 years following the acquisition of the *Varyag*, China went out of its way to negotiate with Turkey for the passage of this hulk from the Black Sea through the Bosporus, with China providing a bizarre insurance for the undertaking and additional lucrative economic incentives to Turkey.[4] In November 2001, the colossus was safely towed through the Istanbul Strait. It continued its nerve-racking journey through the Mediterranean Sea, the rough waters around Africa, the Indian Ocean, and the Southern Pacific, and finally settled in China's northern port city Dalian, next to the Chinese Naval Academy, the cradle of China's naval officers, in March 2002.

It took the Chinese another 10 years to refurbish this warship, with undisclosed additional expenses and tremendous efforts (acquiring the carrier's original blueprint and the main engine from Ukraine, for instance).

The test sail went without incident. Upon the aircraft carrier's return from a 5-day cruise in the Yellow Sea, Chinese Defense Ministry officials stated that "the initial testing objectives had been accomplished" (no details given) and that the *Varyag* would make similar test sails in the future. People's Liberation Army (PLA) commentators speculated that when the carrier becomes fully operational, it will be mostly commissioned to the PLA Navy (PLAN) as a training platform; this diesel- and steam-powered aircraft carrier, after all, has limited capacity for distant combat missions.[5]

Why did China acquire a weapon system that is expensive to build and operate, a war machine of the fading industrial age, and one that is increasingly vulnerable to increasingly advanced anti-ship weapons? What is China's real intent for becoming an aircraft carrier-faring great power? How does the development of aircraft carriers fit into China's national security strategy? Where does the acquisition of aircraft carriers stand in China's ongoing transformation in military affairs? Moreover, as the Chinese military learns extensively from the United States and other Western nations how to build and operate new capabilities and to transform the Chinese war machine in fundamental ways, what impact will this learning have on the Chinese military traditions? How do the Chinese manage these fundamental changes?

It appears that Chinese leaders have thought through these issues. Their decision to pursue carrier-led capabilities is testimony to one of their efforts to meet the challenges and reconcile the contradictions they have encountered in their journey to China's military modernization. This chapter, however, is not about China's acquisition of an aircraft carrier per se, but the use of this anecdote is to highlight the agonies and ecstasies in the Chinese learning from other peoples' wars and military transformation and their efforts to overcome the problems in transforming China's military machine.

A MISSING INSTRUMENT IN CHINA'S NATIONAL SECURITY STRATEGY?

It is understandably gratifying for China to become an aircraft carrier-faring nation. Although it is arguably the last contemporary great power to do so, China surely is delighted to become a member of the "aircraft carrier owner club" rather late than never.[6] Yet, China's real intent is completely practical. It is about augmenting the PLAN's fighting capacity in the Western Pacific and beyond.[7]

Thirty years ago, China made two significant adjustments in its national defense strategy. One was to abandon the concept of "luring the enemy deep into China" ("诱敌深入") within its active defense strategy (积极防御战略).[8] The other was to extend China's coastal defense from a 12-nm (nautical mile) territorial water defense (近岸防御) to a "near sea defense" ("近海防御") strategy.[9] These adjustments ostensibly suggested that China would no longer allow invasion of its homeland, a goal sought by generations of Chinese since China fell victim to foreign invasion in the mid-19th century, and that the Chinese military should be able to "keep any enemy off China's doorstep" ("拒敌于国门外").[10]

Although China has never officially specified the scope of this strategy, *it is increasingly clear that "near sea defense" includes China's territorial waters as well as its claimed 200-nm Exclusive Economic Zones (EEZs) around the nation's extended seashores.*[11] At issue is that China

341

has many disputes in this vast maritime frontier, the most challenging of which is China's avowed mission to reunite with Taiwan—an undertaking that could erupt into large-scale armed conflict should its peaceful efforts fail, and would involve armed conflict with the United States because of the latter's commitment to oppose any forceful attempt to change the status of Taiwan.

In recent decades, China has also had intense conflict with the United States over U.S. military activities in the Chinese-claimed exclusive economic zones (EEZs) and other conflicts of interest in the Western Pacific. China's territorial disputes with Japan in the East China Sea and with several Southeast Asian nations in the South China Sea have drawn much international attention as well.[12]

The Chinese have long held that they could not keep enemies off China's maritime frontier and settle disputes in their favor largely because they did not have an aircraft carrier-led blue-water navy. Therefore, acquiring this capability, to borrow a popular Chinese expression, is to fill in this blank (填补这项空白).[13]

Moreover, in the last 30 years, as a result of its phenomenal economic growth, China's interests have greatly expanded. Its reach is now global. At the same time, China has also become increasingly reliant on global sea lanes for its supply of resources and commercial trading. The need for protecting these growing interests has expanded accordingly. A few years ago, Chinese President Hu Jintao put forward a new mission for China's military in the new century: the PLA is to protect China's interests wherever they go.[14] With the change of time and circumstances, China's demand for an aircraft carrier battle group-capability has become stronger and more urgent.

A NECESSARY STEP IN CHINA'S MILITARY MODERNIZATION?

China set its military modernization in motion in the mid-1990s, ahead of its prescribed schedule and out of great urgency.[15] The most-telling reason for the change was the Taiwan Strait Crisis of 1995-96, because of which China felt a desperate need to acquire credible capabilities for the PLA to prevent Taiwan from seeking formal independence and to deal with an almost-assured U.S. military intervention. The two U.S. aircraft carrier battle groups dispatched by the Bill Clinton administration to the troubled waters during the crisis were perceived by the Chinese as quite insulting.[16]

The other impetus for change stemmed from the challenges presented by the U.S.-led Revolution in Military Affairs (RMA) in the evolving information age. The display of U.S. military power in the Gulf War of 1991, the Kosovo air campaign of 1999, and the anti-terrorist operations in Afghanistan and Iraq in the early-2000s shocked the Chinese leaders. They saw that China must take urgent measures or be marginalized in military affairs for good.

China's answer to these challenges took a two-pronged approach. On the one hand, China accelerated the improvement of its military's so-called industrial-age fighting capabilities—namely, war planes, battleships, missiles, and mechanized land power capabilities,[17] which, among other things, allowed China to establish a creditable deterrence against pro-Taiwan independence drives. On the other hand, the Chinese military simultaneously learned to develop capabilities of the unfolding information age. China took these two approaches as complementary efforts: advances in the latter would accelerate the development of the former; and, at the end of the day, military hard power would still be the decisive factor in war. Therefore, modernizing its industrial-age military capability was a necessary step in China's military modernization.

Nevertheless, the acquisition of aircraft carrier battle groups is still a controversial issue. It is clear now that the proponents of aircraft carriers prevailed in China's debate.[18] Chinese leaders are apparently convinced that although aircraft carriers are products of the fading industrial age, they have not lost their usefulness and are still a powerful battle platform, most likely to remain so throughout the 21st century and beyond. Indeed, Chinese analysts have noted that the United States is still building nuclear-powered aircraft carriers and expecting them to serve beyond the end of the century.[19] Moreover, the United Kingdom, France, Russia, India, Japan, and other great powers are also building aircraft carriers. Against this backdrop, there is no reason that China should forego this option.[20] The purchase and refurbishing of the *Varyag*, therefore, are China's timely investments. They give China an opportunity to learn about the construction as well as the operation of aircraft carriers. Many also see that aircraft carrier building reflects a nation's core industrial capability. It is a drive engine that can lead the development of many other related industries. Its spillover effect can be extensive. This undertaking thus fits nicely in China's modernization mission.

In the next 15 years, unless China finds its efforts totally fruitless, which is highly unlikely, we can expect China to build several aircraft carriers of its own. There is no reason to dismiss the possibility that China could build nuclear-powered warships as well. This missing instrument of China's national security strategy will come in time to help China pursue its expanding interests in the Western Pacific and beyond.[21]

ANOTHER FAILURE IN CHINA'S QUEST FOR MILITARY MODERNIZATION?

China has failed several times in its quest for military modernization in the past 150 years.

China's First Attempt at Military Modernization.

China's first attempt at modernizing its military took place in the aftermath of China's humiliating defeat by the European colonial powers in the mid-19th century. Faced with challenges and strong enemies "not seen in thousands of years of Chinese history" (in the words of Li Hongzhang (李鸿章), a prominent statesman of the late Qing Dynasty),[22] China launched a reform mission known as the "*Yang-wu* Movement" ("洋务运动"). The thrust of this movement was to open up China to the outside world and learn from the European powers in order to modernize the nation. At the top of the reform agenda was the call to restore China's greatness and develop a formidable defense force to safeguard the Middle Kingdom. To Chinese disappointment, however, several fatal problems condemned this reform to failure from its beginning in the mid-1870s to its end 30 years later.

The first of these problems was the absence of central government initiative and support. When the European powers forced their way into China, the Qing Dynasty was corrupt and in the midst of China's cyclical dynastic decline. In the face of external invasion and internal turmoil, the Qing rulers did not take measures to save the nation, but rather continued to indulge in their corruption. Even worse, they did many things to undermine the reform efforts (diverting defense spending funds to build their lavish vacation retreats is a case in point).

The second problem was the incorrect decision the *Yang-wu* reformers (those reform-minded high officials of the Qing government and government-sponsored scholars) made regarding reform in general and the development of China's military power in particular. This decision was based on an erroneous judgment regarding the European powers and a misguided assessment of Chinese capacity. The *Yang-wu* reformers believed that the European intruders were merely superior in their fighting capabilities, in terms of their warships, firearms, and better-trained soldiers, but still inferior culturally and politically to Chinese civilization.[23] China, according to them, should preserve its traditions as fundamentals and use Western imports for practical use; hence went the infamous call for "中学为体, 西学为用" ("Chinese learning for substance; Western learning for utility").[24]

Moreover, they argued that China should learn and acquire advanced capabilities and skills from the West and use them to check the West—it was "师夷长技以制夷."[25] These misguided views ensured that China's learning from the Europeans was haphazard at best and distorted at worst.[26]

The third problem follows from the first two. As a result of central government corruption and misguided learning from the West, there was no genuine economic, political, and cultural development in China. The outmoded government and defunct military organizations did not go through transformations.

346

Although China purchased many advanced weapons from the West, Chinese officials did not make an effort to train the soldiers. Of note is the fact that the *Yang-wu* officials furnished four sizable modern fleets by the late-1880s, totaling 80 advanced warships, ranking sixth in the world and first in Asia in terms of size.[27] To China's misfortune, these poorly managed imports were soon to have their flaws exposed in a war, though ironically not against the Western powers, but rather a fellow developing Asian nation, Japan. China suffered a catastrophic defeat. Among the heavy losses on land and at sea, its entire elite North Sea Fleet (北洋 舰队) had vanished. It is worth mentioning that Japan embarked on its modernization mission under very similar external and internal circumstances to those of China, and generally within the same time span. But Japan's Meiji Emperor was instrumental in the reform. Japan whole-heartedly embraced Western technology as well as the economic, political, and cultural fundamentals. Japanese reformers transformed Japan's government and its military. Moreover, they trained their soldiers and mobilized the nation to strive for the rise of Japan as a great power.

China's Second Attempt at Military Modernization.

Following the fall of the Qing Dynasty in 1911 and in the early decades of the new Republic of China (ROC), the Chinese government resumed the quest for China's military modernization. It first turned to Germany, but then quickly switched to Japan for answers to China's ambitions. Unfortunately, the wars between the government of the Republic of China and the Chinese Communist forces and later against the Japanese rendered learning and development impossible. At the end of World War II, the ROC government turned to the United States for assistance. However, it was soon engulfed again in the fight against the Communists for the fate of China. The attempt at China's military modernization did not even get off the ground.

China's Third Attempt at Military Modernization.

Following its victory over the ROC government in 1949 and a war against the United States in Korea from 1950 to 1953, the Chinese Communist Party (CCP) under the leadership of Mao Zedong attempted for the third time to modernize China's military. This time, the Chinese turned completely to the Soviet model. In 10 years, China literally "carbon-copied" the Soviet political, economic, and military systems (全盘苏化) and had large numbers of Soviet advisors in China to help with the transformation. The Soviet transplant to China, however, was not an innovative or viable system. Worse off, China had to cut short the transformation when the two "communist comrades" became enemies in the late 1950s. The Soviets withdrew all their support and advisors from China following the split. The Chinese had no alternative but to rely on themselves to continue the ill-advised military transformation. To China's credit, it still managed to develop a nuclear arsenal, a missile and space program, and a colossal Soviet-style military industry. But to China's misfortune, Chairman Mao soon put all of these developments in jeopardy through his ruinous "Great Cultural Revolution" from 1966 to 1976. By the time he passed away (in 1976), Mao left behind a nation with a dysfunctional economy, an oversized population exhausted by repeated political movements, and a military with no credible fighting power. China's military modernization was as remote as ever.

China's Fourth Attempt at Military Modernization.

In 1978, 100 years after the disastrous *Yang-wu* movement, China tried again to reform and modernize the nation. Unfortunately, the new Chinese reformers were no better than their *Yang-wu* predecessors. They continued to reject Western political institutions and used the ploy of "Chinese learning as fundamentals and Western import for practical use" ("中学为体, 西学为用") as a cover to preserve their authoritarian rule in China. Indeed, the modernization mission included only four areas: industrial, agricultural, science and technology, and national defense modernizations. Chinese leaders refused to face squarely the need for the so-called "5th Modernization"—namely, political system transformation in China. Their refusal to embrace Western political institutions has made China's reform tortuous.[28] In the midst of their winding journey to modernity, Chinese leaders launched China's fourth attempt on military modernization (in the mid-1990s). The ideological barriers just mentioned are making this mission meandering as well. In the meantime, Chinese leaders have once again found themselves in a situation that their forbearers faced more than a century ago: they have to learn from their enemies to improve China's military machine. Can China succeed this time? Now that China is following the footsteps of the United States to develop aircraft carrier battle groups, will China's gamble end in another failure in its quest for military modernization?

349

A TRANSFORMATION IN MILITARY AFFAIRS WITH CHINESE CHARACTERISTICS?

The Chinese learned about RMA mostly from the United States. (Though the Soviets were the first to advocate the cause and coin the term, the Americans were the ones who put RMA in action and the United States is undisputedly the leader in RMA). The Chinese, however, prefer to call their undertaking "transformation in military affairs" or "military transformation" ("军事变革"). They hold that while the U.S.-led efforts have brought revolutionary changes to the business of war, the Chinese act is only an adaptation to those changes.

Chinese leaders nevertheless are well aware of the roadblocks and pitfalls in their military transformation. To deal with the challenges, Chinese leaders employ the "tricks" they have used in their economic reform—to "cross the river by reaching the rocks" ("摸着石头过河")—that is, to muddle through one problem at a time, and keep China's military transformation in line with Chinese characteristics. That is a code word for the gambit of learning selectively from the U.S.-led West and avoiding the changes that can undermine the CCP's control of the military and China's military tradition (more on this in the latter part of this chapter).

Sun Kejia (孙科佳), a professor at China's National Defense University, provides perhaps the best "deciphering" of this peculiar undertaking.[29] Several key factors, as Sun argues, make China's military transformation special. First, China and the U.S.-led West are essentially different nations with qualitatively different agendas on international relations. Their military transformations therefore have different strategic objectives. The United States and the West want to continue their domination of the international system. Their military transformation aims to ensure that they have the military power to support their political objective. The U.S.-led military transformation reflects the basic needs of imperialism. China, however, is a socialist country. It has no hegemonic design. Its military transformation reflects only its need to protect China in a hostile environment. These differences are essential.

Second, the U.S.-led military transformation builds on the lessons learned from America's past war experiences (the Vietnam War, for instance) and is designed to avoid similar mistakes in its future military actions. China has no such burden to bear. Its military transformation is merely an attempt to keep pace with the changes and a response to the threats posed by the Western powers.

Third, the U.S.-led military transformation builds on a well-developed military machine. It follows new breakthroughs in science and technology to produce new weaponry, introduce new war theory, conduct new forms of military training and education, and eventually bring about the revolutionary changes in military affairs. China, however, does not have the material and technological conditions to do those things. Chinese leaders learned about the RMA late. They set China's military transformation as a national goal to try to catch up in all aspects.

Fourth, the military transformations of the U.S.-led West and China operate in different ways. The former assumes a leading position, operates in a gradual manner, and has an "exploratory" character. The latter, however, starts late, and operates in an exceptional manner with leap-forward moves. The U.S.

351

military made its transition to an information-centric force on the basis of its highly mechanized capabilities. China, however, started its transformation when its military was only halfway into mechanization. Yet China cannot wait until it completes the development of its industrial-age capabilities to engage in the information-age military transformations. It must do both at the same time and make leap-forward moves when necessary.

Finally, the U.S.-led West and China launched their military transformations under very different economic conditions. The West made its transformation on the basis of a well-developed economy and social environment. China, however, undertook its changes while its economic reform and development were still at their early stages. China had to make economic and military transformations at the same time. The challenges are monumental.[30]

Professor Sun, however, argues that China has a good chance to achieve its goals for four main reasons. First, the transformation is moving in the right direction. In 1993, Chinese leaders made a strategic switch from "preparing to deal with local wars under normal conditions" ("应付一般条件下的局部战争"), to "preparing to fight and win local wars under high tech conditions" ("打赢高技术条件下的局部战争"). This watershed adjustment allowed the Chinese military to march into the age of information-centric warfare.

Second, China has made a timely decision to promote the "two fundamental changes" ("两个根本性转变") in the military: the PLA is to change from a manpower-centric force to a science and technology-intensive, and quality and effect-based organization (科技密集型和质量效能型的军队).[31] These changes prepare the PLA to meet the requirements of information-centric warfare. They will ultimately lead to the transformation of the PLA's force structure and overall organization (more on this point later in the chapter). Third, the transformation is in concert with China's overall modernization timetable. China has made a long-range plan for its military transformation. It is a three-step schedule stretching well into the middle of the 21st century: first, lay a solid foundation for the transformation by 2010; second, complete the mechanization of all the armed services and make substantive progress on the infrastructure for information-centric warfare by 2020 (the two-pronged change discussed earlier); and third, reach the goal of national defense and military modernization by 2050.[32]

Finally, China has picked the right path for the transformation. It is to pursue the completion of mechanization of the PLA and simultaneously develop information-centric capabilities. Western military powers naturally went through the path from semi-mechanization to mechanization and now informationization. As the CCP put it in its 16th Party Convention Platform, China has to accomplish the two tasks of mechanization and informationization (again, the two-pronged approach discussed earlier; the purchase of *Varyag* is part of this undertaking) at the same time and achieve "leap-forward development" ("跨越式发展"). Nevertheless, Chinese leaders are confident that these goals are within their reach.[33] With continued economic reform and development, advances in science and technology, and maturation in industrial production, China will have little problem furnishing better weapons systems for the PLA and will have bountiful funding and resources to support this mission.

While pointing out the key characteristics of the Chinese military transformation, Professor Sun also cautions that Chinese leaders must free themselves from some long-held dogmatic views (僵化教条) so that they can carry out China's military transformation. Military transformation, as Sun contends, starts first and foremost with the change of views on the fundamentals in military affairs. Material change in armaments and organizations is secondary. History has shown repeatedly that the ones with backward weaponry suffer from defeats, but the ones with advanced weaponry, yet operate on backward concepts, can still get beaten badly. For China, a break from the following outmoded thinking is essential:

- Dogmatic adherence to Marxist military theory (马克思主义军事理论的僵化教条);
- Conception of warfighting under industrial-age conditions (工业时代战争背景下的观念, 如陆战第一 [land power first, for example]);
- Way of thinking under planned-economy conditions (计划经济体制条件下的思维方式);
- Parochial organizational interest and stove piping (狭隘权力和利益观念);
- Lack of initiative for innovation (因循守旧, 不思变革);
- Self-indulgence of China as "the great power of strategy and stratagem" ("谋略大国 的自我欣赏");
- Historical burden of the PLA as a "triumphal force"("胜利之师 的历史包袱");
- The urge to make a leap forward (急于求成) in military transformation.[34]

INTEGRATED JOINT OPERATIONS:
ONE MODEL FITTING ALL?

Professor Sun certainly deserves praise for his call for the "emancipation of the mind" ("解放思想观念"). Yet, old habits die hard, and the CCP's ideological requirements are formidable obstacles. China's long-called-for reform of the military system (军事体制), which is widely considered to be the starting point of China's military transformation, has been put off repeatedly.

The current Chinese military organization is a legacy of the Chinese learning from the Soviets and Mao's misuse of the PLA as an instrument for the control of the Chinese government and people (the so-called "military rule" ["军管"] during the Cultural Revolution). The current seven Military Regions (MRs) are in essence political strongholds. The central military organization and its extended provincial military garrisons (中央军事组织和地方省军区) are political bureaucracies, but not combat organizations for the conduct of military operations against foreign enemies. If the PLA is to become an effective fighting force, it must abolish or transform this system. However, such a change touches upon two sensitive nerves of the Chinese leaders. One is the ideological requirement the CCP imposes on the military. The other is about the vested interests (corruption, in plain language) of the senior political and military officials.[35] This problem is similar to the tortuous experience China has had with its reluctant political change in other branches of the Chinese government over the past 30 years. Indeed, the CCP has continuously waged ideological battles to keep the PLA in check; it can get new and better weapons, but it cannot turn itself into a "nationalized service" ("国家化军队") like those in the United States and the West.[36] Thus, as long as China's overall political system reform (政治体制改革) continues on its winding path, the PLA's call for organizational reform (军事体制改革) is likely to remain in word, only.

However, the modernization drive, once set in motion, cannot be stopped. In its effort to move forward, the PLA has propitiously found a roundabout way to make systematic reform without stepping on the political landmines. The vehicle for change is the U.S. model of integrated joint operations (IJO).

In their study of U.S. military transformation and its conduct of war, the Chinese were quick to grasp the "changing face of war." As former PLA General and Vice Chief of Staff Xiong Guangkai (熊光楷) put it in a presentation to Chinese military and civilian leaders, there are five key features of war in the information age. They are:

- Artificial intelligence for weapon systems (武器装备智能化), such as precision-guided munitions;
- Streamlining of armed forces and military organization (编制体制精干化);
- Computerization of command and control (指挥控制自动化);
- A multidimensional battle space that expands from the traditional land, sea, and air to include outer space and magnetic space (作战空间多维化); and,
- Integration of combat systems (作战样式体系化).[37]

While studying the new features of war, Chinese military analysts also pay close attention to the way the U.S. military prepares and conducts wars in the new age. They see that the first four features in General Xiong's presentation are about the revolutionary changes in weapons systems and battlegrounds that are a direct result of the ongoing technological innovations since the late-1970s and early-1980s. The last feature is about the nature of war in the information age: it is no longer isolated military confrontation on land, at sea, or in the air, but contests between systems involving all elements of national power and in all dimensions and spectrums simultaneously. The U.S. military has made a timely transformation to fight wars under these new conditions. It has become an "integrated joint force," and its military actions are called "integrated joint operations."

It did not take the Chinese long to reach the consensus that IJO is the U.S. answer to wars in the information age and that it should be the model for China to follow as well.[38] PLA Lieutenant General Liu Jixian (刘继贤) goes so far as to assert that the model of combat in the information age can only be integrated joint operations, which are combat operations employing all necessary forces, seamlessly connected by systems of information networks, focusing on an integrated goal, and taking place in a multidimensional battlefield involving land, sea, air, outer space, and the magnetic and electronic spaces. General Liu also points out that the U.S. military has more than 30 years of experience in developing and practicing IJO; thus, China can learn from the United States' experience and avoid many mistakes.[39]

Another noted analyst of IJO, PLA Major General He Lei (何雷), has stated that combat operations in the information age are a contest between systems of national power (系统对系统). No one military service

357

can single-handedly control the course of war; there will be no future combat without the use of joint operations (无战不联), and if a military cannot conduct joint operations, it will not be able to win in combat (无联不胜).[40]

The highest endorsement of IJO comes from the CCP central leadership. At both the CCP's 16th and 17th Party Conventions, President Hu Jintao put these calls in his reports. China's *National Defense White Papers* of 2008 and 2010 have also stated that IJO is the model for the PLA's transformation.

Moreover, while PLA analysts have gained a good understanding of the new conditions in war and the model of IJO, they also understand that IJO covers more than combat operations in war; it is a "system of systems" ("系统的系统") that requires:

- An integrated understanding of IJO (思想观念 一体化) by the officers so that they can conduct IJO on the same principles and rules;
- Integrated services and fighting power (作战 力量一体化) so as to avoid interservice conflict (军种之间内斗和作战力量不集中);
- Integrated command systems (指挥机构一体 化);
- Integrated information systems (信息系统一体 化);
- Integrated weapon systems (武器装备一体化);
- Integrated logistics systems (后勤保障一体化);
- Integrated quality for officers and soldiers (人员素质一体化); and,
- Integrated education and training (教育训练一 体化).[41]

In short, everything in the war business goes the integrated way.

LEARNING BY DOING: THE PLA'S IMPLEMENTATION OF IJO

The PLA's embrace of IJO has become a driving force for changes in all of the related areas. The aircraft carrier is a perfect example. It requires an integrated operation of naval, air, space, intelligence and reconnaissance, logistics, and many other services. It is an excellent platform for the PLA to learn about IJO.

IJO takes place mostly at the operational level. Most of the changes involve only junior officers. The vested political and economic interests are presumably less developed at this level, thus making it easier for the Chinese leaders to embrace this model and make organizational changes. The following are a few of the landmark changes in recent years.

- On January 10, 2006, the first all-service integrated logistics interactive supply and protection system was inaugurated in the Beijing War Zone (北京战区). This indicates that the Beijing War Zone has achieved initial success in information exchange, resource sharing and interservice interaction (首个三军联勤保障互动平台在北京战区正式启动, 这标记着北京战区联勤保障初步实现了信息互通, 资源互用, 优势互补, 三军互动).[42]
- On February 15, 2007, the Chinese Central Military Commission (CMC) approved the implementation plan for the Jinan War Zone to have integrated logistics system reform (济南战区正式实行三军大联勤体制).[43]
- During the 11th Five-Year Plan, the PLA tried reforming military logistics. On June 21, 2010, a meeting of several departments took place in

Beijing.[44] The Chinese government also passed multiple military transportation regulations (交通沿线军交运输现代化建设规定) and (交通战备现代化建设工作规定).[45]

- In November 2001, the CMC set the reform of the PLA procurement system in motion by approving a pilot plan (试点计划). In 2005, the CMC finalized the reform by authorizing a regulation on military logistics purchases (军队后勤采购规定).[46]

- The China *National Defense White Paper* of 2010 states that China has established a "civil-military integrated military equipment (weapon and supply) study and production system" ("完善军民结合寓军于民的装备科研和生产体系").[47]

- In June 2006, at a PLA conference on military training, President Hu Jintao urged the PLA to practice integrated joint operations. This was a turning point in PLA military exercises.[48] The major exercises are listed in the table in the Appendix. (Note: There are numerous regional and smaller-scale military exercises that are not listed there.)

- While the PLA is learning by "doing" the current changes, Chinese leaders are also making efforts to transform China's armed forces in the long run. In April 2011, Chinese President Hu Jintao signed the new guidelines for developing PLA command officers.[49] The guidelines emphasize the development of officers capable of commanding integrated joint operations, managers capable of integrated information management, engineers capable of developing new technology, and operators capable of conducting new equipment (联合作战指挥人才, 信息化建设管理人才, 信息技术专业人才, 新装备操作和维护人才). As PLA analysts put it, integrated joint operation is a form of war; its historical position in war is unshakable; and to a great extent, integrated joint operations have become the criterion for a strong military power.[50]

In addition to its learning from the U.S. military, the Chinese military also pays close attention to changes taking place in other great powers' militaries. Chinese military analysts have noted that Russia has eliminated the service head posts. In their place, the Russians have created unified war zones. Chinese military analysts have also noticed that the Germans have also abolished the services. In their place, the Germans use special operation units to carry out policy objectives in integrated joint operations.

China finds the war zones (战区) especially useful for the PLA's transformation. While a Goldwater-Nichols-like legislation is difficult to come by in China, the creation of those war zones offers the Chinese another roundabout way to promote IJO and transform the PLA's organization without stepping on political and ideological landmines. By the time these new generations of well-educated and well-trained technocrats come into the services, the old generation will be long gone, and the PLA will be changed for good.

WHAT ABOUT THE CHINESE WAY OF WAR?

Since the Chinese military is learning about the U.S.-led integrated joint operations and transforming the "Chinese war machine" the U.S. way, will it then conduct wars as the U.S. military does? Along the same line, when the Chinese put their aircraft carriers in operation, will they use them as the Americans do? Or to put it a different way, will learning and practicing the U.S.-created IJO render the PLA's traditions and the Chinese way of war obsolete?

The answer is "no." The transformation of military affairs in China and the Chinese military's learning and practicing of IJO only informs us that the PLA will become a joint force and be able to apply its fighting power in integrated ways on the battleground. We also know that the PLA will have many more advanced capabilities from a more robust weapons production and supply system and logistics support, all of which will be nested in an integrated system.

However, this transformation does not change the Chinese views on the nature of war, their justification for the use of force, or the conduct of war. PLA analysts argue that the transformation in military affairs and changing war conditions in the information age are giving the Chinese way of war a new lease on life. They believe that with the modernization of China's military forces, they can bring the Chinese way of war to a new level.

What is the Chinese way of war, anyway?[51] It is one with the following characteristics. First, the Chinese way of war has three identifiable sources: 1) classical Chinese political and military thought; 2) 2,000 years of Chinese strategic culture (权谋文化); and, 3) Mao Zedong's military experience and writings. Chinese leaders constantly tap into these three sources for answers to their national security problems.

Second, the Chinese way of war maintains "Mao's view on the nature of war," namely a Marxist-Leninist assertion that war is an offspring of private ownership of property — in other words, capitalism is the evil origin of war. The Chinese used to have a mixed view on the nature of war from observations made in classical times. Sun Zi (孙子), Lao Zi (老子), Wu Zi (吴子) and Xun Zi (荀子), for instance, took war as the natural state of affairs. Confucius (孔子) and Mencius (孟子), however, believed that peace is the rule and wars are aberrations. These observations all became irrelevant when Mao introduced the Marxist view to China.

A key aspect of the Marxist view is that if human societies are to eliminate war, they must put an end to capitalism. During the heyday of the communist movement, the Soviet Union, China, and other communist states advocated in various ways to pursue this course of action. Although China today has no intention to continue the communist mission of ridding mankind of war by "wiping out capitalism" ("消灭资本主义"), the Chinese nevertheless continue to view the main reason for war in the Marxist way. They have always held that U.S. hegemony is the continuation of capitalism at its highest stage and is the main source of contemporary international conflict.

Third, the Chinese way of war follows a Confucius tradition to justify the use of force. It is a ruler's means to maintain and restore order, both internally and externally. Internally, Chinese governments, central as well as provincial, have used force to preserve or restore order from time to time. Externally, the Chinese also waged wars against their neighbors to restore the "Chinese order." China's periodic expeditions against its neighbors in ancient times are cases in point. Teaching Vietnam a lesson in 1979 is a more contemporary example. This China-centric and authoritarian rule-based justification for the use of force is a point of concern for other nations, for China looks at its territorial disputes—most notably those in the East and South China Seas—as disorders created by China's neighbors "stealing" China's territories when the Middle Kingdom was undergoing dynastic decline and internal fragmentation (civil wars, for instance). It is therefore justifiable from the Chinese perspective for China to use force to "recover those stolen properties."[52]

In addition to the Confucian influence, Chinese leaders also follow Mao's teaching to "define" wars on ideological grounds.[53] Mao argues that all revolutionary and "People's Wars" are just wars. But these assertions suffer from definitional problems and ideological bias. What is "revolution"? Who are the "people"? Mao's "theories" provide no answer. Chinese leaders, nevertheless, follow Mao blindly to justify the use of force in Mao's way. Moreover, since the United States is a capitalist nation, any war it wages will be unjust. This ideological judgment is routinely taken as a given by the Chinese leaders. The Chinese also hold the fallacious view that since China is not a capitalist state and has people everywhere, China is always on the just side when it comes to waging war. This is a dangerous proposition.

Fourth, the Chinese way of war has a tradition of "post-emption" ("后发制人"); that is, to prevail in war with calculated reactive and deferred moves. This is a tradition that goes all the way back to Sun Zi's *Art of War*. Of note is that China's *National Defense White Papers* of 2008 and 2010 have made this an official stand for China in dealing with foreign enemies.[54]

However, one should see that China's post-emption principle applies only to strategic-level moves; that is, whether to take action in wars. The Chinese are in essence saying that China will not be the one to initiate wars against other nations. Yet, once the war threshold is crossed, the Chinese will do whatever it takes to win, including preemptive strikes. Mao's experience and teaching are full of examples of making surprise and preemptive strikes, using overwhelming force against isolated enemy forces, deceptions, and many other tactics at the operational level.[55]

Finally, the Chinese way of war closely follows Sun Zi's teaching to pursue the pinnacle of war—subjugating the enemy without the use of force (不战而屈人之兵). To approach this ideal state of war, Sun Zi prescribes that the first step in war is to attack the enemy's strategy (上兵伐谋) and then to derail the enemy's alliances (次伐交). If these first two efforts are successful, one can destroy the enemy's fighting will, and one may not have to fight to win. Under these circumstances, charging the troops into the battlefields (伐兵) is only to consolidate the victory. From Sun Zi's perspective, the worst thing to do in war is to attack the opponent's strongholds and slaughter the opponent's people (攻城).

In addition, Sun Zi advocates the use of deception—war is a matter of deception (兵以诈立) and emphasizes intelligence and calculation—know yourselves and your enemy, and you will prevail in war (知彼知己百战不殆). The hallmarks of the Chinese way of war are the extensive use of strategy, stratagems, and deception.

Chinese military analysts argue that changes in technology, weaponry, and military organizations have not affected the Chinese way of war. On the contrary, they allow for a more meaningful use of Sun Zi's art of war. Indeed, strategic targeting under the new conditions is no longer the destruction of the enemy's territory or complete annihilation. The emergence of high-tech weaponry allows a nation to achieve war goals without the use of mass-killing force. With air-power and long-range precision strike capability, one can surgically strike targets deep in the enemy's territory and implement "noncontact and indirect attack" ("脱离接触间接打击").[56]

WHAT ABOUT THE PEOPLE'S WAR DOCTRINE?

Perhaps, the one Chinese tradition that gets most hard hit is the People's War doctrine. A group of researchers at the PLA National Defense University led by Li Menghe (李梦鹤) have noted that the People's War doctrine has met with an unprecedented challenge in four ways: 1) war under high-tech conditions makes the employment of untrained people difficult; 2) the short duration of war also makes the mobilization of people difficult; 3) due to changes in war, traditional trench warfare, attrition, and other people's wars have become increasingly irrelevant; and, 4) with advanced information technology, battlegrounds have become crystal clear, making it more and more difficult for ordinary people to make an impact.[57] In addition, past wars were fought in China. It made good sense to mobilize the people to fight against the enemy. However, future wars are likely to be away from China's homeland, along its maritime frontiers or on other nations' soil. It is difficult to conduct People's War in these faraway areas.

Chinese leaders and analysts are aware of these problems. They have made calls to find ways to uphold the People's War principle and find ways to continue this so-called "magic weapon" ("克敌制胜的法宝") of the Chinese Communist Party and military. Deng Xiaoping (邓小平), for instance, stressed that Chinese leaders must adhere to Mao's thoughts, study

People's War under modern conditions, and develop Chinese military science (要继承毛泽东思想, 研究现代条件下的人民战争, 发展我国的军事科学).[58] Former Chinese President Jiang Zemin (江泽民) also stresses that no matter how much weaponry and forms of war have changed, People's War is the key to defeating enemies (无论武器装备如何发展, 战争形态如何变化, 人民战争都是我们克敌制胜的法宝).[59] Current Chinese President Hu Jintao has also emphasized the importance of the People's War doctrine time and again. With heavy pressure from above, Chinese may eventually find ways to make the People's War doctrine relevant to the military conflicts under high-tech and information conditions.

MIRROR, MIRROR ON THE WALL ...

There is an old saying that a nation develops its military and acquires arms to prepare for the war it anticipates. How does this apply to China? It fits perfectly with Chinese military modernization.

China is not modernizing its military to make it look better. It is not developing aircraft carriers to build ocean amusement parks. China pursues military modernization to safeguard its homeland, to support its quest for national unity (read as unification with Taiwan) and territorial integrity (read as "recovering the stolen territories" in the East and South China Seas).

In its pursuit of these interests, China has to prepare to deal with the U.S. military, for the United States is involved in every aspect of China's so-called "core interests," some of which have the potential risk of drawing China and the United States into armed conflict. China's military modernization is designed to meet these challenges.

Complicating the specific conflicts between China and the United States in the Western Pacific is a power-transition process taking place at a more fundamental level between the two great powers. This is a contest for the future of international relations. Both the United States and, increasingly, China take military power as a key component of their national strategy.

Ironically, the Chinese military has no alternative but to learn from the U.S. military how to improve its fighting power. In fairness, the Chinese military has seized the opportunity to learn from the world's most powerful military and kept up with the changes in military affairs. China's investments in weaponry improvement and efforts at organizational transformation (i.e., integrated joint operations construction) are on the right track.

However, China's learning from the United States is about hard power and factors at the operational level. China continues to reject the political aspects of U.S./Western military affairs and to preserve Chinese traditions as fundamentals, only taking Western imports for practical use according to the aforementioned centuries-old fallacious doctrine of "中学为体, 西学为用." Moreover, China also continues to follow Mao's teaching to view the nature of war, the justification for the use of force, and the conduct of war in ideological terms. These efforts unavoidably put China in a perpetual state of antagonism with the United States and the West. Although China has repeatedly asked the United States to abandon its so-called Cold War thinking on China, Chinese leaders themselves are unable to get out of their self-imposed ideological trenches. The result is that China perceives everything the United States does in international affairs as a U.S. imperialist and hegemonic undertaking, and therefore as something unjust that must be opposed. Although China can cooperate with the United States when the two countries' national interests coincide, this ideological divide will ensure that the cooperation will be simply a matter of convenience.

The key elements of the Chinese way of war have largely remained intact in the midst of the transformation in military affairs in China. The Chinese way of war places a strong emphasis on the use of strategy, stratagems, and deception. However, the Chinese understand that their approach will not be effective without the backing of hard military power. China's grand strategy is to take the next 30 years to complete China's modernization mission, which is expected to turn China into a true great power by that time. One can expect that with the integration of its strategic tradition and its increasingly sophisticated hard comprehensive national power, China will become a much more formidable global power by the middle of the 21st century.

ENDNOTES - CHAPTER 9

1. The primary reason for this low-key undertaking is China's attempt to avoid another round of China threat outcry in the Asia-Pacific region and beyond. The Chinese government reportedly was to have instructed the PLA and other institutions to keep the reports and discussion of the aircraft carrier to the minimum. See Li Guang (黎广) and Sun Lei (孙磊), "中国航母低调前行" ("Chinese Aircraft Carrier Took a Low-key Move Forward"), 新闻天地 (*Newsdom*), No. 9, 2011; and Liu Yan (刘妍) and Yang Fan (杨帆), "从航母试验的舆论引导谈起" ("Thoughts on the Efforts to Guide the Reports on the Aircraft Carrier Test Sail"), 对外宣传 (*Foreign Propaganda*), No. 11, 2011.

2. It was purchased at auction for U.S.$20 million by Chong Lot Travel Agency, a Hong Kong-based company widely believed

to have close ties to the PLAN. Chong Lot initially stated that the ship would become a floating entertainment center and casino in Macau, but it eventually turned the hulk over to the Chinese government.

3. The Chinese believe that Ukraine removed the parts under heavy U.S. pressure. See Xiong Songce (熊崧策), "不远万里来到中国的瓦良格号" ("The Varyag's Long Journey to China"), 文史参考 (*Literature and History*), No. 14, 2011.

4. Promising several million Chinese tourists to spend money in Turkey, for example, was part of the deal. See China Central Television (CCTV) interview with Chinese Ambassador to Turkey Yao Kuangyi (姚匡乙), "深度揭秘瓦良格来华曲折斡旋两年通过土耳其海峡" ("Inside Story on *Varyag*'s Tortuous Journey to China, Two Years of Difficult Negotiation on the Ship's Passing of Turkey Strait"), August 8, 2011.

5. 中评社 (China Review News), "中国为何改建废旧航母而不造一艘全新航母？" ("Why China Refurbished an Abandoned Aircraft Carrier But Not Build a New One?"), July 28, 2011, available from www.chinareviewnews.com. The news agency interviewed such PLA commentators as 张召忠 (Zhang Zhaozhong), 曹卫东 (Cao Weidong), 李杰 (Li Jie), and others.

6. Many Chinese celebrated the test sail of *Varyag* as the first step toward turning China's dream for an aircraft carrier and, by extension, a carrier-led blue-water navy, into reality. The celebration, however, was guarded for two main reasons. First, the *Varyag* is an import and a refurbished warship. China's celebration would have been much bigger in scale had it been a home-made and much-more-capable aircraft carrier. Second, and more importantly, the Chinese government exercised control of the celebration, or, in the words of Chinese government's "foreign propaganda" and "guided reports" ("对外宣传" and "舆论引导"). The Chinese government did not want the test sail of this aircraft carrier to generate another round of "China threat" outcry. See Liu Yan (刘妍) and Yang Fan (杨帆), "从航母试验的舆论引导谈起" ("Thoughts on the Efforts to Guide the Reports on the Aircraft Carrier Test Sail"), 对外宣传 (*Foreign Propaganda*), No. 11, 2011. There are many other writings to celebrate the coming of the Chinese aircraft carrier, but there is no need to list them here.

7. See the debate about China's intent for having the aircraft carrier (s) between Michael A. Glosny, Phillip C. Saunders, and Robert S. Ross in "Debating China's Naval Nationalism," *International Security*, Vol. 35, No. 2, Fall 2010. Ross's argument, which generates this debate, is that China will develop carrier capabilities more for security reasons than for military operations other than war, as the other two authors have contended. I support Ross's observation. See also Nan Li and Christopher Weuve, "China's Aircraft Carrier Ambitions," *Naval War College Review*, Vol. 63, No. 1, Winter 2010. Li and Weuve hold a position similar to that of Ross.

8. See Xia Mingxing (夏明星) and Xiao Tebing (肖特兵), "中国军事战略中 '诱敌深入' 方针的谢幕" ("Bidding Farewell to the 'Luring the Enemy Deep into China' in Chinese Military Strategy"), 党史纵横 (*CCP History*), No. 2, 2010. Yuan Dejin (袁德金) and Wang Jianfei (王建飞), "新中国成立以来军事战略方针的历史演变及启示" ("The Historical Evolution of New China's Military Strategy and Its Significance"), 军事历史 (*Military History*), No. 6, 2007.

9. See Li Jie (李杰), "中国海军战略: 60年变与不变" ("Chinese Naval Strategy: Change and No Change in 60 Years"), 世界知识 (*World Knowledge*), No. 8, 2009; Liu Jie (刘杰) and Lin Shihua (林世华), "新中国60年人民海军发展战略的演进及启示" ("60 Years of Evolution in New China's Navy and Its Significance"), 军事历史研究 (*Studies of Military History*), No. 3, 2009.

10. See Yuan Dejin (袁德金) and Wang Jianfei (王建飞), "新中国成立以来军事战略方针的历史演变及启示" ("The Evolution of Military Strategy since the Founding of the New China and Its Implications"), 军事历史 (*Military History*), No. 6, 2007. See also Li Deyi (李德义), "毛泽东积极防御战略思想的历史发展与思考" ("An Analysis of the Evolution of Mao Zedong's Idea of Active Defense"), 军事历史 (*Military History*), No. 4, 2002.

11. Nan Li writes that China's concept of "near sea" is beyond the 200 nautical mile EEZ, stretching all the way to the so-called first island chain. Li's assertion is based on the former Chinese PLA Navy Commander Liu Huaqing's conception and proposal. However, there is no official Chinese government endorsement of this conception and scope. See Nan Li, "The Evolution of China's

Naval Strategy and Capabilities: From 'Near Coast' and 'Near Seas' to 'Far Seas'," *Asian Security*, Vol. 5, No. 2, 2009.

12. The most significant ones are arguably remarks by Secretary of State Hillary Clinton at the ASEAN Regional Forum, Hanoi, Vietnam, in July 2010, and at the joint press conference with the Japanese Foreign Minister in Honolulu, HI, on October 27, 2010. Both texts are available at the State Department website.

13. See Wei Yuejiang (魏岳江) and Sun Hailong (孙海龙), "我国实现航母梦的风雨之路" ("The Touch Journey toward Fulfilling Our Dream for Aircraft Carrier"), 文史月刊 (*Literature and History Monthly*), No. 8, 2011. Dai Xu (戴旭), "航母载起强国梦" ("The Aircraft Carrier Carries the Dream of A Strong Nation"), 时政 (*Politics*), No. 9, 2011; and many other Chinese writings.

14. See David Lai's discussion of the PLA's new mission in the new century in Roy Kamphausen, David Lai, and Andrew Scobell, eds., *The PLA at Home and Abroad: Assessing the Operational Capabilities of China's Military.* Carlisle, PA: Strategic Studies Institute, U.S. Army War College, 2009, "Introduction."

15. Military modernization has always been one of the missions China pursues. However, at the beginning of China's current modernization mission 30 years ago, Deng Xiaoping, the architect of this mission, put military modernization on the back burner. Deng gave priority to the other three modernizations, namely, industrial, agricultural, and science and technology developments. He figured that by the end of the 20th century or at the beginning the 21st century, the size of China's economy should be quadrupled. By that time, China would have bountiful economic resources to support its military modernization.

16. See Wei Yuejiang (魏岳江) and Sun Hailong (孙海龙), "我国实现航母梦的风雨之路" ("The Touch Journey toward Fulfilling Our Dream for Aircraft Carrier"), 文史月刊 (*Literature and History Monthly*), No. 8, 2011; Dai Xu (戴旭), "航母载起强国梦" ("The Aircraft Carrier Carries the Dream of A Strong Nation"), 时政 (*Politics*), No. 9, 2011; and many other Chinese writings.

17. For more than 10 years following the Taiwan Strait crisis, China topped the world in spending the most to purchase

conventional weapons, exclusively from Russia, and mostly advanced fighter jets and destroyers. See *SIPRI Yearbooks* from 1995 to 2008, Stockholm, Sweden: Stockholm International Peace Research Institute.

18. Much of the debate centers around China's quest for maritime interests and power, the latter of which includes calls for the development of aircraft carrier(s) and a blue-water navy. It is beyond the scope of this writing to provide a detailed presentation of the debate and references. Suffice it to say that the debate is rather extensive and open. There are also numerous Chinese publications. In fact, the debate is still going on in China.

19. Shi Shiping (石世平), "航母带动军工发展" ("Aircraft Carrier Leads the Development of Military Industry"), 人民网 (*people. com.cn*), September 7, 2011.

20. Li Jie (李杰), "航母是海上浮动棺材论是一种偏见" ("It Is Misunderstanding to See Aircraft Carrier as a Floating Coffin"), 环球网 (*Global Times*), June 9, 2011.

21. See again the debate on China's naval strategy by Michael A. Glosny, Phillip C. Saunders, and Robert S. Ross in "Debating China's Naval Nationalism" *International Security*, Vol. 35, No. 2, Fall 2010. Ross' argument, which generates this debate, is that China will develop carrier capabilities more for security reasons (than MOOTW, as the other two authors have contended). This writing supports Ross' position in this remark. See also Nan Li and Christopher Weuve, "China's Aircraft Carrier Ambitions," *Naval War College Review*, Vol. 63, No. 1, Winter 2010, for similar arguments to Ross' analysis.

22. Li Hongzhang (李鸿章), "筹议海防折" ("On Coastal Defense"), in 李鸿章全集 (*Complete Works of Li Hongzhang*), Tianjin, China: Baihua Wenyi Chubanshe, 2000.

23. The most outspoken one is perhaps by Zhang Zhidong (张之洞) in his writing 劝学篇 (*On Study*), Beijing, China: Zhonghua Shuju, 1991, in which he argued that Confucianism had been the core ethical and virtual code for China; its teaching was close to perfect and allowed no revision; this Chinese core value was unshakable; China did not need to learn from any other nation;

what China needed was the means to manufacture, which the West could provide; and China should make use of the West's technology on the basis of preserving the Chinese fundamentals.

24. See Wang Weiyu (汪维余) and Zhang Qiancheng (张前程) 论中国特色军事理论创新 (*On Making New Military Theories with Chinese Characteristics*). Beijing, China: PLA NDU Press, 2009, for a discussion of the problem with this approach. The two authors argue that it is a no-brainer to do so. The so-called "learning the skills from the enemy and use that to check the enemy" is only wishful thinking. One cannot succeed without also learning about the ideas behind the skills (所谓"师夷长技以制夷"，只不过是"学其形而未学其神." 所谓"神"即先进的军事理论和军事思想), p. 102.

25. Key reform-minded officials Feng Guifen (冯桂芬) and Shen Shoukang (沈寿康) were the first ones to put forward this concept. Zhang Zhidong (张之洞) provided a comprehensive explanation of this concept in his influential book 劝学篇 (*On Learning*). See Wang Zhaoxiang (王兆祥) "'中体西用' 再论" ("Chinese Learning as Fundamental and Western Learning for Practice Reconsidered"), 广西社会科学 (*Guangxi Social Sciences*), No. 8, 2008.

26. See also Xu Zhigong (许志功), Zhao Xiaomang (赵小芒) and Shang Jinsuo (尚金锁), 中国特色军事变革的哲学思考 (*Philosophical Thoughts on China's Transformation in Military Affairs*). Beijing, China: PLA Press, 2007.

27. Wang Zhaohui (王兆辉), "晚清军工战略与近代中国的军事现代化进程" ("Military Industrial Strategy and Contemporary Chinese Military Affairs Modernization in the Late Qing Era"), 湖南科技学院学报 (*Journal of Hunan Science and Technology College*), Vol. 29, No. 3, 2008.

28. China's economic achievements can easily cause many to overlook the tortuous process Chinese leaders have muddled through in the past 30-plus years. See David Lai, *The United States and China in Power Transition*, Carlisle, PA: Strategic Studies Institute, U.S. Army War College, 2011, for a discussion of China's tortuous road to modernity.

29. There are numerous Chinese writings on military transformation with Chinese characteristics. Sun's works are argu-

ably the most straightforward and comprehensive analyses of the special features of China's military transformation with Chinese characteristics.

30. See Sun Kejia (孙科佳), "试论中国特色军事变革" ("On Military Reform with Chinese Characteristics"), 中国军事科学 (*China Military Science*), Vol. 16, No. 1, 2003; and "中国特色军事变革 '特' 在哪? ("What Are the Special Features of Military Transformation with Chinese Characteristics?") 学习时报 (*Study Times*), Issue 251. Sun lists the special features differently in the two writings, but some of them are repetitive. The presentation in this writing does not translate Sun's characterization word by word. It does not list the features the same way accordingly.

31. The two fundamental changes policy was promulgated by Chinese President Jiang Zemin. See Jiang Zemin (江泽民), 论国防和军队建设 (*On National Defense and Armed Force Building*), Beijing, China: PLA Publishing, 2003, p. 82.

32. Chinese President Jiang Zemin put forward the three-step concept in his report to the 15th CCP National Congress in 1997. This approach has been reaffirmed and further specified in China's *National Defense White Papers* of 2006, 2008 and 2010.

33. Sun Kejia (孙科佳), "试论中国特色军事变革" ("On Military Reform with Chinese Characteristics").

34. Sun Kejia (孙科佳), "思想解放是中国特色军事变革的先导 (上中下)" ("The Emancipation of the Mind Must Be a Precondition for the Military Transformation with Chinese Characteristics, [Parts 1, 2, and 3]"), 学习时报 (*Study Times*), Issues, 293, 295, and 297.

35. See, for example, the timely and revealing analysis of corruption in the senior Chinese political and military leadership by John Garnaut, "Rotting From Within," *Foreign Policy*, April 16, 2012.

36. See *PLA Daily*, "总政治部主任李继耐: 坚决抵制 '军队国家化' 那一套" ("Director of General Political Affairs Department Li Jinai: Resolutely Reject the Call for 'Nationalizing the Military'"), June 20, 2011; Qi Biao (齐彪), "'军队国家化' 剖析" ("An Analy-

sis of 'Nationalizing the Military'"), 政治学研究 (*Political Studies*), No. 4, 2009; Liu Xinru (刘新如) and Qi Biao (齐彪), "西方军队国家化制度在中国行不通" ("Western-style Nationalized Military Does Not Apply in China"), *PLA Daily*, June 29, 2010.

37. General Xiong's presentation was later turned into a book and an article. See Xiong Guangkai (熊光楷), "关于新军事变革问题" ("About New Transformation in Military Affairs"), 军事历史 (*Military History*), No. 4, 2003; and Xiong's book 国际战略与新军事变革 (*International Strategy and New Transformation in Military Affairs*). Beijing, China: Qinghua University Press, 2003. There are many other Chinese analysts' publications about the features of war in the evolving information age. Yet they are more or less along the lines of Xiong's works cited here.

38. See Guo Wujun (郭武君), 联合作战指挥体制研究 (*A Study of the Command System in Joint Operations*), Beijing, China: PLA NDU Press, 2003; Yan Muxian (鄢慕先) and Li Menghe (李梦鹤), 高技术局部战争中联合作战 (*Joint Operations in High Tech Local Wars*), Beijing, China: PLA Press, 1996; Sun Baolong (孙宝龙) and Han Pizhong (韩丕忠), 信息化条件下联合作战通用装备保障 (*Joint Operation General Equipment Supply and Protection under Information-Centric War Conditions*), Beijing, China: Military Science Press, 2008; PLA NDU Scientific Studies and Services Studies Departments (解放军国防大学科研部和军兵种教研室), 高技术条件下联合战役与军兵种作战 (*Joint Operations and Service Operations under High Tech Conditions*), Beijing, China: PLA NDU Press, 1997; Cui Shizeng (崔师增), 美军联合作战 (U.S. Military Joint Operations), Beijing, China: PLA NDU Press, 1995; Feng Zhaoxin (冯兆新), 美军联合作战理论研究 (*Studies of U.S. Military Joint Operations Theory*), Beijing, China: PLA NDU Press, 2001.

39. Liu Jixian (刘继贤), "一体化联合作战与系统化建设" ("Integrated Joint Operation and Its Systematic Development"), 军事运筹与系统工程 (*Military Operations Research and Systems Engineering*), Vol. 22, No. 4, 2008.

40. *PLA Daily*, "专访军事科学院作战理论和条令研究部部长何雷少将: 联合作战将成为未来战争基本作战形式" ("An Exclusive Interview with Major General He Lei, Director of Combat Theory and Doctrine Studies Department of the Academy of Military Science: Joint Operation Will Become the Basic Form of Combat in

Future Wars"), September 9, 2010. There are many other studies by the PLA Academy of Military Science (AMS) researchers about the transformation in military affairs with Chinese characteristics and integrated joint operations. PLA Major General Wang Baocun of the AMS is one of the most dedicated pioneers in studying and writing about RMA. See Wang Baocun (王保存), 世界新军事变革 (*The World's New Military Revolution*). Beijing, China: PLA Publishing, 1999; (王保存), 世界新军事变革新论 (*New Analysis on the World's New Revolution in Military Affairs*), Beijing, China: PLA Publishing, 2003; Min Zhenfan (闵振范) and Wang Baocun (王保存), 构建信息化军队的组织体制 (*Constructing the Organization for a Information-Centric Military*), Beijing, China: PLA Publishing, 2004; (王保存), 外国军队信息化建设的理论与实践 (*Theory and Practice by Foreign Militaries on Developing Information-Centric Forces*), Beijing, China: PLA Publishing, 2008. See also other works such as Li Bingyan (李炳彦), 论中国军事变革 (*On China's Transformation in Military Affairs*), Beijing, China: Xinhua Chubanshe, 2003; Lin Jianchao (林建超) and Ji Wenming (吉文明), 世界新军事变革概论 (*On the New Transformation in Military Affairs in the World*), Beijing, China: PLA Press, 2004; Mu Yongmin (穆永民), Hu Bin (胡滨) and Tang Xiaohua (汤晓华), 军事高技术与新军事变革 (*Military High Tech and New Transformation in Military Affairs*), Beijing, China: PLA Press, 2004. Liang Biqin (梁必骎), 军事革命论 (*On Revolution in Military Affairs*), Beijing, China: Military Science Press, 2001; Li Qingshan (李庆山), 新军事革命与高科技战争 (*New Revolution in Military Affairs and High Tech War*), Beijing, China: Military Science Press, 1995; Zhang Shuguang (张曙光) and Zhou Jianming (周建明), 以军事力量谋求绝对安全: 美国新军事革命与国防转型文献选编 (*Seeking Absolute Security through Military Might: Selected Works on U.S. New Revolution in Military Affairs and National Defense Transformation*), Beijing, China: PLA NDU Press, 2003; Wang Pufeng (王普丰), 信息战争与军事革命 (*Information-Centric Warfare and Revolution in Military Affairs*), Beijing, China: Military Science Press, 1995.

41. Hu Junhua (胡君华) and Bao Guojun (包国俊), "联合作战应强化'八个一体化'" ("Combined Operations Requires 'Eight Integrations'"), *PLA Daily*, October 28, 2010.

42. Chen Hui (陈辉), "全军首个三军联勤保障互动平台在北京战区启动" ("The First Three-Services Integrated Logistics Supply and Support Platform of the PLA Started in the Beijing War Zone"), *PLA Daily*, January 11, 2006.

43. Zhang Yuqing (张玉清) and Xu Jinzhang (胥金章), "中央军委决定: 济南军区正式实行大联勤体制" ("Central Military Commission Decision: Jinan War Zone Formally Implements Integrated Logistics System"), 新华网 (*Xinhuanet*), February 15, 2007.

44. Song Yongchao (宋永朝), "深化军队财务管理体制改革的思考"("Deepen Reform on the Military Accounting System"), 军事经济研究 (Studies of Military Economics), No. 3, 2011.

45. Zhang Xiangdong (张向东), Li Songqing (李松青), and Wei Tongbing (韦统兵), "军交运输现代化建设驶入快车道" ("Military Transportation Modernization Got in Fast Track"), 中国交通报 (*China Transportation*), June 23, 2010.

46. Zhong Xianwen (钟先文), "总后军需物资油料部领导就物资采购改革答记者问" ("Officials of General Logistics Department Oil Supply Branch Interview with Media"), *PLA Daily*, July 18, 2005.

47. San Mu (三木), "中国完善军民结合、寓军于民的装备科研生产体系" ("China Has Established Civil-Military Integrated Research and Production System on Weapon and Military Supplies"), 中国网 (*china.com.cn*), March 31, 2011; "胡锦涛主持政治局学习 强调推动军民融合式发展" ("Hu Jintao Presided Over Polibureau Study and Stressed Civil-Military Development Model"), *Xinhua News Agency*, August 23, 2010.

48. Cao Zhi (曹智), "胡锦涛主席要求推进军事训练向信息化转变" (President Hu Jintao Urges Transition of Military Exercises to Information-Centric Practice"), 新华网 (*Xinhuanet*), June 27, 2006; Jia Yong (贾永) and Cao Zhi (曹智), "全军军事训练会议在京召开, 胡锦涛会见会议代表" ("All PLA Military Meeting Took Place in Beijing, Hu Jintao Met with Delegates"), 新华网 (*Xinhuanet*), June 24, 2006; Li Xunliang (李宣良) and Wu Dengfeng (吴登峰), "全军各部队打抓军事训练整体作战能力提高" ("PLA Implements Exercises Everywhere and Integrated Fighting Power Enhanced"), 新华网 (*Xinhuanet*), June 24, 2006.

49. Chinese Defense Ministry, "2020 前军队人才发展规划纲要颁发施行" ("Issuance and Implementation of the Guideline for Developing Military Talents before 2020"), available from 国防部网 (Ministry of National Defense Website, *www.mod.gov.cn*), April 18, 2011.

50. Zheng Wenhao (郑文浩), "解放军提出重大专项建设人才超前培养工程" ("The PLA Has Put Forward an Important Project to Develop Talented Personnel"), 新华网 (*Xinhuanet*), April 23, 2011.

51. Early study of the Chinese way of war goes to John King Fairbank, *Chinese Ways in Warfare*, Harvard University Press, 1974. Over the years, there have been many more publications about this subject. Andrew Scobell's analysis, "Is There a Chinese Way of War," *Parameters*, Vol. 35, No. 1, 2005, puts those studies in perspective. It is beyond the scope of this writing to provide a comprehensive presentation of the literature. Suffice it to say that there is no agreement in the field. The analysis here is my attempt to provide another perspective on this controversial issue.

52. Calling those disputed territories "stolen territories" is a common expression in Chinese.

53. Chinese have no tradition for scientific definitions. That is why the term "define" is in quotation marks.

54. See the Chinese articulation of "post-emption" ("后发制人"), in the section of "National Defense Policy" in China's 2008 and 2010 *National Defense White Papers*.

55. The most notable Mao teaching is the so-called Mao's Ten Military Principles. See Yuan Dejin (袁德金), "论毛泽东十大军事原则" ("The Evolution of Mao Zedong's Ten Military Principles"). 军事历史研究 (Studies of Military History), for a good discussion of the evolution of Mao's 10 military principles.

56. Wang Xin (王新), "新军事革命赋予军事研究与实践的逻辑观" ("The Logic on Military Study and Practice following the New Revolution in Military Affairs"), *PLA Daily*, April 23, 2004.

57. Li Menghe (李梦鹤) *et al.*, ed., 新军事变革中的战术理论创新 (*Advocating New Operational Theories in the New Military Transformation*), Beijing, China: PLA NDU Press, 2004.

58. "牢记小平教诲, 搞好军事科研" (Never Forget Xiaoping's Teaching, Making Good of Military Research"), *People Daily*, February 23, 2003.

59. Jiang Zemin, 江泽民论有中国特色社会主义 (*Jiang Zemin on Socialism with Chinese Characteristics*), Beijing, China: CCP Archive Press, 2002, p. 454.

APPENDIX I

Exercise Name	Host	Significance
前卫 (Front Guard)-2011	济南军区 (Jinan MR)	大型信息系统首次使用 (First use of large-scale information systems.)
先锋 (Vanguard)-2011	济南军区 (Jinan MR)	工程兵混编跨区联训 (Engineer troops cross-military region joint exercise.)
使命行动 (Mission)-2010	北京兰州成都3集团军 (Beijing, Lanzhou and Chengdu MRs)	信息一体化，跨区机动实兵演习，首次联合战役军团战略投送演习，首次总部统一筹划 (Integrated information-centric exercise, cross-military region mobile life-fire exercise, first strategic power projection by joint campaign groups, first exercise under unified control of the General Staff.)
砺剑 (Sharp Saw)-2010	北京军区 (Beijing MR)	信息一体化 (Integrated information-centric operations.)
先锋 (Vanguard)-2010		
前卫 (Front Guard)-2010	济南军区防空部队 (Jinan MR Air Defense)	防空演习侦查预警 (Air defense, intelligence, and early warning.)
防护 (Protection)-2010	北京军区核化防护部队 (Beijing MR)	核生化防护 (Nuclear and bio-warfare protection.)
交战 (Engagement)-2010	东海舰队 (East Sea Fleet)	海上应急保障 (Maritime emergency operation.)
黄海 (Yellow Sea)-2010	南京军区 (Nanjing MR)	UAV

Exercise Name	Host	Significance
南海 *(South China Sea)*-2010	北海，东海，南海舰队 (North, East, and South Sea Fleets)	对美"亮剑" (Counter U.S. naval exercises.)
西藏 *(Tibet)*-2010	兰州军区 (Lanzhou MR)	陆空联合军演 (Air-land joint operation.)
跨越 *(Stride)*-2009	沈阳兰州济南广州军区 (Shenyang, Lanzhou, Jinan, and Guangzhou MRs)	北斗GPS，首次跨战区 (Employment of Beidou GPS and first cross-war zone exercise.)
联合 *(Joint Operations)*-2009	济南军区 (Jinan MR)	首次战区级联合战役训练包括陆海空二炮等军种 (First war zone-level joint operation exercise involving land, air, naval, and Second Artillery forces.)
砺剑 *(Sharp Saw)*-2009	广州军区 (Guangzhou MR)	多样化军事任务 (Diversified military operations.)
先锋 *(Vanguard)*-2009	济南军区 (Jinan MR)	五项演习 (Five tasking exercise.)
北剑 *(North Saw)*-2009	北京军区 (Beijing MR)	实兵对抗系统原理性演练 (Live-fire system confrontation)
前卫 *(Front Guard)*-2009	济南军区 (Jinan MR)	联合作战全方位体系作战 (Joint operations under all conditions.)
铁拳 *(Iron Fist)*-2009	济南军区 (Jinan MR)	远程机动 (Long-range mobile.)
必胜 *(Must Win)*-2009	南京军区 (Nanjing MR)	三界训练基地红军兰军对垒 (Red and blue forces engagement.)
前锋 *(Front Guard)*-2009	济南军区 (Jinan MR)	联合作战，精确作战 (Joint operations and precision strike, with 150 foreign officers observing.)

Exercise Name	Host	Significance
空降机动 (Airborne)-2009	空降兵部队（郑州）(Airborne Force [Zhengzhou])	跨区战役机动综合演练 (Cross-war zone mobile campaign.)
火力 (Fire Power)-2009	广州军区 (Guangzhou MR)	炮兵防空演练 (Artillery and air defense.)
西南使命 (Southwest Mission)-2009	成都军区 (Chengdu MR)	信息化作战, GPS (Information-centric operations, with GPS.)
先行 (Advance Dispatch)-2009	总后勤部沈阳军区北京军区 (General Logistics Department, Shenyang and Beijing MRs)	首次联合作战后勤保障综合实兵, 野战医疗救护, 饮食技能, 运输, 供油, 抢修 (First joint operations for logistics including medical operation, food supply, transportation, oil supply, and emergency repair.)
卫勤使命 (Medi-Logis)-2009	兰州军区 (Lanzhou MR)	最大规模非战军事行动, 最大规模联合医疗救援 (Largest-scale non-combat operation and joint medical rescue operations.)
铁骑 (Iron Cavalry)-2009	济南军区 (Jinan MR)	装甲师演习, 20个合成战斗团, 信息化指挥 (Armor Division with 20 combined regiments, information-centric command and operations.)
联合 (Joint Operation)-2008	济南军区 (Jinan MR)	首次跨海峡(辽东半岛), 联合指挥, 情报, 火力打击, 电子对抗, 综合保障 (First cross-strait [Liaodong Peninsula] joint operations with command, intelligence, live-fire strike, electronic warfare, and integrated supply and protection.)
北剑 (North Saw)-2008	北京军区 (Beijing MR)	联合作战, 信息攻击, 火力打击, 作战保障 (Joint operations, information-centric attacks, live-fire engagement, and combat protection.)
砺兵 (Sharp Force)-2008	北京军区济南军区 (Beijing, Jinan MRs)	联合作战, 跨军区作战 (Joint operations, cross-war zone, with 36 foreign national observers.)

Exercise Name	Host	Significance
前锋 (Front Guard)-2008	济南军区 (Jinan MR)	装甲旅，阶段性信息火力打击，综合攻击，夺点控域 (Armor brigades, phased information-centric attacks, integrated offense, and position warfare.)
确山 (Queshan)-2007	济南军区 (Jinan MR)	摩托化步兵师 (Mechanized infantry.)
勇士 (Brave Soldiers)-2007	沈阳军区 (Shenyang MR)	摩托化步兵师实弹演习(Mechanized infantry live-fire exercise with 55 foreign officers, including U.S. officers, observing the exercise.)
铁拳 (Iron Fist)-2007	济南军区 (Jinan MR)	王牌机动师检验部队指挥，机动，火力打击，保障防护 (Elite mechanized infantry with tests on command, maneuver, attacks, and protection)
北剑 (North Saw)-2007	北京军区 (Beijing MR)	朱日和合同战术训练基地实兵对抗系统原理性实验演练 (Combined exercises at Zhurihe with system confrontation.)
确山 (Queshan)-2006	四总部济南军区 (4 General Departments and Jinan MR)	Turning Point: 胡锦涛：机械化转信息化，实弹四总部首次联合组织的整建制步兵师演习 (First joint operation exercise with a full division.)
前卫 (Front Guard)-2006	济南军区 (Jinan MR)	联合作战全方位体系对抗 (Joint operation under all conditions.)
北剑 (North Saw)-2006	北京军区 (Beijing MR)	首次由陆军、空军、第二炮兵、武装警察、军区指挥官联合举行的军事操演 (First all-service plus PAP on joint operations.)
Source: From Chinese open sources, compiled by the author.		

ABOUT THE CONTRIBUTORS

DENNIS J. BLASKO served for 23 years in the U.S. Army as a tactical and strategic Military Intelligence Officer and Foreign Area Officer specializing in China. Mr. Blasko served as an Army attaché in Beijing from 1992 to 1995 and in Hong Kong from 1995 to 1996. He also served in infantry units in Germany, Italy, and Korea. He later worked in Washington, DC, at the Defense Intelligence Agency, the Headquarters Department of the Army (Office of Special Operations), and the National Defense University War Gaming and Simulation Center. He is the author of *The Chinese Army Today*, 2nd Ed., New York: Routledge, 2012.

CHIN-HAO HUANG is an Associate Research Fellow with the China and Global Security Program at Stockholm International Peace Research Institute (SIPRI), where he has co-led a study on China's evolving approach toward foreign military activities and peacekeeping operations. Prior to SIPRI, he coordinated the China-Africa project for the Center for Strategic and International Studies (CSIS), a multi-year initiative examining Chinese intentions, policies, and practices in Africa and implications for U.S. strategic interests. He has authored and co-authored several monographs, journal articles, and book chapters on Chinese foreign and security policy and is a contributing co-author (with Robert Sutter) of the chapter on China-Southeast Asia relations for the Pacific Forum CSIS quarterly publication, *Comparative Connections*. A graduate of the Edmond A. Walsh School of Foreign Service at Georgetown University, he is currently completing a Ph.D. in political science and international relations at the University of Southern California (USC).

BERNARD D. COLE is Professor of International History at the National War College in Washington, D.C., where he concentrates on Sino-American relations, the Chinese military, and Asian energy issues. He previously served for 30 years as a Surface Warfare Officer in the Navy, all in the Pacific. He commanded USS *Rathburne* (FF 1057) and Destroyer Squadron 35, and served as a Naval Gunfire Liaison Officer with the Third Marine Division in Vietnam, Surface Operations Officer for CTF 70/77, Plans Officer for Commander-in-Chief Pacific Fleet, and as special assistant to the Chief of Naval Operations for Expeditionary Warfare.

CORTEZ A. COOPER III is a senior international policy analyst at RAND Corporation, where he provides assessments of security challenges across political, military, economic, cultural, and informational arenas for a broad range of U.S. Government clients. Prior to joining RAND, Mr. Cooper served as the Director of the East Asia Studies Center for Hicks and Associates, Inc., as a Senior Analyst for the Joint Intelligence Center Pacific in the U.S. Navy Executive Service, and as a senior analyst at CENTRA Technology, Inc. Mr. Cooper's 20 years of military service included assignments as both an Army Signal Corps Officer and a China Foreign Area Officer.

ABRAHAM M. DENMARK is a Senior Project Director for Political and Security Affairs at The National Bureau for Asian Research (NBR). He also serves as an Asia-Pacific Security Advisor at the Center for Naval Analyses, and is a Sasakawa Peace Foundation Nonresident Fellow at CSIS-Pacific Forum. He previously worked as a Fellow with the Center for a New American Security (CNAS) and Country Director for China Affairs in the Office of the Secretary of Defense. He is the recipient of numerous awards and was named a 21st-century leader by the National Committee on American Foreign Policy. He is a member of the National Committee on United States-China Relations, the U.S. Naval Institute, and the International Institute for Strategic Studies. Mr. Denmark has studied at China's Foreign Affairs College and Peking University and holds a bachelor's degree with honors in history from the University of Northern Colorado and a master's degree in international security from the Josef Korbel School of International Studies at the University of Denver.

DANIEL M. HARTNETT is an Asia analyst in the China Strategic Issues Group, Center for Naval Analyses (CNA). Prior to joining CNA, he was the senior policy analyst for security affairs at the congressionally mandated U.S.-China Economic and Security Review Commission. Mr. Hartnett began his career as a Russian and Serbo-Croatian linguist in the U.S. Army, where he employed his language skills during the civil war in Bosnia. He also worked in the Department of Energy's National Nuclear Security Administration, where he assisted the department in nuclear nonproliferation negotiations with Beijing, China. His research interests include China's security and military affairs. Mr. Hartnett has attended several language schools, including the Defense Language Institute in Monterey, California; the Sprachen und Dolmetscher Institute in Munich, Germany; and the Beijing Language and Culture University. He holds a B.A. in Chinese from the University of Massachusetts at Amherst and an M.A. in Asian studies from the Elliott School of International Affairs at George Washington University. He is currently pursuing a Ph.D. in political science at George Mason University.

ROY KAMPHAUSEN is a Senior Associate for Political and Security Affairs (PSA) at The National Bureau of Asian Research (NBR) and an adjunct professor at Columbia University's School of International and Public Affairs. He advises and contributes to NBR research programs on political and security issues in Asia. Mr. Kamphausen previously served as Senior Vice President for Political and Security Affairs and Director of NBR's Washington, DC, office. Prior to joining NBR, Mr. Kamphausen served as a U.S. Army officer, a career that culminated in an assignment in the Office of the Secretary of Defense (OSD) as Country Director for China-Taiwan-Mongolia Affairs. Previous assignments include the Joint Staff as an intelligence analyst and later as China Branch Chief in the Directorate for Strategic Plans and Policy (J5). A fluent Chinese (Mandarin) linguist and an Army China Foreign Area Officer (FAO), Mr. Kamphausen served two tours at the Defense Attaché Office of the U.S. Embassy in the People's Republic of China. He has authored numerous articles and book chapters, including most recently "China's Land Forces: New Priorities and Capabilities" in *Strategic Asia 2012-13: China's Military Challenge*. Additionally, he has co-edited the last six volumes produced from the Carlisle People's Liberation Army (PLA) Conference. Mr. Kamphausen studied Chinese at both the Defense Language Institute and Beijing's Capital Normal University and he holds a B.A. in political science from Wheaton College and an M.A. in international affairs from Columbia University.

DAVID LAI is a Research Professor of Asian Security Affairs at the Strategic Studies Institute (SSI) of the U.S. Army War College. Before joining SSI, Dr. Lai was on the faculty of the U.S. Air War College. Having grown up in China, he witnessed China's "Cultural Revolution," its economic reform, and the changes in U.S.-China relations over the years. Dr. Lai's most recent publication is the book titled, *United States and China in Power Transition* (2011). Dr. Lai holds a bachelor's degree from China, and a master's degree and Ph.D. in political science from the University of Colorado.

REAR ADMIRAL MICHAEL McDEVITT is a Senior Fellow associated with CNA Strategic Studies, a division of CNA — a not-for-profit federally funded research center in Washington, DC. During his Navy career, Rear Admiral McDevitt held four at-sea commands, including an aircraft carrier battle group. He was a CNO Strategic Studies Group Fellow and the Director of the East Asia Policy office for the Secretary of Defense during the George H. W. Bush administration. He also served for 2 years as the Director for Strategy, War Plans, and Policy (J-5) for the U.S. Pacific Command (USPACOM). Rear Admiral McDevitt concluded his 34-year active duty career as the Commandant of the National War College in Washington, DC. He is a graduate of the National War College and holds a Bachelor of Arts degree in U.S. history from the University of Southern California and a master's degree in American diplomatic history from Georgetown University.

TRAVIS TANNER is Senior Project Director and Director of the Pyle Center for Northeast Asian Studies at The National Bureau of Asian Research (NBR). He is co-editor of the past four volumes of NBR's Strategic Asia series. His interests and expertise include Northeast Asian regional security, China's economy and foreign affairs, and Taiwanese politics. Prior to joining NBR, he was Deputy Director and Assistant Director of the Chinese Studies Program at the Nixon Center. He was also a research assistant at the Institute for International Economics in Washington, DC. Mr. Tanner holds a B.A. in Chinese language and literature from the University of Utah and an M.A. in international relations from the Johns Hopkins School of Advanced International Studies (SAIS) and the Hopkins-Nanjing Center in Nanjing, China.